MATERIALS
AND
STRUCTURE
OF
MUSIC

VOLUME ONE

MATERIALS AND STRUCTURE OF MUSIC

Second Edition

William Christ
Richard DeLone
Vernon Kliewer
Indiana University

Lewis Rowell
University of Hawaii

William Thomson
Case Western Reserve University

Prentice-Hall, Inc., Englewood Cliffs, New Jersey

© 1972, 1966 by PRENTICE-HALL, INC.
Englewood Cliffs, New Jersey

Printed in the United States of America
13-560342-0
Library of Congress Catalog Card No.: 70-152713

Current printing (last digit):

10 9

PRENTICE-HALL INTERNATIONAL, INC., London
PRENTICE-HALL OF AUSTRALIA, PTY. LTD., Sydney
PRENTICE-HALL OF CANADA, LTD., Toronto
PRENTICE-HALL OF INDIA PRIVATE LIMITED, New Delhi
PRENTICE-HALL OF JAPAN, INC., Tokyo

To

NELDA, JOANNE, DIANE, ANNETTE, and BETTY

who were so patient

CONTENTS

PREFACE, xiii

Chapter 1

INTRODUCTION TO BASIC PROPERTIES
AND NOTATION OF TONE, 1

*Characteristics of Rhythm. Basic Durations and the Beat. Meter
Signatures; Establishing the Basic Duration's Length and Grouping.
Compound Meter. Subdivisions of the Basic Duration. Notation of
Rhythm. Notation of Pitch. Intervals.*

Chapter 2

TONALITY, 20

Pitch Roots. Interval Quality and Melodic Organization.

Chapter 3

KEY, MODE, AND SCALE, 34

*The Diatonic Scale Systems. Terminology of Scale Degrees. Key
Signatures. Modulation and Mutation.*

Chapter 4

MELODIC CADENCES, 53

*Perfect and Imperfect Terminal Cadences. Transient-Terminal Cadences.
Cadences and Musical Style.*

Chapter 5

FORMAL CHARACTERISTICS OF MELODY: THE MOTIVE AND PHRASE, 65

Motive Structure.   Phrase Structure: Rhythmic Aspects.   Phrase Structure: Pitch Aspects.

Chapter 6

THE EXTENDED MELODY, 79

Chapter 7

BASIC MELODY, 90

Terminal Pitches in Tonal Melody.   Melodic Contour and Step-Progression.   Duration and Metric Locations.

Chapter 8

MELODIC ELABORATION, 104

Chapter 9

TWO-VOICE COMBINATIONS, 116

Texture.   Rhythmic Association.   Pitch Association.   Vertical Considerations in Two Voices; Consonance and Dissonance.   Contrapuntal Motion Between Parts and Approaches to Structural Intervals. Contrapuntal Treatments of Other Consonances.   Summation of Principles of Melodic Movement and Intervallic Succession in Tonal Music.   Basic Contrapuntal Treatments of Unstable Intervals.   Other Unstable Intervals.   Organization of Two-Voice Phrases.   Pitch Material in Tonal Music.   Cross Relation.

Chapter 10

CONTINUATION OF TWO-VOICE COMBINATIONS, 142

Other Interior Cadence Patterns.   Tonal Function Within the Phrase; Root Relations in the Two-Voice Frame.   Implied Triads.   The Two-Voice Framework.

Chapter 11

TWO-VOICE COMBINATIONS; DECORATIVE PITCHES, 164

Passing Tones. Neighbor Tones. Suspensions. Different Forms of Suspensions. Appoggiaturas (Leaning Tones). Escape Tones. Pedal Points.

Chapter 12

CONTINUITY AND RECURRENCE IN TWO-VOICE MUSIC, 184

Imitation.

Chapter 13

THREE-VOICE COMBINATIONS, 197

Rhythmic Association. Rhythmic Unity. Pitch Association of Three Parts. Spatial Distribution of Parts.

Chapter 14

CHORD STRUCTURE, 215

Chord Succession. Chord Position. Chord Inversion. Melodic-Harmonic Synthesis.

Chapter 15

CONTINUATION OF THREE-VOICE COMBINATIONS, 232

Spacing. Crossing Voices. Contrapuntal and Homophonic Textures. Doubling in Three Voices. Decorative Patterns. Suspensions in Three-voice Textures. Ornamental Resolutions of Suspensions. Other Forms of Pitch Decoration.

Chapter 16

HOMOPHONIC TEXTURES: NON-CHORD TONES, 248

Textural Considerations. Spacing of Four-voice Textures. Harmonic Succession. Contrapuntal Considerations (Voice Leading). Non-chord Tones. Pedal Point. Accented Non-chord Tones. Simultaneous Non-chord Tones. Non-chord Tones in Twentieth-century Harmonic Contexts.

Chapter 17

TONIC, DOMINANT, AND SUBDOMINANT CHORDS; HARMONIC PROLONGATION, 276

Tonic and Dominant Triads. Inverted Tonic and Dominant Triads. Other Forms of Tonic and Dominant. The Subdominant Triad. Examples of the Subdominant in Root Position and First Inversion. Harmonic Prolongation. Pedal Point.

Chapter 18

FURTHER STUDY OF HARMONIC RELATIONS; HARMONIC RHYTHM; SECOND-INVERSION CHORDS; THE SUPERTONIC, 292

Harmonic Rhythm. Second-inversion Triads. The Cadential I_4^6. Passing Six-four Chords. Embellishing Six-four Chords. Other Uses of Six-four Chords. The Supertonic Chord.

Chapter 19

THE DOMINANT SEVENTH; DIMINISHED $_3^6$; HARMONIC CADENCES, 313

Melodic Tendencies in V_7. Figuration of V_7 and its Inversions. Inversions of V_7. Summary of Characteristics of V_7. The vii_6° Chord. Harmonic Cadences.

Chapter 20

TERNARY FORM; THROUGH-COMPOSED FORM, 326

Through-composed Form.

Chapter 21

SUBMEDIANT AND MEDIANT CHORDS; HARMONIC SEQUENCE; CHORD RELATIONS; MUTATED CHORDS, 344

The Submediant and Mediant Chords. Harmonic Parallelism. Harmonic Sequence. Tonal Relations in Major and Minor Keys. Mutated Chords: ♭III and ♭VI.

Chapter 22

SECONDARY DOMINANTS, 369

Secondary Dominants of the Dominant (V/V; V_7/V). Dominant of the Subdominant. Dominant of the Supertonic.

Chapter 23

CONTINUATION OF SECONDARY DOMINANTS, 388

Dominant of the Submediant (V/vi; V/VI). Dominant of the Mediant (V/iii; V/III). Dominant of the Subtonic. Irregular Resolutions of Secondary Dominants. Sequential Treatment of Secondary Dominants.

Chapter 24

TONALITY CHANGE, 404

Relationships of Keys. Less Common Key Relations. Modulation. Modulation by Pivot Chord. Pivot Tone Modulation. Modulation by Chromatic Inflection. Enharmonic Modulation. Abrupt Tonality Changes. Mutation.

Chapter 25

BINARY FORM, 435

Baroque Binary Form. The Thematic Design. The Tonal Design. Other Formal Considerations. Binary and Ternary Forms Contrasted. Rounded Binary. Song Form and Trio.

INDEX OF MUSICAL EXCERPTS, 447

INDEX, 454

PREFACE

In these two volumes we have attempted to accomplish two main tasks: (1) To set out in effective pedagogical order a framework of understanding for the materials and structure of music; and (2) to transmit this understanding by means of the actual music produced in the Western world.

To achieve the first goal, Volume I begins with a study of melody. The complexities of the traditional four-part "harmony" work have been deferred until step-by-step knowledge of basic pitch organization in two- and three-voice combinations has been introduced. In this way the learning sequence is realistically geared to student comprehension, and a true ordering from simple to complex is realized.

The format of introducing pitch organization through study of counterpoint in these early chapters (9-12) is more akin to the traditions of sixteenth-century contrapuntal teaching than to any other, for the *interval* is the basis of pitch determination. We believe that the teaching of counterpoint *as a compositional discipline* is more properly within the domain of the composition class than the theory class; in the theory class the work aims more toward comprehension of music than toward demonstrable skill in writing, for the written work is only a means to the more basic and significant goal of understanding. The object of this early introduction to rudimentary counterpoint is not to provide a rigidly disciplined course in contrapuntal skill, but rather to enrich the student's understanding of music.

In these two volumes the different structural elements of music, such as tonality, melody, harmony, texture, and form, are presented as interrelated phenomena without unwarranted emphasis upon the formulation and application of contrived principles. Through this approach, and through his own involvement with *all* of the materials of music, the student develops a wider perspective and a deeper understanding of its organization.

To meet the second goal, an abundance of musical examples accompanies the text of Volumes I and II. These volumes contain more examples from before 1700 and after 1900 than any other basic theory text that is available at this time. There is an emphasis, of course, on the music of the so-called "period of common practice" which is included with the full realization of the significance of this repertoire both to the performing and listening musician.

Materials and Structure of Music I and *II* are designed for a basic music theory curriculum. It is assumed that the materials of the two volumes and accompanying workbooks will be used as the basis for the entire course of study, with the supplementation of melodies for music-reading practice and at least some of the scores for works that are discussed in the texts. Each chapter concludes with suggested *Exercises* designed for the application of information exposed in the text. These *Exercises* are minimal and are intended only as outlines of supplementary work that should be done. Both Workbooks I and II are planned to furnish sufficient materials for a comprehensive course of study, and for maximum efficiency it is highly recommended that they be utilized.

The teacher should by all means plan his use of the texts and workbooks to meet the needs of his own class and his own academic situation. The separate volumes are planned around the thirty-week academic year of a four-semester course, the "freshman and sophomore *theory* classes." The concepts and procedures presented here have been applied successfully in music programs of diverse institutions throughout the United States and Canada.

Some of the chapters might well be dealt with in less than a week of class time, while others conceivably should be granted more time for discussion and assimilation. The experienced teacher should encounter no difficulty in establishing a workable time sequence that will fit the texts and workbooks to the needs of his own classes.

It is intended that Volume I be the basis of a beginning theory program with the primary prerequisites being demonstrable performance skill on an instrument and knowledge of the rudiments of music. Chapter 1 of Volume I is a review of fundamental matters which the music major must know.

Volume II is a logical continuation of Volume I. While Volume I is devoted mainly to the materials of music, Volume II deals more with the organization of these materials. The subjects covered in Volume II represent some departures from the conventional second-year theory text. In addition to the treatment of musical forms, melodic, harmonic, and rhythmic concepts and materials are introduced which exceed the bounds of the "traditional." Their inclusion is essential because the student of music will not be equipped to understand the music of this century if his study is terminated with the materials that were typical of Bach, Mozart, Beethoven, or even Wagner.

These "new" materials are introduced when possible as the extension of matters fundamental to *all* music. For instance, chords are built of intervals: therefore, chords can be constructed of *fourths*, or *seconds* as logically as from thirds, even though the past four hundred years of musical practice might lead one to assume that tertian chords are normative for all music.

There is a shift of basic approach during the final four chapters, a shift necessitated by the fact that the music involved represents a diversity of musical types for which no universal pattern of common practice has been developed. These final chapters are devoted to a systematic and comparative examination of significant musical resources and individual techniques both "old" and "new," with an explanation of the musical logic of each. Though no all-embracing rationale of analysis is offered to elucidate all contemporary music, techniques of analysis and points of view are explained.

We acknowledge the influence, both implicit and explicit, of Hindemith, Schenker, and other twentieth-century writers on our collective efforts.

Finally, we wish to thank all of those who were directly helpful in the preparation of the manuscript and the compilation of musical examples.

THE AUTHORS

There is a certain marvellous order which belongs to the nature of harmony in general; in this order every instrument, to the best of its ability, participates under the direction of that faculty of sense-perception on which they, as well as everything else in music, finally depend.

Aristoxenus
The Harmonics, Book II

MATERIALS
AND
STRUCTURE
OF
MUSIC

1

INTRODUCTION TO
BASIC PROPERTIES
AND NOTATION OF TONE

As performers, listeners, and composers, we deal with patterns of organized sound. Musical sound has four properties: *pitch*, which may be described as high or low: *intensity*, described as loud or soft; *timbre*, or tone quality; and *duration*. In this chapter we shall review some of the important characteristics of two of these properties, pitch and duration.

Characteristics of Rhythm

We often respond to music by tapping our feet, dancing, or snapping our fingers. In doing so we are carried along by a characteristic of rhythm called *pulse*. Rhythmic pulse can be compared to the ticking of a watch or the throbbing of a heartbeat. In a sense, rhythmic pulsations, like heartbeats, indicate "aliveness," and music comes alive through rhythm. We respond easily to rhythmic pulse when it is periodic, or regular. When pulses are not periodic, it is more difficult for us to react or participate through the physical responses mentioned above.

Rhythmic pulses (or beats) are usually grouped (or *metered*) by acknowledging one of a series as a mental accent or "more important" pulse. These groupings are generally made in the form of pairs, or threes, or fours. Any grouping, however, is possible, and units of five, seven, or more beats per group can be found in Western music. Beats, then, are usually regularly recurring pulsations, like the ticks of a metronome, which have a precise speed (tempo). In the three melodies shown as Ex. 1-1a, Ex. 1-1b, and Ex. 1-1c, twelve periodic beats have been grouped differently: first in pairs, second in threes, and third in alternate groups of two and three. Perform the melodies at a moderate tempo (M.M. = 80 per beat) and note that it is through our acknowledgement of accented (strong) beats, as indicated below each melody, that we perceive each successive group.

1

Ex. 1-1.

The particular grouping of beats within a composition is called *meter*. Metric accent is the impetus or inflection created by the accented pulsations of strong beats. Unaccented beats are called *weak beats*. In Ex. 1-1a the ordering of beats creates the pattern *strong–weak* (*S–w*), and the pattern in Ex. 1-1b is *S–w–w*. The irregularity of Ex. 1-1c results from alternate groupings of *S–w* and *S'–w–w*.

Our perception of meter is not limited to the recognition of accented and unaccented beats. In fact, in many compositions meter results more from the grouping of melodic pitches or chords than from the mere ordering of strong and weak beats. To understand better this aspect of rhythm and meter, let us reconsider the term *beat*.

Basic Durations and the Beat

A beat is understood to last until a next beat occurs. But if we imagine beats as instantaneous pulsations or ticks, then it is difficult to view one beat as continuing until the next beat occurs. However, if we regard the beat as only the beginning of a regularly recurring time span, then we can more accurately describe the *total time span* from one beat until the beginning of the next as a *basic duration*. Furthermore, the various durations used in a composition can be related to the *basic duration*. Meter, then, is more accurately described as an *ordering of basic durations* into groups of two, three, or four units per measure, or whatever pattern the composer may wish to establish. Basic duration refers to the time span from the articulation of one beat to the next, and this unit is usually represented in notation by one of the note-values shown in Ex. 1-2.

Ex. 1-2. Basic durational signs (note-values).

Whole note = o   Half note = ♩   Quarter note = ♩   Eighth note = ♪

Sixteenth note = ♪   Thirty-second note = ♪   Sixty-fourth note = ♪

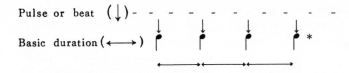

* Basic duration represented here by the quarter note.

We have noted several processes that are involved in creating meter. First a pulse at a particular tempo or speed must be established. And second, the successive beats must be organized into periodic groups, each of which begins with a strong (or mentally accented) pulse.

Meter is a basic kind of rhythm, the rhythm of pulse, or *metric rhythm*. It is important to note, however, that rhythm also occurs in the form of accented and unaccented, long and short durations which organize melodies, accompaniments, chord patterns, and other parts of a musical texture. These varied patterns of duration in most melodies communicate metric organization to the listener. This can be seen in the melody of Ex. 1-3, which is shown without a meter signature. Both the distribution of long and short notes and patterns of durations in threes created by the pitch line, reinforce our notion of a triple meter.

As a rule, then, the structure of a melody (or other parts of a musical texture) confirms the metric organization denoted by the meter signature.

Ex. 1-3a. Beethoven: Symphony No. 3, 1.

(The actual meter signature for the melody in Ex. 1-3 is $\frac{3}{4}$). When a conflict occurs between the accents of melody or chords and the metric accents, *syncopation* results. By notating the melody from Ex. 1-3 in $\frac{2}{4}$ meter, a conflict is created between the implicit triple meter of the melody and the metric accents (S–w) of the notated meter. This is shown in Ex. 1-3b.

Ex. 1-3b. Renotation of Ex. 1-3a.

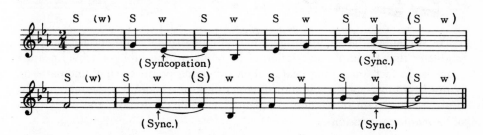

Other factors, too, particularly the placement of high or low notes, or the emphasis created by the use of dynamic accents such as *f* or *szf*, or >, frequently reinforce or agree with metric accents. When they do not, syncopation results.

In Ex. 1-3c dynamic accents (*f*) reinforce the metric organization in measure 1 to the first beat of measure 5; however, the regular pattern of accentuation is broken by syncopation, which is introduced by means of dynamic accents on the third beat of measure 5 and the second beat of measure 6. The particular pattern of displacement used here is commonly called *hemiola*.

Ex. 1-3c. Mozart: Sonata in F Major, K. 332, I.

A further illustration from the same piece noted above reveals displaced accents produced by both dynamic and contoural accents occurring in combination.

Ex. 1-3d. Mozart: Sonata in F Major, K. 332, I.

The strong beat has an importance to rhythmic structure and musical form that is greater than a simple description of its position in a duple or triple measure suggests. In fact, the strong beat is often a rallying point for rhythmic patterns, phrase beginnings, or the initiation of larger musical sections. Furthermore, strong beats are important in relation to cadences, melodic decoration, and many types of harmonic progressions.

Rhythm occurs in many ways. Meter is one form of rhythm in that it involves duration. In addition, any aspect of music that possesses duration, such as successions of pitches that constitute a melody, the duration of a chord, the time span occupied by a clarinet solo, or the total duration of a large section of a symphonic movement, creates rhythm. It is the coordinate activity of both large and small levels of musical action that produces the total effect of rhythm in music.

Meter Signatures; Establishing the Basic Duration's Length and Grouping

The rate at which basic durations occur is usually indicated by a word such as Allegro (fast) or Adagio (slow) or other descriptive words. Since these terms, which are generally chosen from Italian, French, German, or English, are not precise, composers also often assign a metronome marking. The metronome is a clocklike instrument which divides the minute into a precise number of beats ranging from thirty to two hundred. By indicating a metronome speed (M.M. = 120, or M.M. = 80),[1] the composer can set the desired tempo accurately for performers.

The *number* of *basic durations per measure* is shown as the upper part of the *meter signature*. The lower part, a number such as 2, 4, or 8, represents the *basic duration*.[2] For example, the number 2 represents a half note; 4, a quarter note; and 8 indicates that eighth notes equal the basic duration. Meter signatures whose upper numbers are 1, 2, 3, or 4 are called *simple* meters. The prevailing note-values in simple meters generally represent divisions or multiples of the basic duration by two, four, or eight. The conductor's beat patterns for duple, triple, and quadruple simple meters are shown in the diagram of simple meters below.

An interpretation of the meter signature is often subject to the tempo. For example, a fast simple triple measure such as $\frac{3}{4}$, Allegro molto, may be interpreted or conducted "in one," in other words, with one main pulsation (divided by three equal sub-pulses) per measure. And a duple or quadruple meter may be performed "in one," or "in two." By the same token, an extremely slow simple measure may be divided into twice as many beats as are indicated by the signature, where to do so facilitates the performance.

	Duple	Triple	Quadruple
Usual Number of Beats per Measure	2	3	4
Common Basic Durations	♩ ; ♪ ; ♪	♩ ; ♪ ; ♪	♩ ; ♪ ; ♪
Grouping of Strong (S) and weak (w) beats	S w	S w w	S w S w
Conducting Patterns	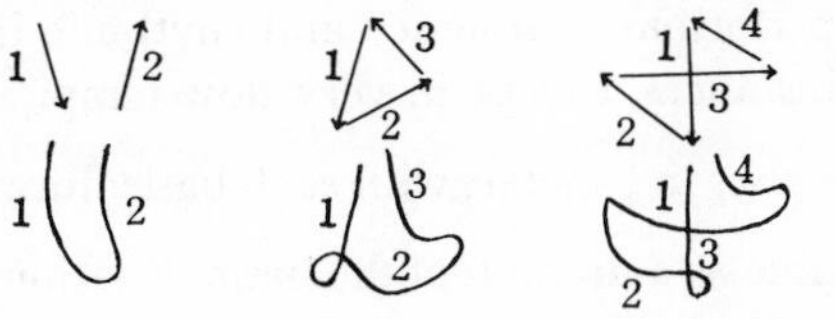		

---

[1] M.M. stands for *Maelzel's metronome*.
[2] We shall note important exceptions to these statements when we study *compound meters*.

Compound Meter

We have noted that the common divisions and multiples of the basic duration in simple meters are duple. Since in a simple meter the division of the basic duration by three (the triplet) is not a usual one, it is generally shown by writing a *3*

above the beam, or by a bracketed *3* above the stems 𝅘𝅥𝅮 𝅘𝅥𝅮 𝅘𝅥𝅮 if a beam is not used.

In contrast to simple meters, triple divisions of the basic duration are common to meters called *compound* meters.

Compound meters, those calling for a triple division of the basic duration, have a *dotted note* as the basic duration, as shown here:

(Common)	*Basic Durations in Compound Meters*	and their	*Normal Divisions*
	𝅗𝅥.		𝅘𝅥𝅮𝅘𝅥𝅮𝅘𝅥𝅮
	𝅘𝅥𝅮.		𝅘𝅥𝅯𝅘𝅥𝅯𝅘𝅥𝅯
	𝅗𝅥.		𝅘𝅥 𝅘𝅥 𝅘𝅥
	𝅘𝅥𝅮.		𝅘𝅥𝅰𝅘𝅥𝅰𝅘𝅥𝅰

Compound meters, like simple meters, are called duple, triple, or quadruple, depending on the number of basic pulses per measure. The family of compound

meters can be shown as $\dfrac{2,\ 3,\ or\ 4}{X}$ 𝅗𝅥., 𝅘𝅥𝅮. 𝅗𝅥. , 𝅘𝅥𝅮. with the upper numbers

signifying the number of beats per measure and *X* representing any of the basic durations shown above (as dotted notes).

Meter signatures for compound time are actually representations of the first (or primary) *division* of the basic duration, rather than the number of main pulses and basic duration, as in simple meter signatures. For example, a common compound meter signature is $\frac{6}{8}$. This signature would seem to denote a meter of six basic durations per measure, each of whose value equaled the eighth note. While such an interpretation can be made, it does not present an accurate picture of general performance practice and rhythmic interpretation. This is true because in most instances, except in very slow tempi, performers acknowledge two, not six, main

pulses in $\frac{6}{8}$ meter, with each basic duration as 𝅘𝅥., (or its equivalent) and the eighth

note as a division of the basic duration. Read the melody that follows and note the analysis of its rhythm shown below.

Ex. 1-4.

Note the essential grouping of each measure into *two* main pulses (duple). The eighth notes divide each basic duration by three and are in fact a division of the basic beat rather than a primary level of accent. Only those eighths that fall as the first or fourth (eighths) of a measure correspond with the main accents of the measure. It can be seen that the signature $\frac{6}{8}$, which accounts for the total number of eighths that occur in a measure of $\frac{6}{8}$ meter, actually refers to a grouping that results from dividing each basic duration by three, thereby producing a total of six eighths (or their equivalent). Six-eight meter could be more effectively shown as $\frac{2}{♩.}$, and has been by some composers.

If we apply the same reasoning to other compound meters we note that $\frac{9}{8}$ is a triple compound meter, easily grasped as $\frac{3}{♩.}$, and $\frac{12}{8}$ is a quadruple meter understood as $\frac{4}{♩.}$. Any dotted note can serve as the basic duration for a compound meter.

The most common compound meter signatures are grouped below:

♩. = basic duration

$\frac{6}{8}\left(\frac{2}{♩.}\right)$ $\frac{9}{8}\left(\frac{3}{♩.}\right)$ $\frac{12}{8}\left(\frac{4}{♩.}\right)$

♪. = basic duration

$\frac{6}{16}\left(\frac{2}{♪.}\right)$ $\frac{9}{16}\left(\frac{3}{♪.}\right)$ $\frac{12}{16}\left(\frac{4}{♪.}\right)$

♩. = basic duration

$\frac{6}{4}\left(\frac{2}{♩.}\right)$ $\frac{9}{4}\left(\frac{3}{♩.}\right)$ $\frac{12}{4}\left(\frac{4}{♩.}\right)$

Subdivisions of the Basic Duration

Although the primary division of the main pulse in compound time is usually triple, the *subdivisions* of the basic duration, that is, divisions of the primary division, are generally *duple*. Triple subdivisions of the basic duration are called *irregular*, as are triple divisions of the beat in simple meter. The first four measures of the melody in Ex. 1-5 contain regular (duple) subdivisions of the basic duration, while the second four measures illustrate both regular and irregular subdivisions. An analysis of the rhythmic content of the example shows:

basic duration = ♩.   primary division = ♪♪♩

regular sub-division = ♫♫♩ ♫♫♩

irregular sub-division = ♫♫♩ ♫♫♩

Ex. 1-5.

Moderato

Notation of Rhythm

Notating rhythm involves the use of the following symbols: 1) a note-head ○ , ● , that is written on the line or space of the pitch to be expressed; 2) a note-stem | , (for all durations except whole notes) which is formed by a straight line that joins the note-head at the left or right, depending upon the location of the note-head on the staff[3] ♩ , ♪ ; 3) a flag ♪ , which joins the note-stem at the farthest point from the note-head ♪ , or double, triple, or quadruple flags ♪ ♪ ♪ , depending on the duration desired. Flags are frequently replaced by beams ♪ ♪ = ♫ , which are used to join series of similar durations that would normally employ flags.

Beamed notes are associated primarily with instrumental notation, while the use of flagged notes is indigenous to vocal music, where the flag is used for notating tones that occur with single syllables of text, as shown in Ex. 1-6.

---

[3] If the note-head is located above the third line of the staff, its stem usually points down, or hangs below the note-head. The opposite is true when the note-head is written below the third line.

Ex. 1-6. Schubert: *Frühlingssehnsucht.*

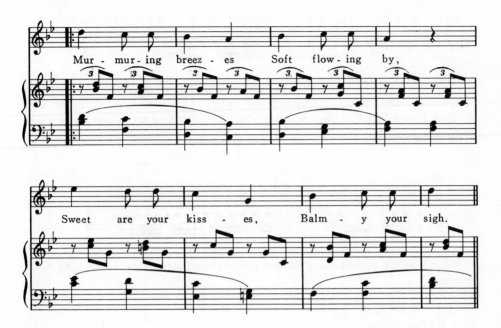

Flags are always used for isolated notes or where single durations of an eighth note or less are preceded or followed by quarter, half, or whole notes (or their equivalent rests). See Ex. 1-7.

Ex. 1-7.

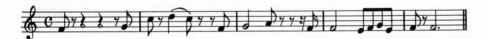

Beams help the reader to group note patterns according to basic durations. In the first group of patterns shown in Ex. 1-8, the location of beats has been obscured by illogical beaming.

Ex. 1-8.

In Ex. 1-9 the same patterns are beamed in groups that reveal the meter's beat structure.

Ex. 1-9.

A general guide for notation is to avoid beaming more than six notes together, unless more are needed to consume the equivalent of one basic duration; and further, beams begin *on the beat* unless the notes they join are preceded by a rest sign.

Ex. 1-10.

When possible, avoid mixing flagged and beamed notes, except in notating vocal music.

Ex. 1-11.

Rests

Absence of tone is indicated by *rests*, and each of the basic durations discussed earlier has an equivalent rest symbol. Rest equivalents for each basic duration are shown as Ex. 1-12.

Ex. 1-12. Basic durations and their rest equivalents.

Note - value	Rest	Name
		Breve (or double whole-note)
		Whole note
		Half note
		Quarter note
		Eighth note
		Sixteenth note

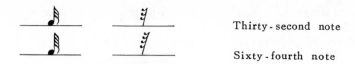

Thirty-second note

Sixty-fourth note

Rests may be used in the same situations as their corresponding note-values, with the following exceptions:

1. Rests are never tied.
2. Half-note rests are not used in $\frac{3}{4}$ meter.
3. The whole-note rest may be used for convenience to indicate a full measure rest in any meter, except in those meters in which the whole note is equal to less than a complete measure's duration.
4. The notation of rests, like note-values, should permit clear understanding of the metric organization.

Ex. 1-13 clarifies the use of rests.

Ex. 1-13.

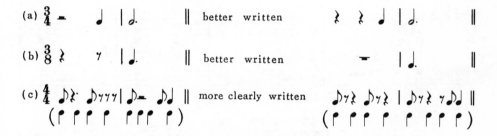

Augmentation Dots, Ties and Slurs

The *augmentation dot* (·), placed immediately after a note-head ($\lozenge$.), extends the duration of the note by one half of its normal duration. This means that $\lozenge \quad \lozenge$ could also be written as $\lozenge$.. Augmentation dots are not used if they would prolong a note into the next measure ($\frac{3}{4}$ $\lozenge$ $\lozenge$.). In such a situation, and where a continuation of sound between two notes of the same pitch is sought, *ties* are used. The *tie* is a curved line which connects two notes of *identical* pitch:

The tie should not be confused with the *slur*, which is used to indicate a smooth connection of two notes of *different* pitch:

Ex. 1-14 illustrates several notational signs and principles of clear notating.

Ex. 1-14. Beethoven: Sonata for Violin and Piano, Op. 23, II.

Notation of Pitch

Pitch results from the sustained, periodic vibrations of a flexible body such as a string, a column of air, or a vocal cord. Pitch is indicated by symbols, most familiarly the first seven letters of the alphabet, *a b c d e f* and *g*. These letter-names represent the different lines and spaces on the five-line staff:[4]

By itself the musical staff is meaningless. However, by placing a *clef sign* at its left edge, a specific letter-named pitch is designated for each line and space. The *treble* clef sign is actually an elaborate script *G* that designates the pitch g^1 on the second line of the staff.

Ex. 1-15. Notes on the staff in the treble clef.

The *bass* clef specifies the note *f* for the fourth line of the staff.

---

[4] For example, the tone that results from a vibration rate (frequency) of 440 vibrations per second (v.p.s.) is known as a^1.

Ex. 1-16. Notes on the staff in the bass clef.

F   G   A   B   C   F   E   D   C   B   A   G   F   E

The question may arise as to the need for more than one clef. If our musical system were limited to only seven or so pitches, there would be no such need. However, the capabilities of hearing are such that a broad range of pitches has been used in most Western music. Consequently, a number of clefs are used, each employed to represent pitches in particular areas of the pitch spectrum, or *gamut*.

The gamut of pitches most used in music is shown in Ex. 1-17, which illustrates the "Great" staff.

Ex. 1-17. The "Great" staff.

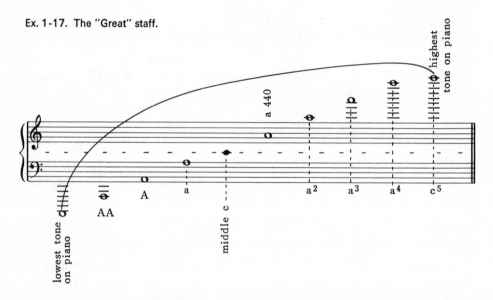

The midpoint of this staff, which joins or links the treble and bass clefs, is a broken line that represents middle *c*, or *c*^{1}. Added line segments above or below either staff are called *ledger lines*, and they are used to notate pitches which lie beyond the staff area of a particular clef.

Although the treble and bass clefs are most used, other clefs are needed for the notation of some music. They are known as "movable clefs," or as the "family of *c* clefs." Using these *c* clefs, it is possible to assign middle *c* to any line of the staff. Four *c* clefs are shown in Ex. 1-18.[5]

---

[5] The two *c* clefs most often found are those that place *c*^{1} on the third and fourth lines of the staff. These are the alto and tenor clefs, and they are used for the notation of parts for alto and tenor instruments (or voices) such as the viola, cello, and trombone. They are also frequently employed as a basis for instrumental transposition.

Ex. 1-18.

Musicians have developed a useful terminology for pinpointing the various pitches of the gamut. This amounts to grouping the pitches of the pitch spectrum into seven-note segments, called "octave segments." Each segment begins with a *C* and includes all possible pitches between *C* and the *B* seven notes above. With the addition of the two tones below the lowest *C* (*CC*) on the piano, *AAA* and *BBB* (the partial segment called "Sub-contra"), the different seven-tone segments are named *Contra* (*CC-BB*), *Great* (*C-B*), *small* (*c-b*), *prime* or 1 (c' or c^1—b' or b^1), *double prime* or 2 (c'' or c^2—b'' or b^2), *triple prime* or 3 (c''' or c^3—b''' or b^3), *quadruple prime* or 4 (c'''' or c^4—b'''' or b^4). The highest note on the piano begins the five prime segment, c''''', or c^5. This nomenclature is illustrated in notation as Ex. 1-19.

Ex. 1-19. The seven-tone segments of the pitch spectrum.

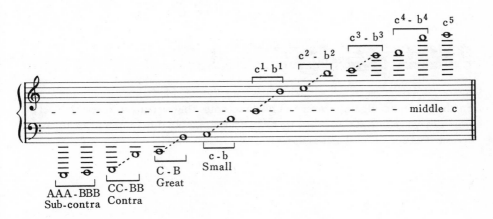

Accidentals

Any of the notes of the gamut may be preceded by accidentals. Sharps (♯) or flats (♭), double sharps (✖) or double flats (♭♭) are placed immediately before the note-head and indicate slight pitch modifications. Sharps indicate a raising of the natural note by one half-step, while flats indicate that the natural note is to be lowered a half-step. Similarly, double sharps indicate a raising of the note by two half-steps, and double flats are used to lower the note by two half-steps.

Natural signs (♮) are used to cancel previous sharps or flats. Proper use of all accidentals may be found in Ex. 1-20.

Ex. 1-20. Correct use of accidentals.

Accidentals are understood to continue throughout the measure in which they appear without being rewritten. Therefore, all of the notated *f*'s appearing in Ex. 1-21 should be performed as *f-sharps*.

Ex. 1-21.

Furthermore, accidentals govern only those notes that occur on the pitch level at which they are introduced; they do not affect pitches in different octaves. A more precise notation of Ex. 1-22a is shown in Ex. 1-22b.

Ex. 1-22.

Intervals

An interval is the spatial relation or gap between two pitches. Numbers are used to describe the total number of letter names encompassed by any two pitches. Thus a fourth denotes an interval that spans four different letter names of the staff; for example, *c'* up to *f'* spans four letter names, *c' d' e'* and *f'*, and *a'* down to *e'* spans four letter names, *a' g' f'* and *e'*. Intervals may be described as *melodic*, which means successively sounded tones, or *harmonic*, which means sounded together.

Whole-Steps and Half-Steps

The *half-step* is the smallest difference of pitch formally recognized in Western music. The *half-step* interval is easily observed by locating adjacent white keys on the piano. The relation between these pairs of keys, *e-f* and *b-c* is called a *half-step*,[6] a *minor second* (m2), or *semitone*. The relation between pairs of white keys separated by black keys comprises a whole-step, or major second (M2).

Although the numerical name of an interval describes the number of different lines and spaces spanned, and this is easily relatable to the positions of two pitches on the staff, it does not account for the *exact size* of the interval. This can be checked by comparing the sound and total number of whole- and half-steps in each of the

following intervals, both of which are fourths: 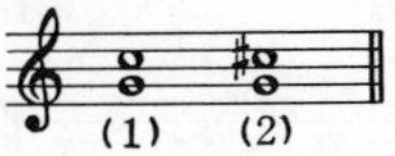 . The first of

these two intervals is one half-step smaller than the second, since it consists of a total of two whole-steps and one half (or five semitones), while the second interval spans three whole-steps (or six semitones). To describe intervals more accurately, musicians use the terms *perfect, major, minor, augmented,* and *diminished.* The abbreviations for these are shown below:

Perfect——P	Augmented——A or (+)
Major——M	diminished——d or (○)
minor——m	

The term *perfect* is applied only to unisons (primes), fourths, fifths, and octaves, while the words *major* and *minor* are applied only to seconds, thirds, sixths, and sevenths. *Augmented* and *diminished* are applied to certain modifications of any type of interval. As a synopsis of the preceding discussion, the following chart may prove useful for reference.

Perfect Intervals	*Major Intervals*	*Minor Intervals*
Octave (8^ve)	Seventh	Seventh
Unison (prime)	Sixth	Sixth
Fifth	Third	Third
Fourth	Second	Second
. . . .	. . . .	. . . .
Enlarged by $^1/_2$ step* becomes *augmented;*	Enlarged by $^1/_2$ step* becomes *augmented;*	Enlarged by $^1/_2$ step* becomes *major;*
Reduced by $^1/_2$ step* becomes *diminished;*	Reduced by $^1/_2$ step* becomes *minor;*	Reduced by $^1/_2$ step* becomes *diminished;*

* Chromatic half-steps.

---

[6] The half-step from *e'-f'* is more accurately called a *diatonic half-step*, which means that different note names are employed in its notation. These same pitches in other instances may be notated as *e'* and *e'* sharp. This notation differentiation calls for using another name, *chromatic half-step*, for a relationship that is identical in sound to that of *e'* and *f'*. By placing sharps or flats in front of notes on the staff, their pitch is raised or lowered by one chromatic half-step. The various available pitches of our musical gamut can be notated different ways, that is, spelled *enharmonically*, and our notational practices are usually determined by specific musical contexts, as we shall note in Chapters 3-8.

Two processes are necessary for the precise identification of any interval. First a generic classification must be made, based on the number of letter-names spanned. This is easily done by noting the relative positions of two notes in terms of lines and/or spaces on the staff. These are illustrated in Ex. 1-23.

Ex. 1-23.

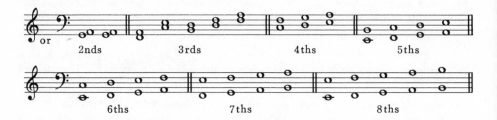

Note that seconds are notated on adjacent lines and spaces; thirds span two lines or two spaces; fourths span two lines and a space or two spaces and a line; fifths span three lines or three spaces; sixths span three spaces and a line or three lines and a space; sevenths span four lines or four spaces; and octaves span four lines and a space or four spaces and a line.

Having determined the generic classification of an interval (as shown in Ex. 1-23), a more precise description, such as *perfect, major, minor, augmented,* or *diminished,* can be made on the basis of the number of whole- and half-steps involved. This is illustrated in Ex. 1-24.

Ex. 1-24.

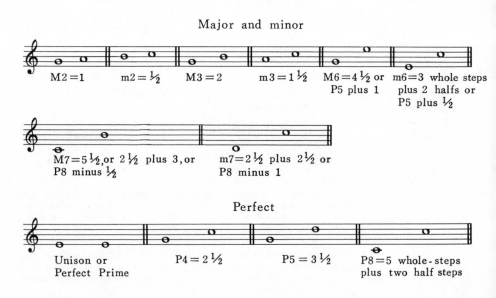

Tritones (TT)

+4 = 3 whole steps

o5 = 2 whole - steps
plus 2 half steps

Exercises

Additional materials are contained in *Materials and Structure of Music I, Workbook,* Chapter 1.

1. Practice drawing treble and bass clef signs.
2. Identify the names of notes written in both clefs, indicating the specific octave (contra, small, 1, 2, etc.) of each note.
3. Locate the different note and rest symbols in a composition.
4. Name the equivalents of different notes in smaller denominations of note-values. For example, how many sixteenths equal a dotted half-note?
5. Correctly rebeam patterns of incorrectly beamed notes.
6. Transcribe a vocal melody of many individually flagged notes into correct instrumental notation.
7. Identify the notes that occur in each part on successive strong beats in Ex. 1-1.
8. Use Ex. 1-14–1-20 for interval identification.
9. Compose eight measures of rhythm in $\frac{2}{4}$ meter, trying to avoid the repetition of any measure's pattern.
10. Make a neat copy of Ex. 1-6.
11. Play any note on the piano (within your voice range) and sing fourths above and below the note played. Apply the same procedure to the practice of other intervals.
12. Write the following intervals above and below g^1:
    P5, M3, m7, °4, +6, m3, M2, P8, °5, M6, °7, M7, +8, m10, +4.
13. Transcribe Example 1-5 into $\frac{6}{16}$ and $\frac{6}{4}$ meters.

2

TONALITY

In Chapter 1 our discussion of meter showed that music can be grouped into regular units of time, or "metered." In this sense the patterns of weak and strong beats form a framework within which groups of tones are organized into rhythms. The total range of pitches we use in music can be ordered in a similar way within still another kind of framework, in this case called *tonality*.

If music were made from only one continuously repeated pitch, the need for such an organizing scheme would not arise; melody would derive its charm from rhythmic play alone. In fact, some very simple music does incorporate a relatively limited set of pitches, thus reducing its attraction primarily to rhythmic motion. The two very primitive melodies of Ex. 2-1 illustrate such a narrow choice of pitch ingredients.

Ex. 2-1. Taulipang melody (after Hornbostel). From Curt Sachs, *The Rise of Music in the Ancient World,* New York: W. W. Norton & Company, Inc.

Ex. 2-2. Uitoto Indian melody (after Bose). From Curt Sachs, *The Rise of Music in the Ancient World,* New York: W. W. Norton & Company, Inc.

It is clear that in each of these melodies one pitch is emphasized so extensively (*a* in melody 1, *c* in melody 2) that it becomes a point of focus around which the other pitches are more or less decorative. Just as all the dots in Ex. 2-3 point to the last dot to the right, all pitches in these simple melodies converge toward one point of focus; in music, this point of focus is called the *tonic*, or center of tonality.

Ex. 2-3.

In the melody of Ex. 2-1 the pitch *a* is stressed, for it is both the beginning and ending pitch, as well as the pitch of longest duration. The numerous *g-sharps* clearly perform a more decorative role as pitch filigrees related to their more basic neighbors, the *a*'s.

The melody of Ex. 2-2 is organized with *c* as its tonic, or focal pitch. *C* is heard first and last, and it is heard more often than its two associates, *b* and *a*. In other words, *c* is dwelt upon as a kind of home base, a frequent point of departure and return during the course of the melodic unfolding.

These examples are simpler in structure than the melodies that we associate with our Western musical heritage. By our melodic standards they are a bit dull in terms of pitch resources, and they move within a pitch range that is narrowly restricted. (The wider melody of Ex. 2-2 covers a span of only a minor third, *a'—c''*.) Nonetheless, the more complicated melodies of our own musical tradition reveal identical principles of organization. Note the repetitions and other kinds of emphases that create the tonality of the melodies in Ex. 2-4.

Ex. 2-4a. German folksong.

Ex. 2-4b. Irish folksong.

Ex. 2-4c. Gregorian Chant: Responsorium, *Libera me* (first two phrases).

The melodic excerpt of Ex. 2-5 begins and ends with the same pitch, *f'*. But unlike the simpler melodies of Ex. 2-1, 2-2, and 2-3, this melody does not confirm its first and last pitch by frequent repetitions, nor does the tonic have excessively greater durations than other pitches. And yet, the melody does not require a full playing to convince us that *f* is the tonic pitch.

Ex. 2-5. Mozart: Sonata in F, K. 332, I.

This leads us to the conclusion that something about tones in a melody—in addition to accents or durations or repetitions or position as first or last or lowest or highest—can create this element of pitch-focus in melody. This further potential source of tonality lies in the interval relations formed between the tones of a melody. In their movement in time, the various pitches create a tonal *framework*, a kind of "floor and ceiling," within which the melodic parts will all sound as related elements of the tonal design. Some pitches are basic to this framework like the beams of a house, while others are more important as decorative overlay.

In the Mozart melody of Ex. 2-5 the longer and metrically stressed notes seem more important to the overall contour of the whole melody. The first pitch, *f'*, is the beginning of the melodic pattern; it performs the vital function of "leading the listener" into the melodic organization. Here the composer's problem is similar to that of the painter who wishes to compose an effective picture: both must immediately attract the attention of an audience and, at the same time, ensure that this first attraction is the beginning of a comprehensible pattern.

To achieve this immediate goal the painter usually organizes color and line in a way that ensures focal points within his canvas. Regardless of which area of the painting we look at first, we are always led into the picture plane (if it is a successful painting) by the arrangements of lines and forms and colors. A clear illustration of this attention-focusing can be seen in the reproduction shown in Ex. 2-6 and the analysis of linear forces that reveals this painting's main scheme of organization.

The composer ushers the listener into a suitable framework of pitch reference—the "auditory picture-plane"—by beginning his music with patterns which establish clearly the kind of frame he desires. One of these potential frames of reference in melody is tonality. Melodies which begin with a downbeat pattern most frequently begin with the pitch that is to serve as tonic, while melodies which begin with an upbeat figure frequently begin with some other pitch, then move to the tonic without delay, usually on the first strong beat.[1]

---

[1] Our discussion here pertains only to melodies which do exhibit the property of tonality. Some melodies are not *tonal* in this sense.

Ex. 2-6.

The Last Supper, Leonardo da Vinci. European Art Color, Peter Adelberg, N.Y.C.

DIRECTIONAL FORCES OF MAIN LINES

Regardless of the relation of the first pitch to the melody's tonality, the first few pitches usually make clear all or a part of the pitch framework that will serve as a basis for the remainder of the melody.

Ex. 2-7a. The National Anthem.

Ex. 2-7b. *Comin' Round the Mountain.*

Ex. 2-7c. Italian folksong.

The idea of a pitch framework within which the tones of a melody are organized has still another facet. Notice that the metric stress we associate with the f^2 of measure 5 of the Mozart melody (Ex. 2-8) invites us to accept this pitch as an important point of arrival within the whole melody. It acts as the basic high point of melodic motion. Though actually higher, the g^2 of measure 3 is rhythmically less forceful and thus sounds like a mere upper neighbor to the more important f^2 that arrives in measure 5.

Ex. 2-8. Mozart: Sonata in F, K. 332, I.

The pitch f' forms the bottom of the pitch framework of this melody, and so the Mozart melody is essentially a pitch line that forms a path from f' up to f^2, then returns to its original point of departure as shown in Ex. 2-5. Its framework of activity is

For this reason alone, *f* assumes an important function within this succession of tones. This particular framework, combined as it is with *f* as the first and last pitches of the melody, creates a tonality that unmistakably bears *f* as its tonic. We shall refer to this relationship, formed by the tonic and the highest and lowest *structural pitches* of a melody, as the *tonality frame*.

Pitch Roots

Within a melody certain special groupings of pitches can confirm or deny a particular pitch as tonic. Just as the words "I am going home" take on a quite different meaning when rearranged to the order "Am I going home?" so the tonality of a melody is affected by the way in which pitches follow one another and by the rhythms they form. Although both melody (a) and (b) below contain the same pitch materials, they represent different "tonal meanings" because they are organized in ways which make *C* the tonic for the first melody, *F* the tonic for the second.

Ex. 2-9.

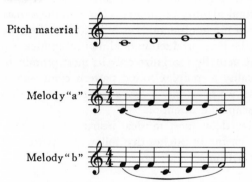

Furthermore, the metric frame affects tonality by imposing a sense of accent on some pitches. By reorganizing the same pitch successions used in Ex. 2-9, we can create different focal points through metric and durational means alone.

Ex. 2-10.

But in addition to these causes of pitch significance, the particular intervals formed between pitches, sounded in succession or simultaneously, produce qualitative effects that influence tonal structure.

The octave has the unusual quality of sounding like the same pitch duplicated at different high-low levels. It is this peculiar effect that leads us to repeat note names of tones at every octave of the musical staff, so that the thirteenth note of any chromatic series always has the same name as the first. For instance, if at the piano we begin with any key and play every successive white and black key, the thirteenth key will always have the same note name as the beginning key.

Ex. 2-11. Octaves.

Other intervals share this quality of pitch identity in lesser degrees than the octave; the octave is the only interval to bear notes of the same name. A clear representation of the decreasing mutual identity of pitches is found in the *overtone* or *harmonic series*. This natural order of pitches functions as a part of our hearing process, and it operates as a part of the tone production of almost all musical instruments. When we hear a tone, we actually recognize only its most prominent characteristic, for the "tone" is in reality a complex sound pattern composed of several different elements. In a sense, we hear only a *generalized tone*, for the less obvious features of its constitution escape our attention.[2]

A tone *D*, for example, when played on most musical instruments, is really only the most prominent part of a scheme of pitches that follows the pattern of overtones illustrated in Ex. 2-12, the *natural harmonic series*.

Ex. 2-12. Harmonic series on D.

Fewer or more parts (or *partials*, as these accompanying sounds are called) are present in the make-up of a tone, depending upon what instrument produces it. A violin normally produces a tone that contains more partials above its fundamental pitch than a saxophone or a flute. But the pattern is duplicated in a greater

---

[2] With training one can learn to recognize some of these other parts of a tone that lie higher in pitch than the note by which we name it.

or lesser fashion by any musical instrument,[3] and except for unusual cases, we recognize only the lowest (or *fundamental*) as *the pitch* of the tone. These additional members of the harmonic series affect the qualitative aspects of instrumental and vocal tone, controlling the *tone color* or *timbre* by their presence or absence and relative strength.

This pattern of pitch relations represented in the harmonic series is imposed upon our every experience of musical tone, and its particular formation (the way the various parts are ordered in relation to one another) has many interesting parallels in the world of sound. The harmonic series of a single tone is itself a kind of "pitch framework," for the fundamental member of the series serves as a nucleus, or *tonic*, for all of its accompanying parts.

We have already noted the unique quality of the octave, the way its separate parts fit together in a relationship that suggests a mutual identity; for this reason the two parts even bear identical note names. The second interval that occurs in the harmonic series after the octave, the *perfect fifth*, shares this mutual identity of its parts to a lesser degree. It is not difficult to hear this interval as two separate pitches, even when played simultaneously. But next to the octave, the fifth is the simplest of all pitch relationships. It is not so simple as to sound like a single tone, but it is simple enough to create a strong effect of tonal focus, this quality causing its lower tone to act as the fundamental pitch of the interval.

Ex. 2-13. Pitch roots.

The first five partials of the harmonic series create five different intervals, including the perfect octave and the perfect fifth.

Ex. 2-14. First five partials and intervals.

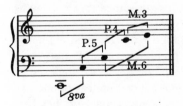

Since the fundamental pitch of the harmonic series is the focal point for the whole pattern, *the root pitch for any one of these intervals is the fundamental pitch of its series.* This means that if we hear one of these intervals apart from any extraneous

---

[3] Only pure tones contain one simple pitch element, and they are quite rare in music.

context, we tend to regard *the fundamental of the series to which the interval belongs as the interval's root.* Whether the interval is melodic (successive) or harmonic (simultaneous), each of these intervals implies a root that can operate in melody. When combined with rhythms, these interval relations create a pitch framework of melodic organization.

The intervals in Ex. 2-15 are arranged in pairs according to their *inversion properties.* Note that turning each interval upside down produces its inversion complement: the inversion of the perfect fifth is the perfect fourth; the inversion of the major third is the minor sixth; and the inversion of the major sixth is the minor third. This similarity is also revealed in the common root that each interval of the pairs shares with its inversion.

This root property of musical tones can best be illustrated by separating each of the five elementary intervals and showing their separate root effects.

Ex. 2-15. Interval roots.

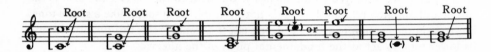

We should remember that this root effect operates with more force for the octave, the perfect fifth, and the perfect fourth than for any other intervals. Implied within the harmonic series itself is a set of dwindling relationships to a fundamental pitch; the higher in the series an interval appears for the first time, the weaker is its root effect.[4] The roots of intervals that lie above the fifth partial become increasingly negligible. For this reason, melodies that span a range of less than a perfect fifth or perfect fourth rely most heavily upon rhythmic details (such as repetition, duration, and accent) to produce an effect of pitch focus.

As can be seen in Ex. 2-15, even the major sixth and minor third are subject to two possible root analyses, depending upon their position within a group of tones. As isolated intervals, the first root possibility is more probable, but in a musical context, melodic emphasis on the upper tone of the major sixth or on the lower tone of the minor third can impart to those tones a significance that outweighs their intervallic effect alone.

Western music since the Renaissance has for the most part consisted of chords comprising fifths, fourths, thirds, and sixths in a way that creates a larger harmonic unit than the mere interval. Called *triad,* this unit can consist (as we shall see in Chapter 14) of any three different pitches which are not octave replicas of one another. Four kinds of triads are of special importance, however, because they best represent harmonic content and melodic configuration in a preponderance of traditional music.

---

[4] Other intervals, such as seconds, sevenths, and tritones, occur less prominently in the harmonic series and exhibit far weaker root effect.

These special kinds of triads are called *major, minor, diminished, and augmented,* the name of each derived from the principal intervals which form them. Each is illustrated below with notations which make clear their most salient features.

Ex. 2-16.

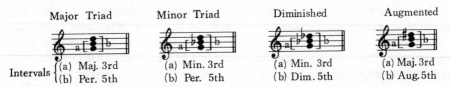

Major Triad	Minor Triad	Diminished	Augmented
Intervals { (a) Maj. 3rd (b) Per. 5th	(a) Min. 3rd (b) Per. 5th	(a) Min. 3rd (b) Dim. 5th	(a) Maj. 3rd (b) Aug. 5th

We shall return for a more detailed study of these four triad types when we discuss three-voice textures. For the present we shall confine our attention to the way two of these—the major and the minor—play a principal role in tonal music by providing a direct means for establishing pitch focus within a collection of different tones.

Interval Quality and Melodic Organization

Returning to the Mozart excerpt of Ex. 2-5 (page 22), we can now see other reasons for the importance of *f* as the tonic.

Ex. 2-17. Mozart: Sonata in F, K. 332, I.

From its first skip, this melody traces a pattern that reinforces *f* as tonic; each new tone of the entire first two measures confirms this relationship to *f* as root tone, therein establishing the F major triad as the tonal basis for the entire melody (*f–a–c*).

Ex. 2-18. Analyses of Ex. 2-17.

These inner relationships within the pitch framework of *f'—c²* pre-establish the basis for this melody's pitch organization. After the first two bars any digressions (such as the *b-flats* and *e*'s of measures 3 and 4) are heard as subservient *in their*

relations to f as tonic. And then the return of *f* in the seventh measure is like the closing of a full circle, for it comes as the return and reconfirmation of the fundamental pitch from which the melody originated.

Other melodies reveal these same characteristics of pitch organization to lesser or greater degrees. The relative simplicity or complexity of any melody is determined to a great extent by the clarity with which the various pitches have been organized in relation to a tonic. Some simple songs of widespread use—hymns, communal songs, children's play chants, and the like—are even more tenacious than the Mozart example in their adherence to a tonic. (Sing through the first six measures of "America" for such an example.) More complicated melodies are comparatively vague as pitch organizations around a tonic, avoiding rhythm and pitch patterns that could confirm and intensify the focal role of any single pitch.

Sing or play through the melodies of Ex. 2-19, which illustrate this less definite kind of pitch organization in melody.

Melody (a) is slightly ambiguous because the initial *C* is not strongly reinforced by interval relations with other pitches or by frequent repetition. After early emphasis (by repetition at the octave and the fifth-fourth formed by *G* in between) no pattern confirms this opening pitch as tonic with any degree of conclusiveness.

Ex. 2-19a. Hindemith: *Theme and Four Variations.* (C) 1947 by B. Schott's Soehne, Mainz. Reprinted by permission.

Melody (b) represents a different kind of problem, for here it is possible to find two plausible tonics, *B-flat* and *F.* The numerous soundings of *F* draw our attention to it as a possible reference pitch, but *B-flat* also is very much in evidence. *B-flat* is the intended tonality (we know this because of what happens in the remainder of the piece and by the accompanying harmonies!), but the patterns of the first few measures of melody alone are not decisive in establishing this pitch as tonic.

Ex. 2-19b. J.S. Bach: Fugue in B-flat Major (*Well-tempered Clavier,* Book I).

Melody (c) is similar to (b), for again there is some question about pitch focus. Is it *B-flat* Mixolydian or is it *E-flat* major? Heard with Mozart's accompaniment there would be little question, for *E-flat* dominates the harmonic structure of the first measure. But removed from its context, this short melody dwells on *B-flat*

to such an extent that even the perfect fourths of *B-flat—E-flat* (mm. 1 and 3) do not convince us that *E-flat* is tonic. Only with the entrance of *A-flat*, with its resolution to *G*, in the final pattern, is *B-flat* made an *improbable* tonic. Once we have heard this melody through measures 3 and 4 it is easier to hear the beginning tones within a framework that has *E-flat* as its tonic, supported by *B-flat* as its upper fifth.

Ex. 2-19c. Mozart: Sonata in E-flat Major, K. 282, I.

When rhythmic and intervallic emphases of a particular pitch are combined in melody, a sense of organization results where aimless, random successions of tones might otherwise prevail. The effect of randomness—without a sense of tonality— can be engaging, for musical tone by itself can be an object of beauty. Tonality provides one of several means of tonal organization (meter is only one other) whereby form can be imposed upon the musical experience. When we sing, play, or listen to music, tonality is one of the most important form-giving elements, helping us to orient our tonal "thoughts" into comprehensible images. We shall learn about other agents of musical organization as our study progresses, but of all those pertinent to the musical experience, tonality is perhaps the most intrinsic to musical tone. It certainly is one of the most crucial in music produced prior to the early twentieth century.

We can isolate five simple questions that are important to any decision about the tonality of a melody. Your study of any particular melody should begin with the answers to each of these questions.

1. Does the melody seem to possess pitch focus or is this property absent? (An affirmative answer makes the following relevant.)
2. What is the last pitch, and what is the first pitch of rhythmic importance (because of metric position or greater duration or both).
3. Is any pitch made prominent because of its frequent occurrence, or its several repetitions, or because of its relatively greater durations and stresses?
4. What intervals occur during the first patterns of pitch motion, and what is their common or most emphasized root, if any?
5. Does the contour of the melody appear to form a frame of activity that is separated by an octave or a perfect fifth, or another interval that could represent a simple tonality frame?

Many melodies incorporate at least three of the above strategies for establishing a tonic, others no more than two, and still others utilize all four. It is the basic problem of the performer and listener to recognize the various clues of pitch ordering, these to serve as guides for musical understanding. Three melodies of relatively simple pitch structure are shown below, each accompanied by its tonality frame. Sing or play each melody, then see how you can justify the tonality frame shown for it.

Ex. 2-20a. Pergolesi.

Tonality frame

Tonic

Ex. 2-20b. Hungarian folksong.

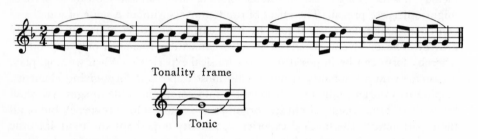

Tonality frame

Tonic

Ex. 2-20c. Scotch folksong: *My Bonnie Lies Over the Ocean.*

Tonality frame

Tonic

Exercises

See Chapter 2 of *Materials and Structure of Music I, Workbook* for more detailed work.

1. Using only the given prescription, write a short melody that fulfills each of the following:

A) Tonality, F: Meter, $\frac{3}{4}$: Pitches:

B) Tonality, A: Meter, C: Pitches:

C) Tonality, E flat: Meter, $\frac{2}{4}$: Pitches:

D) Tonality, D: Meter, $\frac{2}{4}$: Pitches:

E) Tonality, C: Meter, $\frac{6}{8}$: Pitches:

2. a) Find five melodies which exhibit a tonality frame of an octave, tonic to tonic.
   b) Find five melodies which exhibit a tonality frame of an octave, dominant to dominant.
   c) Find five melodies which exhibit a tonality frame of only a fifth, from tonic to dominant.
   d) Find three melodies which in your opinion do not possess tonality.
3. At random, choose relatively simple melodies from a sight-singing collection. Analyze each melody for tonality frame and the relations (step or skip) of all other pitches within the melody to that frame. Then sing the melody.

3

KEY, MODE, AND SCALE

Closely related to the tonality framework discussed in Chapter 2 are the key systems and scales of traditional music. Although pitch focus can be produced with tones in many different ways, the music of Western tradition has developed its own characteristic methods.

We commonly speak of a composition as being "in the key of *C* major" or "in the key of *B-flat* minor." In such statements we establish a relationship between particular pitches of focus (*C* and *B-flat* respectively) and particular patterns of notes (major and minor scales). In other words, *key* combines the factors of tonic and scale.

Many different kinds of scales can be abstracted from music: There are "Hungarian Scales," pentatonic scales, whole-tone scales, chromatic scales, gapped scales, symmetrical scales, and so on, each of which has a unique combination of notes that sets it off from any other. Any one of these scales is nothing more than a particular ordering of notes that can form the basis for the pitch patterns of music. For the present we shall confine our attention to only a few types.

If we extract all of the notes from the Mozart melody quoted in Chapter 2 (Ex. 2-5), then order them in succession following the tonic pitch of the melody (*F*), the result is *the scale* that serves as the pitch basis for this melody; it represents the pitches which are used to fill in the span between the outer limits of the tonality frame, f^1 to f^2.

Ex. 3-1. Mozart: Sonata in F, K. 332, I.

The result of this abstraction is what we call the *major scale of F*.

Any series of pitches that duplicates the same pattern of successive intervals—1, 1, $^1/_2$, 1, 1, 1, $^1/_2$—is a major scale. (The number 1 represents a whole-step, $^1/_2$

represents a half-step.) The note combinations of Ex. 3-2 contain five patterns which are major, five which are not. Check those which are not (√).

Ex. 3-2.

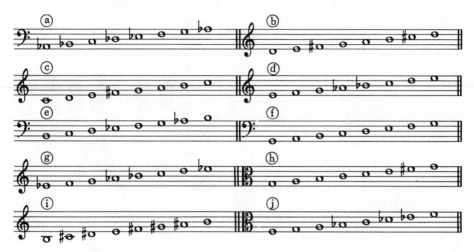

We can transpose[1] each of the scales shown in Ex. 3-2 so that the pattern of intervals remains the same but the initial note is always *c'*. In this way the similarities and the differences in the various arrangements become more apparent.

Ex. 3-3.

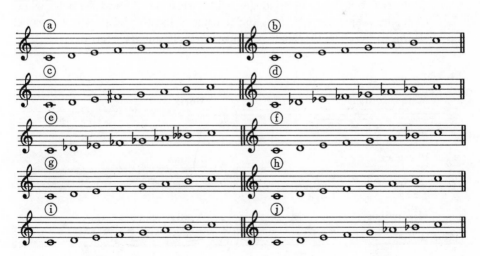

Each of the scales in Ex. 3-3 is a "*C* scale," although half do not qualify as "major scales."

---

[1] *Transpose* literally means to "change position." In music it refers to a change of pitch level. Thus, any series of notes can be transposed if the series is kept intact but changed to a higher or lower pitch register.

Our literature of music reveals that certain arrangements of pitches have been most favored by composers during the past several hundred years, and for this reason we shall pay particular attention to these. We might note in passing that our musical staff, with its alternating lines and spaces, and the black and white key-pattern of the piano both have a simple relationship with the *C* major scale pattern.

Ex. 3-4.

Thus a scale of all successive notes beginning on *C* and extending up or down an octave *automatically* creates a major scale pattern on the staff of any clef; playing the successive white keys of the piano from *C* to *c automatically* results in the *C* major pattern.

The Diatonic Scale Systems

If we begin a scale on any note other than *C* (written on the staff or played at the keyboard), and if we use only unaltered pitches, different kinds of scales are produced. As in major, there will still be a pair of minor seconds at some two points within the series, but they will no longer fall between the 3-4 and 7-8 notes where they fell in the major pattern. It is the shifting of location of these two smaller intervals within the series of scale tones that determines the scale form.

Ex. 3-5.

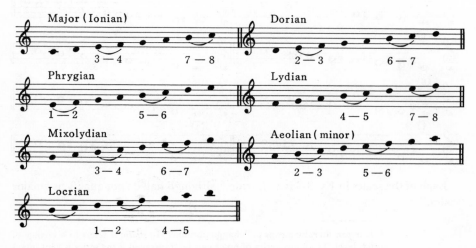

Each of these different arrangements of seven notes is called a *scale* or *mode*.[2] If we again use *C* as a common tonic, we can see more readily how changes of mode are brought about with the relocation of the two half-steps in relation to the tonic note.

Ex. 3-6.

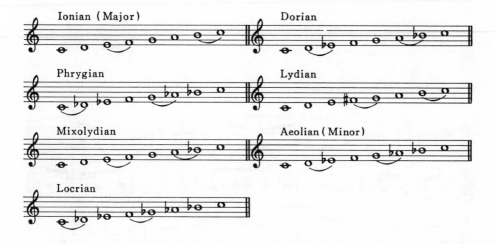

Since scales "1" and "6" of Ex. 3-6 are better known today as *major* and *minor*, we shall henceforth drop their impressive Greek names in favor of the more familiar names.

It is significant that six of the seven modes contain a perfect fifth interval between their tonics and their fifth scale degrees. As we can recall from our study of the tonality framework in Chapter 2, the diminished fifth is not one of the intervals that produces a strong root effect. For this reason, the Locrian mode (which contains a diminished fifth between 1 and 5) is regarded as a "theoretical mode" (i.e., not used in music), and it is rarely found as the true pitch basis for a composition.

The melodies of Ex. 3-7 are labeled according to the mode their pitches form. Sing or play each, making certain to produce all pitches accurately in order to recreate the true modal character. Note also the tonality frame for each melody.

---

[2] The word *mode* is derived from the same word root as *mood*. Each of the traditional mode names is of Greek origin: *Ionian, Dorian, Phrygian, Lydian, Mixolydian, Aeolian,* and *Locrian*. In most instances the word *mode* is interchangeable with *scale*.

Ex. 3-7a. Greek: Epitaph of Seikelos.

Ex. 3-7b. United States: Folksong.

Ex. 3-7c. Spain: Chant to the Virgin.

Composers and folk singers have not always created melodies limited to the pitches of any one of these scales. In this sense, scales or modes are really basic patterns that sometimes represent the full pitch complement of a melody, at other times represent only a generalized pitch complement. In many melodies it is impossible or difficult to represent melodic content by a single seven-note (*hepta-tonic*) scale. For instance, the melody in Ex. 3-8 seems to be Aeolian in its first five measures, but notice that the sixth and seventh scale degrees are raised by a semitone in measure 6.[3]

Ex. 3-8. Dufay: *Le jour s'endort.*

Mode (Aeolian?)   Tonality frame

Through the raising of these notes one semitone (particularly the *c* to *c♯*) the melody line leads with even greater impetus into the tonic pitch, *D*. This strong melodic tendency of *c♯-d*, the melodic half-step below tonic pitch, gives this seventh scale degree the name *leading tone.*

Two modes contain this relation between their seventh and eighth notes without note alterations: Major and Lydian. To contain the leading tone, the remaining modes would require the raising (by sharp or natural accidentals as the case may require) of the seventh scale member. Without this change their seventh degrees are called "subtonics," to distinguish them from the semitone step of the leading tone—tonic relation.

When the seventh degree of the Dorian mode is raised by one half-step, a pattern very similar to the major mode results. It is different from major only in that its lower half-step falls in a different location.

Ex. 3-9.

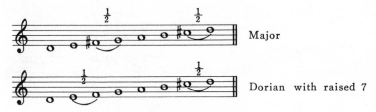

Major

Dorian with raised 7

---

[3] Melodies which contain only the pitches of a single seven-tone scale are called *diatonic*. Thus, the Dufay melody here is not, strictly speaking, diatonic.

This scale is better known by still another name, *melodic minor*. It shares the minor second placement between pitches 2 and 3 of the Aeolian mode, but it is different in that its other minor second occurs between 7–8 rather than 5–6.[4] This whole scale, then, consists of the interval succession of $1—\frac{1}{2}—1—1—1—1—\frac{1}{2}$.

A third kind of minor scale results if the seventh note of the Aeolian (natural minor) pattern is raised a semitone to create a leading tone. This new pattern differs from the other modes discussed in that it contains three minor-second intervals rather than the usual two. Such an arrangement leaves an unusual interval, the augmented second, between 6–7.

Ex. 3-10.

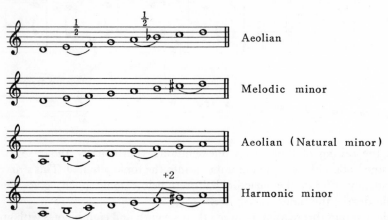

Aeolian

Melodic minor

Aeolian (Natural minor)

Harmonic minor

The fourth scale of Ex. 3-10 is traditionally called *harmonic minor*. Along with the *melodic* and *natural* patterns, it occurs frequently in the music most familiar to us.

It is important to remember that each of the modes derives its unique character from the particular intervals which are formed between its pitches, both successively and between any two members that are not adjacent. For this reason it is helpful to note carefully in each scale type the most significant intervals, those which in actual melody impart its characteristic *modality*. Study below the statements which best differentiate the various modes, regarding these as efficient clues for determining the particular mode of any melody.

Ex. 3-11a.

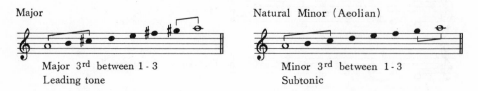

Major

Major 3rd between 1 - 3
Leading tone

Natural Minor (Aeolian)

Minor 3rd between 1 - 3
Subtonic

---

[4] One tradition regards melodic minor as actually consisting of two different scale patterns, one the ascending form (as shown here in Ex. 3-9), the other what we shall call *natural minor*.

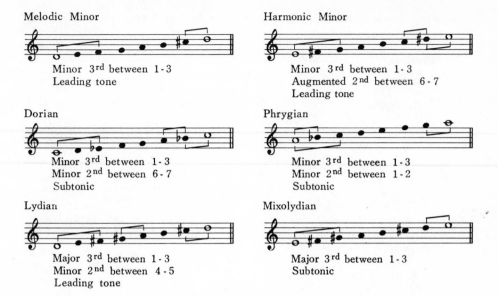

Melodic Minor

Minor 3rd between 1-3
Leading tone

Harmonic Minor

Minor 3rd between 1-3
Augmented 2nd between 6-7
Leading tone

Dorian

Minor 3rd between 1-3
Minor 2nd between 6-7
Subtonic

Phrygian

Minor 3rd between 1-3
Minor 2nd between 1-2
Subtonic

Lydian

Major 3rd between 1-3
Minor 2nd between 4-5
Leading tone

Mixolydian

Major 3rd between 1-3
Subtonic

Terminology of Scale Degrees

In addition to the *tonic*, which is the central tone of any scale of pitches, the tones of all scales are named in a way that classifies their particular function within the total scale system. This gives us an additional name for reference. Ex. 3-11b shows a *C* major scale and the various symbols which are commonly used to represent each degree.

Ex. 3-11b.

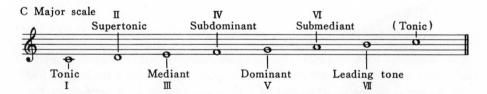

C Major scale

This set of names is applied to every scale or mode, no matter what its structure, except when the seventh degree is not a semitone below tonic; in this case the pitch of *seven* is called *subtonic* rather than *leading tone*.

The name for each scale degree is derived from its functional relationship to tonic. The set of definitions that follows explains the distinction of each name as it relates to the scale set.

    Tonic: Tone of focus for the scale
    Dominant: The tone a fifth *above* (or fourth *below*) the *tonic*

Tonic Dominant

Mediant: The tone between (the "medium" or "halfway" tone) the *tonic* and its *dominant*

Subdominant: The tone a fifth *below* (or fourth *above*) the tonic (the *under-dominant*)

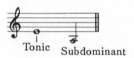

Submediant: The tone between (the "medium" or "halfway" tone) the *tonic* and its *subdominant*

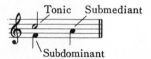

Supertonic: The next tone above *tonic*
Leading-tone: The tone a semitone below tonic
Subtonic: The tone (when present) a whole step below tonic

Each of these names is a normal part of the trained musician's vocabulary. We shall use them even more when we deal with chords. At that time we shall use both the numerical distinction (such as I (for "one") and V (for "five")) and the functional distinction, such as *tonic chord* (or pitch) and *dominant chord* (or pitch).

Key Signatures

Our system of music notation developed concurrently with the gradual adoption of our major-minor scale systems.[5] One effect these scales have had on our notation has been the development of a shorthand method for previewing the pitches encountered in a composition. Such is the essential function of the *key signature* that appears at the beginning of many compositions. These collections of sharps or flats (or their absence) indicate the alterations of the "natural" note system that must be made to achieve the desired pitches. Without sharps or flats the musical staff represents a set of notes that renders a major scale possible only from *C*, a natural minor scale only from *A*.

---

[5] Most of our current music notation practices were established during the seventeenth and eighteenth centuries. Earlier music requires considerable deciphering to be made readable by modern performers.

Ex. 3-12.

Since the lines and the spaces of the staff have "built-in" half-steps and whole-steps, untransposed modes result from successions of unaltered pitches. A beginning on any note other than *C* or *A* will produce one of the modes, Dorian, Phrygian, Lydian, Mixolydian, or Locrian. (See Ex. 3-5.)

A composer writing a composition for soprano voice based on the natural minor scale could, by pitch alterations, shift the intervals of the unaltered *C* scale so that minor results. The required alterations are those which produce minor seconds where they occur in the pattern of natural minor, between 2–3 and 5–6.

Ex. 3-13.

As a convenience to the composer and the performer, the three flats (*B-flat, E-flat,* and *A-flat*) required to make this shift of pattern can be indicated as a "signature" at the beginning of the line after the clef sign. This relieves the composer of inserting necessary alterations every time these notes occur within the melody.

Ex. 3-14.

In the same way, the key signature of three flats can be used to produce the major mode from a scale that begins on the note *E-flat.*

Ex. 3-15.

The order in which flats or sharps are placed in the key signature follows a set pattern; it is based on the sequence of pitch changes required to produce relocations of the scale.

Using the unaltered mode based on *F*, one alteration is needed to create the major scale: the lowering of *B* to *B-flat*. Since this is the first flat demanded in the notational system, it is always the first flat to the right of the clef sign of any signature containing flats. Ex. 3-16 shows the successive alterations required to produce major scales from the natural notes of the musical staff.

Ex. 3-16.

Notice that after *B-flat* is introduced, *E-flat* follows: *A-flat* next; then *D-flat* and *G-flat*. A progressive series by fours is established that can be represented as:

$$\overset{\frown}{BCD}\ \overset{\frown}{EFG}\ \overset{\frown}{ABC}\ \overset{\frown}{DEF}\ \overset{\frown}{GAB}\ \text{etc.}$$
$$\ \ _1\ \ \ \ \ _2\ \ \ \ \ _3\ \ \ \ \ _4\ \ \ \ \ _5$$

With the addition of sharps for the creation of major scales, the series follows a sequence by fives. The first sharp alteration required is *F-sharp*; the second *C-sharp*; the third *G-sharp*; and so on.

$$\overset{\frown}{FGAB}\ \overset{\frown}{CDEF}\ \overset{\frown}{GABC}\ \overset{\frown}{DEFG}\ \text{etc.}$$
$$\ \ _1\ \ \ \ \ \ _2\ \ \ \ \ \ _3\ \ \ \ \ \ _4$$

Ex. 3-17.

This series of pitch alterations has historical significance as the *circle of fifths*, which is a circular scheme that pictorially represents the system of keys for our major-minor scale system.

Ex. 3-18. Circle of Fifths.

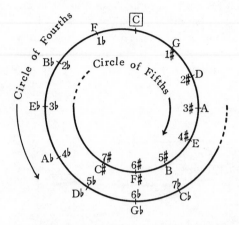

Two scales which have the same tonic but which do not contain identical pitches on every scale degree are called *parallel scales*. For instance, the keys of *B-flat* minor and *B-flat* major are *parallel keys*. On the other hand, two scales (or keys) which contain identical pitches but do not have the same tonic are called *relative scales*. Thus *G* minor and *B-flat* major are *relatives*, and *D* major is the relative major of *B* minor.

Ex. 3-19.

Since double sharps (**✖**) and double flats (♭♭) are not generally used in key signatures, the system of keys normally is extended no further than seven sharps (for *C-sharp* major or *A-sharp* minor) and seven flats (for *C-flat* major or *A-flat* minor). But the progression by fifths can be continued until the original pitch, spelled enharmonically[6] as *B-sharp*, is reached.

The key signatures of our music are usually derived from the diatonic scale structures. As a result, music based on the pitch resources of some other scale does not readily fit our traditional signatures. A composition that makes free use of the twelve tones of the chromatic scale gains little of practical use from a key signature. If used, the composer and the performer are kept busy staying abreast of alterations and, ultimately, their frequent cancellation.

Ex. 3-20. Chopin: Waltz in A-flat Major, Op. 64, No. 3.

Compositions based on scales unlike the traditional modes might conceivably use signatures that look strange. The melody in Ex. 3-21 incorporates such a scale, and the composer fabricated a special key signature that indicates to the performer the pitch materials to be expected within the composition.

Ex. 3-21. Bartók: *Cradle Song* (Violin Duets, No. 11). Copyright 1933 by Universal Edition, Vienna. Renewed 1960. Copyright & Renewal assigned to Boosey & Hawkes Inc., for the U.S.A. Reprinted by permission.

---

[6] Enharmonic tones are those which bear different *note names* but which have the same *pitch*. For example, *F-flat* and *E*, *A-flat* and *G-sharp*, *B-sharp* and *C* are all enharmonic pairs.

Modulation and Mutation

Our foregoing discussion of keys, modes, and scales must be amplified somewhat to account for the pitch organization of many melodies. For the sake of variety, more than one pitch framework is often used within a composition.

The word *modulation* refers to this shifting from one pitch focus, or tonic, to another. Thus we can say that a modulation occurs at section "Y" of Ex. 3-22, the initial tonic of *C* replaced by the new tonic of *G*.

Ex. 3-22. Russian folksong.

Sections "X" and "Y" both utilize simple scale materials within their respective boundaries, each incorporating only four different notes. It is the new focus on *G*, following the focus on *C*, that constitutes the modulation or *change of key*.

Change of *mode* alone does not achieve the same result as change of *tonic*. On the contrary, we can best describe the pitch organization of Ex. 3-23 by noting that a common tonic, *F*, persists throughout. The change of mode from minor to major at section "Y" represents *mutation* rather than modulation. In this case, mutation refers to scale change as distinct from tonic change. In this example the contrast is effected by a change to the parallel major scale.

Ex. 3-23. Swedish folksong.

Ex. 3-23 continued.

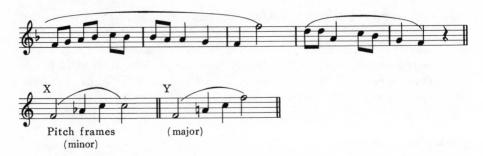

Pitch frames   (major)
(minor)

Modulation usually is closely allied with the sectional divisions—the phrases of musical form—which we shall discuss later in Chapters 4 and 5. For the present, however, we can observe that the melody of Ex. 3-22 illustrates this formal division by shifting tonics halfway through the melody. In a similar way, Ex. 3-23 is sectionalized by the change of mode—the *mutation*—that occurs after measure 8.

It is this psychological shift from the old tonic to the new that makes modulation an element of variety, for only the relation of the orginal tonality to another establishes a condition of change. Either one without the other would represent merely one particular tonality, and thus provide no contrast.

In establishing a new pitch focus, the same techniques of repetition, duration, metric placement, and strong interval embellishment are used. The melodies which follow incorporate these various methods of establishing a new tonic. It is interesting to see that several techniques can be combined, as in Ex. 3-25, to create an immediate and unmistakable shift of pitch focus.

Ex. 3-24. Schumann: *An den Sonnenschein,* Op. 36, No. 4.

Ex. 3-25. Chopin: *The Maiden's Wish.*

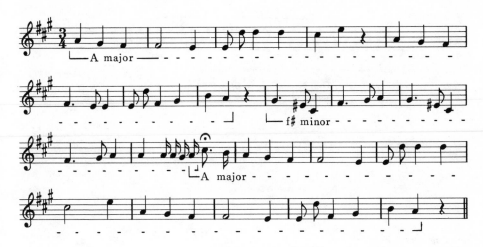

It would be unrealistic, however, to regard all shifts of pitch emphasis, no matter how brief, as key changes. In this sense we are dealing with an organizational matter that is subject to relative judgments. Pitch focus is itself a product of our psychological response to tone patterns, so it is reasonable to assume that one person's reaction might be slightly different from another's. For instance, one person might regard the "Y" section of Ex. 3-26 as an interesting *diversion within the tonality* of *D*; another might hear the passage as a definite modulation to the new tonic of *A*.

Ex. 3-26. German chorale: *Valet will ich dir geben.*

As a general rule, we can judge melodies as modulating if the apparent shift of tonic is confirmed by *at least two consecutive sections* of the melody.[7] Thus the melody of Ex. 3-27 does not contain a change of key; the emphasis on *E-flat* in the bracketed section represents emphasis on the dominant within the tonality of *A-flat*. On the other hand, the melody of Ex. 3-28 modulates, for the emphasis continues long enough for the new pitch frame to be established clearly in the listener's mind.

---

[7] We shall make our definition more precise in Chapter 4 by regarding the *phrase*, with its attendant cadence, as the unit of measurement for modulation.

Ex. 3-27. Beethoven: Trio in E-flat Major, Op. 1, No. 1, II.

Ex. 3-28.

Some melodies use a modulatory scheme to create a series of shifting tonics, each new section creating a new reference point. These *transitory modulations* (or *tonal regions*) usually occur between sections of clear tonal focus, the shifts of tonics creating a tonal variety as compared to the definite, unchanging pitch frameworks of the beginning and ending sections. Once again, it is quite possible to hear such melodies as organized around a single tonic, the changing pitch frames representing changing stress upon different pitches belonging to the single overall tonality. In cases where a beginning and ending are clearly grounded in a single tonality, it is perhaps more accurate to favor the latter interpretation.

Ex. 3-29. Froberger: Gigue.

The melody in Ex. 3-29 contains a beginning section based within the tonality frame of e'—e^2. The leading tone—tonic (d^2-*sharp*—e^2) pattern in measure 8 is the final substantiation of this tonic before a change occurs, in the section marked "X". This second section revolves around the pitch frame of g^2—g', with emphasis on the fifth (d^2). From measure 15–17 d^2 and f^2-*sharp* are emphasized by repetition and by the leading tone created by the sharped c. Measures 18 and 20 relate these two pitches (d^2 and f^2-*sharp*) to a new pitch frame based on a tonic of *B*. Thus section "Y" brings a new tonic to the fore, followed by a return (Section "Z") to the beginning tonality frame of e'—e^2. We can digest this tonal movement into a simple diagram.

Section	"W"	"X"	"Y"	"Z"
	1–8	9–14	14–20	21–30
Tonics	E	G	B	E

Overall Pitch Frame

Principal Tonic: E

Exercises

See Chapter 3 of the *Materials and Structure of Music I, Workbook* for more detailed work.

1. Look in a collection of melodies (for sight-singing, perhaps) and find examples of Dorian, Aeolian (or natural minor) Phrygian, Mixolydian, and Lydian scales. Copy the total melody and then show the pitch frame and scale in notation after the melody.
2. Write a melody according to each of the following prescriptions:
    a) Six measures long, range *d—d'* in bass clef, tonic *D*, in Mixolydian mode.
    b) Four measures long, range from *g—g'*, tonic *C*, in major mode.
    c) Four measures long, range from $e'—e^2$, tonic *E*, in Phrygian mode.
3. Find examples of melodies which begin and end clearly in the same key but which contain a modulation to another tonic within interior parts.
4. Write a melody eight measures long that emphasizes *F* as beginning and ending tonic, but stresses *C* at some point within.
5. Transpose relatively simple melodies in major or minor keys to new pitch levels. (For example, transpose at sight a melody in the key of B-flat major to E-flat major.) Play at the piano. Practice the same procedure with other instruments.
6. Practice writing every possible major scale, beginning with *C* and ending with *B* as tonics.
7. Practice spelling scales orally.
8. Write the proper key signatures for all major and minor scales.

4

MELODIC CADENCES

A fundamental characteristic of human behavior is our inability to sustain a peak level of attention or participation in any activity. Whether in work or play, our patterns of involvement are normally marked by periods of successive intensity and relaxation. Such behavior is required for maximum efficiency, whether in reading a book or in physically more taxing pastimes.

Even our speech reflects patterns of rise and fall, slow and fast, motion and rest, hard-accent and soft-accent, all of which, when combined, transmit more effectively what we wish to communicate; they create the *cadence* of our phrases and sentences. The result is an organization of sounds into meaningful language.

The cadence in music provides pause amidst activity that gives form to the unfolding of tonal ideas. Even if composers did not mold such articulations of movement-repose into their music, listeners would seek them as aids to the listening process. A continuous series of identical clicks is heard as grouped into accents of twos or threes; and melodies are heard as patterns of tones grouped around certain structural rallying points.

The cadence is that point in melody that provides momentary pause to the onward flow of musical pattern or, at the melody's end, signals permanent conclusion. It is, therefore, a sign for the listener of relative degrees of termination; it separates one melodic unit from another. Like the speech effect represented in language by commas and colons and periods, the cadence is a *heard* signal that helps us organize our world of tones into comprehensible forms.

The cadences of music are named according to the roles they play in tonal organization. In regard to melody alone we shall discuss only two basic types: the *terminal cadence*, denoting a partial or total cessation of melodic activity; and the *progressive cadence*, marking a break in tonal flow but with the suggestion of continuation. Compared with the punctuation marks of language, the terminal cadence resembles the period, while the progressive type is more like the break in a sentence marked by a comma.

The Beethoven melody in Ex. 4-1 contains each of these cadential types, *progressive* at the midway point in measure 4, *terminal* at the end. Sing this melody.

Ex. 4-1. Beethoven: Symphony No. 9, IV.

Progressive
cadence

Terminal
cadence

Rhythm and pitch combine to produce the cadence effect. Although each of the two segments of the melody in Ex. 4-1 closes with the same rhythmic unit (), the two cadences create different expectations because of the positions of their cadence pitches within the melody's tonality. The *e* of measure 4 is foreign to the *d—a* frame established in measures 1–3. Since it does not create an effect of repose, it sets the stage for continued activity. By contrast, the *d* of measure eight, as tonic of the melody, provides an effect of closure.

In addition to the increased note durations in measures 4 and 8, another aspect of rhythm confirms the arrested motion at these two cadence points. Notice that the pitch contour of this melody consists of a two-measure arch that rises gently in measure 2, falling to a low point at the beginning of measure 3.

Ex. 4-2.

The same shape is repeated in measures 3 and 4, creating a balance of melodic contour, a musical statement modeled from the repetition of a two-measure unit. The continuation of this pattern into measure 4, combined with the longer durations (dotted quarter and half), implies that the close of a definite musical section has been reached.

Ex. 4-3.

While these rhythmic groupings create the cadential *caesura*—the pause effect—, it is the *cadence pitch* that determines the kind of punctuation.

It is interesting and informative to experiment with other pitches as cadential notes in the middle of the Beethoven melody, to observe the punctuative effects produced by different relations. Since the second four measures duplicate the first four (excepting the cadence pattern itself), separation of the two by a terminal cadence produces a monotonous, disjunct effect, as illustrated in melody *a* of Ex. 4-4. Play or sing each of these versions to observe the contrasting cadential effects.

Ex. 4-4.

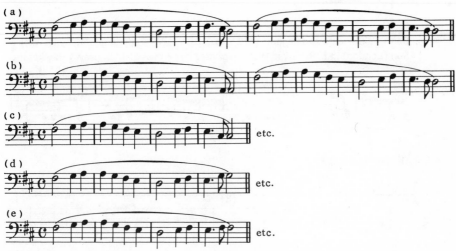

With the exception of *d* and *f-sharp*, the alternate cadence pitches perform about the same role as *e* of the original. They imply, in varying degrees, the continuation of melodic flow. However, all would not be successful choices for this melody because some, such as *f-sharp* and *g*, destroy the two-measure shape established as a pattern of contour in measures 1 and 2.

Cadences frequently lie at equally spaced locations within a melody, thus giving a simple continuity to the flow of tones. But not all melodies follow the same four-measure pattern of Ex. 4-1, and some melodies are notably free of the regularity imposed by phrases of equal lengths.

Melodies "a," "b," and "c" of Ex. 4-5 have balanced pattern lengths; but melodies "d," "e," and "f" deviate from this regularity of formation. The last two examples are interesing because their cadences establish unbalanced melodic units as the basis for melodic form.

Ex. 4-5a. American folksong.

Ex. 4-5b. Schubert: Trio in E-flat Major, Op. 100. III.

Ex. 4-5c. Bartók: "Staccato and Legato" (*Mikrokosmos,* Vol. V). Copyright 1940 by Hawkes & Son (London) Ltd., Renewed 1967. Reprinted by permission of Boosey & Hawkes Inc.

Ex. 4-5d. German folksong.

Ex. 4-5e. German folksong.

Ex. 4-5f. Brahms: Variations on a Theme of Haydn, Theme.

The patterns that span the distance from one cadence to the next are called *phrases*. This unit of melodic form will be discussed in greater detail in Chapter 7, but no discussion of the melodic cadence could be clear without some attention to its nature. We might turn to language again for comparison to note that the melodic phrase is similar to the "clause" or "phrase" of the sentence. And like its language counterpart, the musical phrase can usually be reduced further into smaller units called *motives*. For instance, the third phrase of the melody of Ex. 4-5d consists of the rhythm: ($\flat$ ♩ ♩ ♩ ♩) and its immediate repetition, both squeezed into the span of three measures.

The Brahms-Haydn melody (Ex. 4-5f) yields a similar result in that the five-measure phrase units can be reduced to two-part units, the first unit of three measures, the second of two. In this case the divisions are represented by *different* patterns rather than the repetition of a single motive.

Ex. 4-6.

For this reason a break occurs between the patterns of measures 3 and 4 which, in a limited sense, is a cadence; only after hearing the continuation of measures 6–11 can the listener decide that the important melodic units are five measures long. The combination of the two phrases results in a ten-measure section.[1]

Perfect and Imperfect Terminal Cadences

As we noticed earlier (page 54), it is the particular pitch at the cadence that determines the cadential effect by implying or denying continued motion. A strong *progressive cadence* forcefully suggests continuation, while a strong *terminal cadence* unquestionably marks finality. The tonic as cadence pitch most appropriately fulfills this latter function, while its scale relatives a major or minor third

---

[1] This combination of two phrases separated by a progressive cadence and ending with a terminal cadence is sometimes called a *period*.

or perfect fifth above can also, under most circumstances, imply closure to a limited degree.

The third cadence of the Brahms-Haydn melody in Ex. 4-5 is an *imperfect terminal cadence*. Since the ultimate pitch *d* is preceded by the tonic *B-flat*, and since *B-flat* is the root of this melodic relation *B-flat—d*, the cadence pattern does not unequivocally demand continuation. And yet, it also does not suggest that melodic motion has concluded; such a cadence lies in the never-never-land between the *weak progressive cadence* and the *strong terminal cadence*.

The cadences of the melody in Ex. 4-7 are similar. Here there are two based on *a*, the perfect fifth above tonic *d*. In measure 4 the *a* acts as a point of brief rest. It fits into the frame of the *D*-tonality (since the tonic, *D*, is also the root of the relation *d—a*), so it does not demand resolution to the same extent as other pitches, such as *e*, *c-sharp*, or *g*. Compare the relative intensification of this cadence when these other pitches are substituted for *a*. Play or sing each version several times to realize the precise cadential effects.

Ex. 4-7.

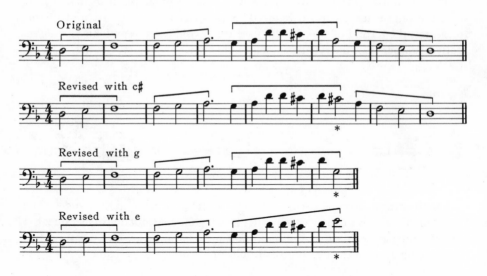

In a later chapter we shall discuss the ways accompanying chords and melodic activity in other parts can emphasize or weaken the cadential effect of a particular pitch. This is one of the ways chords can add variety and alter the function of pitches within a melody. Without chordal underpinnings a melody must depend on rhythm and pitch relations alone to create the nuances of cadence.

Transient-Terminal Cadences

If melodies always hovered within a single tonality frame and scale, the foregoing discussion of cadences would suffice for all music. But since many melodies fluctuate in their obedience to a single pitch focus,[2] some cadences momentarily create the effect of closure, and yet they do not meet the other specifications demanded by our definition of the *terminal cadence*.

The middle portion of the melody in Ex. 4-8 pauses momentarily on *d*, a tone made prominent by its leading tone, *c-sharp*. If the initially established tonality were *d*, then this would be a simple terminal cadence. But since *G* is the tonic of the tonality frame (g'—d^2), the pause on *d* does not represent a *perfect terminal cadence*.

Ex. 4-8. German chorale: *Ermuntre dich, mein schwacher Geist.*

We shall call such a cadence *transient-terminal*. Only if the motion to the cadential *d* is interpreted as a modulation from the tonality of *G* to the tonality of *D* can it be associated with full termination.

Transient-terminal cadences can occur on any degree of a scale other than tonic. The *dominant* (V) is one of the most common, as illustrated in Ex. 4-8. Other pitch degrees that frequently function in this way are the *subdominant* (IV), the *mediant* (III), and the *submediant* (VI).

Each of the melodies in Ex. 4-9 contains at least one transient-terminal cadence. Of particular importance to melodic structure is the way each of these "temporary tonics" is established as a pitch of emphasis, either by association with its leading tone, with pitches a fifth or third above, or by its successive repetitions.

Ex. 4-9a. German chorale: *Valet will ich dir geben.*

Ex. 4-9b. Irish folksong.

---

[2] See the earlier section of Chapter 3 that deals with modulation, pp. 47–51.

Ex. 4-9b continued.

Submediant

Ex. 4-9c. Dunstable: *Sancta Maria.*

Dominant

Ex. 4-9d. Handel: Air with Variations, Var. 3.

Mediant

A more detailed discussion and precise classification of cadence patterns must wait until harmonic features can be added to the rhythm and pitch elements that create the cadential effect.[3] The present limitation of basic types to the *progressive*, the *terminal* (both perfect and imperfect), and the *transient-terminal* suffices for a comprehension of the usual patterns found in melody.

Cadences and Musical Style

Since the cadence is a fundamental determinant of musical form, it is not surprising to find that composers consistently have made use of individualized cadence patterns in their music. Stereotyped formulae can be found, used repeatedly by one

---

[3] This further discussion appears in Chapter 19.

composer or by a group of composers who share a common musical heritage. These cadential "cliches" run the gamut from the strong terminal cadences in music of the eighteenth and nineteenth centuries to the actual suppression of cadential effect in some works of the twentieth century.

We mentioned earlier that the cadence acts as a "signal" in musical form. Like the other signs of everyday life—the green light, the siren, the waved hand, the raised eyebrow—the melodic cadence can function as a clear, absolute *signal*, or, at the other extreme, as a weak *symbol* or hint of musical organization. Music literature contains melodies whose cadences operate at both of these extremes, as well as at levels in between.

It is not difficult to follow the melodic structure of some fourteenth-century music, for instance, because many of the outlining cadences use a specific scale formula, 7–6–1 as their pitch content.

Ex. 4-10a. Ciconia: *Et in terra pax.*

Ex. 4-10b. Landini: *Amor dal tuo suggétto.*

Ex. 4-10c. Machaut: *Mes esperis.*

Although the name "Landini cadence" (after the fourteenth-century Italian composer) has been coined for this pattern, it was actually used as the common property of many earlier and later composers.

In music of the sixteenth century the fusion of a set rhythm and pitch formula provides the cadential basis for many compositions, particularly the choral sacred music of Palestrina. Ex. 4-11 shows this pattern, a rhythmic syncopation combined with the 7–1 scale degrees, both as a terminal and as a transient-terminal cadence.

Ex. 4-11a. Palestrina: *Missa Vestiva i colli,* Kyrie.

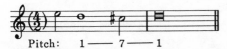

Ex. 4-11b. Palestrina: *Missa In dominicus quadragesima.*

Ex. 4-11c. Lassus: *Cantiones,* No. 1.

The use of these established "signals" of cadence goes somewhat beyond the mere "rhythmic pause" of the cadential effect as we discussed it earlier; their repeated use in music established them as the powerful "road signs" of musical form. The appearance of a conventionalized pitch-rhythm pattern reinforces the mere durational and tonal ingredients in differentiating the parts of melodic form.

Bach, Handel, Haydn, Mozart, and Beethoven shared as common property the perfect terminal cadence of 7–1, the leading tone resolving to tonic, with a weak-to-strong metric location. It is the power of this simple pitch-rhythm pattern to confirm tonality relations that makes it a significant cadential formula in the entire history of music. Aside from its frequent appearances in music written by composers of the classic and Baroque eras, this cadence pattern can be found in the bulk of popular and community music whose most conspicuous features are simplicity of tonality and phrase organization.

One special adaptation of the 7–1 figure became a cadential trademark in the music of Haydn, Mozart, and Beethoven, whereby the usual weak-strong rhythmic placement of the two parts of the 7–1 pitch pattern were regrouped into a strong-weak relation of syncopation. The leading tone of such a cadence is suspended from a preceding weak position, thus delaying resolution to the tonic pitch.[4]

Ex. 4-12a. Haydn: Sonata in E-flat Major, II.

Ex. 4-12b. Mozart: Sonata in F Major, K. 533, I.

---

[4] This delay is further enhanced, as we shall see later in Chapter 19, by the underlying chords.

In our own day, some composers have used certain cadential patterns frequently enough to justify their identification with the composer's personal style. Since harmony plays a crucial role in determining the character of most recent music, it is increasingly difficult to identify cadential patterns as melodic formulae alone. However, composers whose music emphasizes melody as a dominant ingredient use melodic cadences of some uniformity.

Ex. 4-13a. Hindemith: *Theme and Four Variations.* (C) 1947 by B. Schott's Soehne, Mainz. Reprinted by permission.

Ex. 4-13b. Hindemith: *When Lilacs Last in the Dooryard Bloomed.* (C) 1948 by Schott & Co., Ltd., London. Reprinted by permission.

It seems clear, then, that in addition to its role as a determinant of form, the cadence can be elevated to a position of significance and individuality, thereby recognizing its contribution to the "personality" of a particular work, the works of a single composer, or even the compositions from an entire era of music-making. In this latter role the cadence is a prime element that suggests, perhaps in a more direct way than other musical elements, the peculiar flavor that makes one melody utterly and uniquely different from another.

Exercises

See Chapter 4 of the *Materials and Structure of Music I, Workbook* for more detailed work.
1. Write several melodies, each of which fits one of the following schemes:

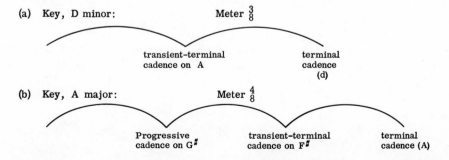

(c)   **Key, G Mixolydian:**   **Meter** $\frac{3}{8}$

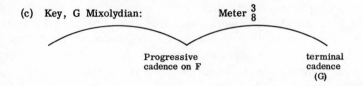

Progressive   terminal
cadence on F   cadence
                               (G)

Compose other melodies with similar characteristics.

2. Copy several complete chorale tunes from a collection such as the 371 Bach Chorales. Using only the melody as a basis for determination, name the cadence types.

3. Write one- or two-measure fragments which illustrate each kind of cadence type. Use a variety of keys, major, minor, and modal.

Example: 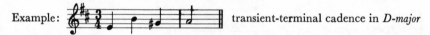 transient-terminal cadence in *D-major*

4. Analyze the melodies of any chosen composition for scales. Having determined the tonic pitch for a passage, arrange the pitch materials in an ascending scale that begins with the lowest note and extends to the highest. From this determine the basic scale.

5

FORMAL CHARACTERISTICS
OF MELODY :
THE MOTIVE
AND PHRASE

In Chapter 4 we saw how cadences impose form on tonal ideas by setting off one melodic unit from another. In this sense cadences form still another kind of musical framework. The span between cadences is "filled-in" by various related and contrasted melodic patterns. Even in the most complex melody, these patterns are combined to create recognizable units between the cadential boundaries.

Since music takes place in time, we hear musical patterns in succession. Musical patterns may be repeated immediately; may be restated after a contrasting unit or units; or may be varied slightly or a great deal. It is succession of tonal units that produces form in music.

Such a description of musical form is very general; however, a close look at several melodies will show what is meant by musical form. The terminal cadence in measure 6 of Ex. 5-1 divides the whole melody into two smaller sections. These two sections complement one another tonally and rhythmically, even though they are not of equal length.

Ex. 5-1. *America.*

Each of these two melodic sections is a *phrase*. As each unit is succeeded by another, the unfolding of the melody takes place and its form is delineated. As Ex. 5-1 illustrates, the phrases need not be of equal length; however, it is not until we count the measures that we become aware of unequal phrase lengths.

Both phrases of Ex. 5-1 are formed from successive statements of smaller patterns, each of which is two measures long. Thus, just as this melody is made up of two phrases, so each of its phrases is made up of smaller units. These subphrase units are simple pitch and rhythm patterns such as those seen in measures 1 and 2 (♩ ♩ ♩ | ♩. ♪♪). When subphrase units appear consistently in a musical context they are called *motives*.

The rhythmic pattern (♩ ♩ ♩ | ♩. ♪♪) is the essential binding force of the tune in Ex. 5-1. In many melodies a short pattern may form the basis for the unfolding of the initial musical phrase and subsequent phrases as well. In some melodies this is not as easily observed as in the tune "America," and in still others no short unit or section is repeated (see Ex. 5-2). However, some characteristic pattern often appears as a formal binder.

Ex. 5-2. Beethoven: Sonata in C Minor, Op. 13, II.

Motive Structure

A motive is a short and distinctive melodic pattern, often characterized by simplicity of rhythm and pitch design. Because of its brevity, the motive is easily recognized and frequently plays an important role in melodic organization.

Both pitch and rhythm produce the distinct qualities that characterize a particular motive. Either the pitch or the rhythmic structure can be the dominating factor, or both can be combined and equally important. The motive illustrated in Ex. 5-3 does not have a noteworthy rhythm, and yet its pitch outline forms a striking pattern of great melodic potentiality.

Ex. 5-3. Mozart: Symphony in C Major, K. 551 (*Jupiter*), IV.

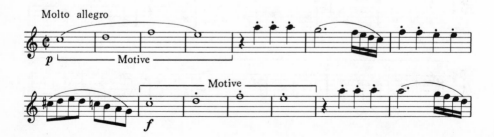

On the other hand, rhythm may be the dominant feature of a motive. In Ex. 5-4, repetition of the rhythmic motive (♪♪♪ | ♪) dominates the whole phrase until the change at the cadence. As is frequently the case, this motive has an up-beat beginning, its first stress falling on the relatively longer duration of the first measure. The restatement of the pitch pattern at different levels, as well as at the same level, counterbalances the persistent character of the rhythmic motive.

Ex. 5-4. J.S. Bach: Brandenburg Concerto No. 3, I.

In many melodies the motive's pitch pattern is varied when it is repeated. The repetition of the rhythmic motive in Ex. 5-5 is associated with a *melodic inversion* (e.g., measures 2 and 4) of the initial pitch pattern. Chopin not only repeats the motive of measure 1 as a unit but also repeats the subphrase (measures 1 and 2) unit as measures 3 and 4. Measure 5 begins as a variant of measure 1, but with the upward leap a new dimension is introduced—repetition at a different pitch level (*sequence*).

Ex. 5-5. Chopin: Valse brillante, Op. 34, No. 2.

When a motive is repeated both pitch and rhythmic changes may occur. Ex. 5-6 shows some changes a motive might undergo when it is repeated. Notice that the characteristic rhythm of the first part of the motive (♩ ♩ ♩) is retained. In addition, the varied repetition is shorter, three beats instead of four.

Ex. 5-6. Piston: Symphony No. 4, I. (C) 1953 by Associated Music Publishers, Inc., New York. Reprinted by permission.

Piacevole

Successive repetitions of a motive often occur in the same metric position. Such periodic statements are typical of musical phrases that contain few contrasting motives. In Ex. 5-7 the chordal motive unifies the melodic phrase and provides the harmonic direction for the phrase.

Ex. 5-7. Schubert: Symphony No. 5, I.

Allegro

Subsequent statements of a motive may appear in a different metric position, as in Ex. 5-8. The repetition of the five-beat motive is an interesting example of variety created by metric relocation; the repetition of the motive begins on the second instead of the first beat in measure 2. A secondary motive is heard in measures 4-6. This motive is repeated in the same metric position and occupies the same amount of time in the repetitions shown but undergoes rhythm and pitch changes, from three articulations to five and from an interval span of a minor third to a perfect fifth.

Ex. 5-8. Prokofiev: Violin Concerto No. 2, I. By permission of the International Music Company, New York.

Allegro moderato

Phrase Structure: Rhythmic Aspects

At a larger level of structure, the phrase is a distinctive agent of musical form. Motives are relatively short and are sub-units of the phrase. Even though an all-encompassing definition of *phrase* is difficult to formulate, an examination of music shows that there are numerous possibilities for constructing phrases.

A common type of phrase structure is seen in Ex. 5-9. Each of the four phrases is marked off rhythmically by a tone of longer duration and a rest (♩. ♪ ♪). When the two elements of greater duration followed by rest are combined, a rhythmic cadence is unquestionably established. Therefore, at the beginning of measure 5 we recognize, in retrospect, a complete rhythmic structure, a phrase. The succession of shorter rhythmic figures shapes the entire phrase. In this melody the shortest durations occur in the first measure of each phrase, and the second longest duration occurs in the second measure. Even if the phrases are performed without the assigned pitches, we recognize them as a complete rhythmic structure; nothing else is needed to complete them as a balanced rhythmic design.

Ex. 5-9. German folksong: *Die Lorelei.*

Cessation of activity does not by itself shape phrases. In Ex. 5-9 the first part of each measure always contains a longer duration, and an upbeat precedes each durational accent. The rhythmic motion from a lesser to a greater accent also occurs between measures, as from measure 1 to the durational accent of measure 2. Considered in this light, each phrase consists of two rhythmic subphrases that complement one another but are not rhythmically identical. The rhythmic subphrases are restated in each of the phrases with the exception of the negligible pattern change in measure 14. The result is a rhythmically unified melody.

Phrases formed from two rhythmic subphrases occur frequently in music. Ex. 5-10 illustrates other possibilities. Here the first phrase consists of two subphrases each of which is a complete statement of a motive. In both statements of the motive the rhythm is identical, but the pitch level changes forming a sequence. The second phrase is formed in a similar fashion with two repetitions of a one-measure rhythmic motive and closing with a contrasting, cadential rhythmic figure in measure 8.

Ex. 5-10. Beethoven: Quartet in C Minor, Op. 18, No. 4, I.

Although the rhythmic shaping processes are similar in the first two phrases of Ex. 5-10, their effect is quite dissimilar. The two-bar motive of the first phrase gives the impression of being able to stand alone rhythmically, whereas the one-bar motive of the second phrase does not exhibit such independence. The rhythmic dependence of the secondary motive results principally from its syncopated structure, which leads us to expect a rhythmic realization on an accented beat.

Phrases produced by motivic or other subphrase repetitions occur frequently in some musical styles. Quite often these repetitions or subphrase divisions are by twos, or multiples thereof. On the other hand, in some styles such rhythmic groupings or divisions are not the norm or as readily apparent. Rhythmic repetition and restatement are not characteristic features of some of the following melodies; neither are their phrase lengths always predictable. It is quite apparent that such aspects of rhythmic organization do not distract, but enhance. Rhythm does not stand alone, however; other factors, such as pitch, also enter into the shaping processes. Pitch factors are discussed in the next section.

Ex. 5-11a. Alec Wilder: Concerto for Oboe, String Orchestra and Percussion, I. (C) 1957 by Associated Music Publishers, Inc., New York. Reprinted by permission.

Ex. 5-11b. Bartók: "Boating" (*Mikrokosmos,* Vol. V). Copyright 1940 by Hawkes & Son (London) Ltd., Renewed 1967. Reprinted by permission of Boosey & Hawkes Inc.

Ex. 5-11c. Schumann: Symphony No. 1, II.

Ex. 5-11d. Trouvére Song: Virelais, *Or la truix.*

Phrase Structure: Pitch Aspects

Pitch also influences phrase structure. We often speak of a melodic "line," which is an analogy to the graphic arts. For example, if we perform only the rhythm of any of the preceding excerpts without a change of pitch, their pitch contour would be analogous to a horizontal line. A complete rhythmic structure still remains; however, most of us would agree that such phrases are comparatively dull, that they are really not melodies. When changes of pitch are added to our performance a different kind of "line" results. Such a line generally corresponds to a wavy pattern, with the high points, low points, final note, etc., delineating the contour of a melody.

Phrase contour is produced by the rhythmic placement of the high and low pitches. In the first phrase of Ex. 5-12 the pitch apex is in measure 4, the highest point of the entire melody. After this highest point the predominant pitch motion is down to tonic. The phrase forms one broad arch that includes several smaller waves.

Ex. 5-12. Trouvére Song: *C'est la fin.*

The contour of the second phrase forms an inverted arch and it contrasts with the first phrase because of its length and its range. The rising inflection raises a "question," similar to the way the pitch of a spoken word rises when we ask a question, producing an expectation of something to follow. Notice also that a progressive cadence is used. Thus, ascending contour, combined with progressive cadence, results in anticipation of continuation.

In Ex. 5-13 the pitch apex apears at the beginning of each phrase. However, both phrases differ in contour and range. Considering the number of waves in the line, it is "complex," each phrase consisting of several secondary arches.

Ex. 5-13. Tansman: "Berceuse" (*Pour les Enfants, Set 4*). (C) 1934 by Editions Max Eschig, Paris. Renewed 1962. Reprinted by permission.

The five-tone melody in Ex. 5-14 forms another type of contour. The wave pattern is characterized by descending motion until the rise to the metrically stressed *b* (measure 5). The appearance of this basic pitch (*b*) coincides with a change of tonal emphasis. The opening of the phrase outlines a *D* tonality (the perfect fifth, *a—d*). However, the tonality of the excerpt is *E*. The tonal center of *E* is created by using *b*, the dominant degree, as the apex of the phrase and *e* as the final pitch.

Ex. 5-14. Bartók: "Playsong" (*Mikrokosmos,* Vol. IV). Copyright 1940 by Hawkes & Son (London) Ltd., Renewed 1967. Reprinted by permission of Boosey & Hawkes Inc.

The arch formed by the phrase in Ex. 5-15 is a common one. Notice that the highest pitch is reached around the middle of the phrase and that this pitch is the dominant scale degree. Notice also that the leaps centered around *c* in measures 2 and 3 slightly disguise the tonality of *a*.

Ex. 5-15. Brahms: *Salamander.*

The possibilities for different types of phrase contour are numerous. Ex. 5-16 illustrates other possibilities.

Ex. 5-16a. J. C. Bach: Symphony in B-flat Major, II.

Ex. 5-16b. J.S. Bach: *St. John Passion,* "Ruht wohl, ihr heiligen Gebeine."

Ex. 5-16c. Bloch: Concerto Grosso for String Orchestra with Piano Obbligato, IV. Copyright by Universal Editions. Used by permission.

Ex. 5-16d. Ravel: String Quartet in F, I. By permission of the International Music Company, New York.

Ex. 5-16e. Maschera: Canzona.

Ex. 5-16f. Mozart: Concerto for Two Pianos, K. 365, III.

Generally, the apex of a line will be a pitch that is basic to the tonality frame: the dominant, the tonic, or the mediant scale degrees. Other parts of the scale also appear as highest points, but they frequently have clearly decorative relationships to pitches that are basic to the tonality.

Pitch climax is also associated with the contour of phrases. As a phrase unfolds, the pattern of motion to the highest pitch directs our attention to that pitch. In a manner of speaking, the "energy" of the directional pattern is concentrated in the pitch apex or in its opposite, the low point. Since we know that a "build-up" of energy is usually followed by release, we expect the same to happen in a phrase of music. The pitch apex and the low point, then, are important factors that outline the contour of a phrase or section of music.

A description of melodic contour represents the beginning stages of the study of pitch organization in relation to phrase structure and inter-phrase relations. Detailed study of pitch organization takes place in subsequent chapters. Here we continue with some of the pitch aspects that delineate, shape, and relate phrases as wholes.

Cadence pitches signal the ends of phrases and serve as connecting links to phrases that follow. The two phrases given in Ex. 5-17 both have the tonic for cadence pitch, but their musical effect is not the same. At the end of the first phrase the cadence ascends and ends in a weak metric position, both factors contributing to the suggestion of continuation. The second phrase has a stronger impression of closure because the overall pitch motion of the phrase leads to the tonic which now occurs in a stronger metric position.

Ex. 5-17. Beethoven: Piano Concerto No. 3, Op. 37, III.

The cadential activity of the preceding two phrases also is important for establishing the *antecedent-consequent* effect. This question-answer relation is complemented by the relation that results from the sharing of melodic material.

When adjacent phrases share the same material, the phrase relation is called *parallel phrase construction*. In such a phrase relation the sharing of material occurs at the beginning of the phrases. The cadences are different, for if they were identical they would be merely repeated.

Ex. 5-18 is another illustration of parallel phrase construction. In this instance only the last measure of the second phrase differs. The first raises the question by remaining tonally and rhythmically "open," whereas the second phrase answers by closing on the tonic on a strong metric position.

Ex. 5-18. Mozart: Sonata in A Major, K. 331, I.

Inter-phrase sharing of melodic material does not always occur. When adjacent phrases do not share material the relation is called *contrasting phrase construction*, as Ex. 5-19a and 5-19b illustrate.

Ex. 5-19a. Schubert: *An die Leier.*

Ex. 5-19b. Dufay: *Craindre vous vueil.*

Both of the excerpts are balanced two-phrase structures, as are those in Ex. 5-17 and Ex. 5-18. In one respect, however, the balanced structure of Ex. 5-19b differs: the phrase lengths are unequal, 4 +3, instead of 4 + 4.

When adjacent phrases are the same length they form a *symmetric* structure; when the adjacent phrases are of unequal length, the result is *asymmetric.* In Ex. 5-20 the phrases also vary in length. Nevertheless, the melody is highly coherent because of its motivic and figural unity.

Ex. 5-20. Hovhaness: *Prayer of Saint Gregory,* for Trumpet and String Orchestra. Copyright 1952 by Peer International Corporation. Reprinted with permission of the copyright owner.

Formal units containing phrases of equal duration are common, for they create an easily understood musical form. In Ex. 5-21 both phrases are four measures long. Moreover, each phrase is a complete rhythmic unit. However, the parallel phrases are dependent upon one another tonally; a terminal cadence does not appear until the end of the second phrase.

Ex. 5-21. Beethoven: Piano Sonata, Op. 31, No. 3.

Both phrases in Ex. 5-21 form a musical *period.* In a period, two or more phrases are joined by avoiding an implication of finality at the close of the interior phrase or phrases. In Ex. 5-21 this is accomplished by the progressive cadence at the end of the first phrase. The two-phrase formal unit, then, is understood when the terminal cadence appears at the end of the excerpt.

Many melodic periods consist of only two phrases. However, this is not always the case. In Ex. 5-22 three phrases combine to form a period. Each of the phrases contains similar melodic elements. Since the second phrase does not have a strong rhythmic close, there is no suggestion of finality until the end of the third phrase.

Ex. 5-22. Beethoven: Symphony No. 8, I.

Formal sections consisting of four or more dependent phrases occur frequently. In Ex. 5-23 a larger formal unit is not heard until all four phrases have been stated. Not only are the first and third, and the second and fourth, phrases rhythmically similar, they are also alike in pitch contour. Notice the subtle pitch changes in the last phrase which provide variety and delay the arrival of tonic. The second cadence (measure 8) binds the first phrase pair to the last by closing on supertonic. Each of the phrase pairs forms a period. In this example, however, the two periods are dependent upon one another both tonally and rhythmically. Such joining of phrase pairs is often called a *double period*.

Ex. 5-23. Haydn: Symphony No. 93, I.

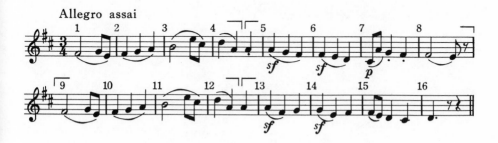

It is impossible to exhaust all the possibilities for constructing phrases, for every composition presents new solutions. However, certain principles are present in all compositions.

1. A phrase is a rhythmic-pitch unit marked off by a cadence. The stress patterns produced by rhythm and pitch generally reinforce the meter of a phrase as indicated by the meter signature.

2. The length of phrases, considering only the number of measures, is variable. In part, the length is determined by tempo; more precisely, it is completely influenced by our psychological span of attention. Certain phrase lengths predominate, e.g., in a slow tempo, two measure phrases; in a faster tempo, four or more. Other phrase lengths, such as three, five, etc., are also possible.

3. The shape or contour of a phrase is the result of the placement of high and low pitches. The apex and the lowest pitch of a phrase are usually either the tonic, mediant, or dominant.

Exercises

For more detailed assignments see *Materials and Structure of Music I, Workbook*, Chapter 5.

1. Perform each of the examples in this chapter. Listen for the larger formal sections. Isolate the motive, or motives, and describe the rhythmic structure and pitch structure of each motive found.

2. Use several of the motives contained in examples cited in this chapter as the principal unifying factor in two-phrase melodies.

3. Devise three or four original motives. Then use these motives to organize original three-phrase melodies.

4. Listen to and analyze the phrase structure of songs by Schubert, Schumann, and Brahms. Describe phrase lengths, pitch structure, and rhythmic structure of the melodies selected.

5. Find examples of melody in the literature for your voice or instrument containing parallel phrase construction, contrasting phrase construction, and period construction.

6. Listen to the first movement of Mozart's Symphony No. 40 in *g* minor, K. 550. Compare the prominence given to the initial motive with the use of the motive in the first movement of Beethoven's Symphony No. 5.

7. Find examples of melodies in a collection such as the *Historical Anthology of Music* in which motive repetition, phrase repetition, etc., play a small organizational role. Describe how unity is achieved.

6

THE EXTENDED MELODY

In a broad sense, a melody may be regarded as the joining together of several phrases. One-phrase melodies are possible; however, most of the melodies we hear are longer. The principles of repetition and contrast form the core of our musical experience in extended melody.

Repetition of a musical unit produces emphasis, but excessive repetition can be boring. For this reason, contrasting ideas usually mark off the various parts of a melody, thereby contributing to musical balance and variety.

Contrast and repetition are opposites. In between these two extremes changes can be wrought that combine features of both. In other words, rhythmic and tonal patterns can be *varied* to produce contrasts that are still within the bounds of similarity.

Repetition

A simple way of extending a melody is to repeat complete phrase units. The repetition of the initial phrase in Ex. 6-1 immediately focuses our attention on that phrase. In this excerpt the repetition is almost exact.

Ex. 6-1. Schumann: *Dichterliebe,* "Im Wunderschönen Monat Mai."

More frequently the repetition of a pattern will contain some change, usually at the cadence. In Ex. 6-2 two changes appear: the progressive cadence (measure 4) is replaced by a terminal cadence in measure 8, and the pitch contour of measure 7 is slightly altered from its prototype in measure 3. This relation is typical of a two-phrase period in parallel construction.

Ex. 6-2. Brahms: Symphony No. 1, IV.

In many melodies extension is achieved by the repetition of a phrase at a different pitch level. This type of repetition is called *sequence*. In Ex. 6-3 the intervals are not precisely the same in both phrases because the change of pitch level in the second phrase is not an exact transposition of the first. A sequence that is not an exact transposition of its model is called a *modified* or *tonal* sequence. The following illustrates such a sequence.

Ex. 6-3. Prokofiev: Rigaudon, Op. 12, No. 3. Reprinted with permission of Robert Forberg (Sole agents: C.F. Peters Corporation, New York).

Sequential repetition is an important procedure for extending a melody: it provides both continuity and variety, as well as simplicity and economy. In Ex. 6-4 both four-measure phrases use the same material but not in precisely the same manner. The first phrase consists of two subphrases, the second subphrase forming a tonal sequence of the first. The end of the sequence is signalled by the change of the perfect fourth skip in measure 2 to a minor sixth skip in measure 4.

Ex. 6-4. Beethoven: Sonata in C Major, Op. 2, No. 3, I.

Ex. 6-5 illustrates a sequential section that is not diatonic. Note that the melodic pattern remains identical because it is an exact transposition. Such sequences are called *exact* or *real* sequences.

Ex. 6-5. Elliott Carter: Piano Sonata, II. Used with the permission of the copyright owner, Mercury Music Corporation.

In Ex. 6-6 the motive that begins in the last portion of measure 2 is treated sequentially, spinning out an extended contrasting phrase.

Ex. 6-6. Mozart: Quartet in D Major, K. 499, I.

Repetition need not be as obvious as in the previous examples. Some compositions repeat only the rhythm or motive of a phrase. In the melody of Ex. 6-7 none of the pitch patterns are exactly the same, but the phrases that have the same rhythmic shape contribute to the unity of the balanced design.

Ex. 6-7. Anonymous: *Sumer Is Icumen In.*

Just as melodies can be lengthened by sequence, so a phrase may be lengthened by adding material. One characteristic procedure is the repetition of a small melodic unit at the end of a phrase. The cadential *extension* in Ex. 6-8 lengthens the third phrase by reiterating the closing figure. The extended length of six measures better counterbalances the two preceding four-measure phrases.

Ex. 6-8. Beethoven: Sonata in F Minor, Op. 2, No. 1, III.

Another type of cadential extension delays the appearance of the cadence pitch. We expect the cadence to occur at measure 8 in Ex. 6-9. But we are deceived, for the motion to tonic is temporarily halted by a *fermata*, followed by the repetition of measure 7 in a stretched out version in measures 8 and 9 and measures 10 and 11. This delay intensifies our expectations and emphasizes the finality of this section.

Ex. 6-9. Beethoven: Sonata in C Major, Op. 53, I.

A phrase also may be lengthened by *internal extension*.[1] As in the cadential extension, the internal lengthening is accomplished by the repetition of some melodic unit, as in Ex. 6-10.

Ex. 6-10. Brahms: Symphony No. 3, II.

(Original version)

(Extended version)

The recognition of this type of phrase extension is dependent upon previously recognized phrase lengths. Thus a phrase built from motive repetitions or a phrase

---

[1] Also referred to as a lengthening by *interpolation*.

in which a motive fragment is repeated does not necessarily represent internal extension.

Internal extension is another possibility for extending a phrase or melody. In Ex. 6-11 the first phrase establishes the phrase length we expect to hear continued, but the second phrase is stretched considerably through an internal sequence.

Ex. 6-11. Wagner: *Die Meistersinger,* Prelude to Act III.

Succeeding phrases may also be shortened, as in Ex. 6-12. Again an expectation of a four-measure phrase has been established; however, the second phrase is only three measures long. In this case the compression results from the omission of one measure in the second phrase. This type of compression is called *truncation.* Since truncated phrases result from shortening phrase duration, the effect of compression will be understood only if the phrase lengths have been previously established, and if the truncated phrases are easily relatable to an earlier phrase.

Ex. 6-12. Schubert: Sonata in A Major, II.

Still another type of compression occurs when the close of one phrase is the beginning of the next phrase, as in Ex. 6-13. Such phrase interlocking is called *elision.* When phrases elide, continuity is produced by avoiding a cadential "breathing point." Elision also creates a shorter total time span for the interlocked phrases than when a separation occurs between phrase endings and beginnings.

Ex. 6-13. Bach: Sonata No. 3 for Flute and Harpsichord, II.

Contrast

Successive repetition of a single musical pattern provides rather limited possibilities for extending a melody. Generally, the repetition of a first phrase unit is "interrupted" by the introduction of a contrasting pattern, which makes later restatements of the initial pattern more interesting and welcome.

In Ex. 6-14 the second phrase forms a contrast to the first by a change of contour, by slight changes in rhythm, and by the transient-terminal cadence.

Ex. 6-14. Beethoven: Symphony No. 2, II.

The third and fourth phrases are repetitions of the first two. The two-part sequence of the fifth phrase contrasts with the preceding phrases, and the sixth phrase adds still further variety to the whole melody.

For convenience, a letter system of diagraming is used to designate the various parts of a melody. If we call the first phrase of the preceding melody *a*, the form representation of the total melody would be *ab ab cd cd'*. There are four sections, each resulting from the combination of two phrases. Since each of these sections forms a larger unit, it is helpful to "reduce" the diagram to its lowest common denominator, A   A   B   B'[2]

      ab   ab   cd   cd'

A change of tonality may coincide with other contrast-producing elements, such as change of contour and pitch motion. Tonality change frequently is introduced at the end of a section, announcing that a new formal unit will follow. A return to the orginal tonality and a restatement of the opening material coincide in the following excerpt. Generally, changes of tonality are more essential to an extended composition than to a short melody. In either case, a new tonal center provides contrast.

---

[2] The designation *B'* (*B*-prime) is used because the last phrase (*d'*) is not the same as its model. *Prime* thus denotes similar but different.

Ex. 6-15. Schubert: *Der Alpen Jäger.*

Variation

In their simplest forms, repetition and contrast are easily understood. Of greater interest are those melodic procedures which combine elements of both, *i.e.*, gradations of contrast and repetition brought about by varying the materials. The fourth phrase of Ex. 6-16 is obviously related to the second phrase. By inverting the perfect fifth in measure 3, the resulting perfect fourth produces a change of pitch contour in measure 7. Note also that some of the pitches in measure 4 are eliminated in measure 8 to create a clearer cadential motion. As a whole, phrase four is a *variation* of phrase two.

Ex. 6-16. Schubert: Impromptu, Op. 142, No. 3.

We have already observed that phrases in parallel construction share material but that the pitch structure frequently is changed. In Ex. 6-17 the second phrase begins like the first, but the pitch structure is a variant of the first phrase.

Ex. 6-17. Schubert: Trio in B-flat Major, Op. 99, II.

Ex. 6-17 continued.

Notice that each of the phrases is three measures long, containing a three-measure and a one-measure extension. Both measures 4 and 8 are *variants* of measures 3 and 6, respectively.

Some forms of varying a melody normally occur when melodic units are restated in the later portions of a melody. In Ex. 6-18 both the pitch and rhythm patterns of the phrases are slightly ornamented, producing a more active variation of the initial statement.

Ex. 6-18. Le Bégue: Bourrée.

Frequently only parts of a phrase are varied in a later appearance. In Ex. 6-19 the approach to the final cadence of the excerpt is the same rhythmically in both versions. However, the varied version contains figurations not hinted at in the original.

Ex. 6-19. Satie: Fifth Nocturne. (C) 1920 by Editions Max Eschig, Paris. Renewed 1948. Reprinted by permission.

In variation movements melodic embellishment sometimes becomes the principal procedure of melodic organization. Ex. 6-20 shows typical changes a phrase might undergo in a variation movement.

Ex. 6-20. Beethoven: Symphony No. 5, II.

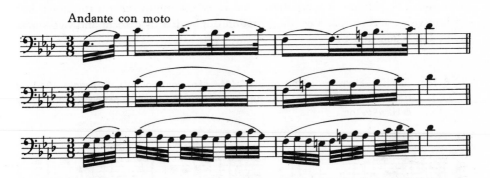

To a greater or lesser extent these procedures of variation could be used in any composition, either forming the basis for an entire movement, or appearing less consistently as an extension procedure. In any event, the relation of a variation to the original is usually apparent. However, the embellishments could reach a state of complexity in which the original melody is no longer recognizable.

In some melodies rhythms are varied by changing the durational values of all or parts of a phrase. In Ex. 6-21 the pattern of measures 9–12 is an *augmented* (lengthened) version of the preceding patterns in measures 5–6 and 7–8.

Ex. 6-21. Beethoven: Quartet in G Major, Op. 18, No. 2, IV.

The pattern that begins in measure 11 of Ex. 6-22 is a *diminished* (shortened) version of the pattern that begins in measure 5. If the tempo remains the same, augmentation lengthens a phrase; conversely, diminution shortens a phrase.

Ex. 6-22. Beethoven: Quartet in G Major, Op. 18, No. 2, IV.

Sometimes a melody is extended by *inverting* the contour of the whole or a part of a phrase. The rhythm of the pattern that is *inverted* might remain the same, but its intervals are reversed, ascending motion duplicated by descent and vice-versa, as in Ex. 6-23a and b.

Ex. 6-23a. Bartók: "From the Island of Bali" (*Mikrokosmos,* Vol. IV). Copyright 1940 by Hawkes & Son (London) Ltd., Renewed 1967. Reprinted by permission of Boosey & Hawkes Inc.

Ex. 6-23b. Brahms: *Ein deutsches Requiem,* "Wie lieblich."

Since change of contour creates only pitch contrast, the *inversion* of a pattern is easily recognized. Notice that only the first portion of Ex. 6-23a is inverted. Note also that measure 5 is a partial augmentation of measure 2.

Variety of phrase structure frequently is produced by *mutation.* In Ex. 6-24a, the fourth phrase repeats the third phrase in the parallel minor key; the third phrase in Ex. 6-24b also is in the parallel minor. In the latter, mutation coincides with the beginning of a new section, while in Ex. 6-24a phrase repetition is involved.

Ex. 6-24a. Beethoven: Sonata in C Major, Op. 53, III.

Ex. 6-24b. Schumann: *Carnaval,* "Reconnaissance."

Varying all or part of a motive or phrase is an important means for creating the extended melody. As a matter of fact, variation in some form is nearly always present in any musical composition.

Exercises

For more detailed assignments see *Materials and Structure of Music I, Workbook,* Chapter 6.

1. Extend Ex. 6-1 for four more measures. Use one of the procedures discussed in the chapter.
2. Find examples in music for your instrument or voice that contain sequence, variation, and change of tonality.
3. Write a melody that has as its basis the rhythmic structure of Ex. 6-7.
4. Listen to and analyze the phrase combinations of various works from Bartók's *Mikrokosmos,* Volume IV.
5. Use one of the motives invented for previous assignments as the basic unifying factor of a three-phrase melody. Create variety through the use of the procedure of inversion.
6. Write an experimental melody four phrases long that contains no repetition of pitch or rhythm patterns.
7. Listen to the first movement of Beethoven's Piano Sonata, Op. 2, No. 3. List and describe the ways in which Beethoven varies the motive and the phrase lengths.

7

BASIC MELODY

In the last five chapters our attention has been drawn to various aspects of melody—tonality, scale, cadence, phrase, and motive—that constitute the organizational procedures and materials. It is now possible to study the full melody and reduce its total pitch structure to a skeletal outline. Through this procedure many melodies can be seen as elaborations of essentially simple tonal plans. We shall call these fundamental outlines *basic melody*.

The pitches of a basic melody differ from less structural pitches because they receive special emphasis through their placement and function. In other words, the total pattern of tones is formed so that some individual parts are more important than others.

Strip an automobile of all its parts except its motor and drive mechanism, its chassis and wheel assembly, and, strictly speaking, an *automobile* still exists. The thousands of additional parts are in varying degrees elaborations or ornamentations of the core, the fundamental mechanism. No one would seriously advocate a return to such "fundamental autos," but clear knowledge of any object—car or melody—begins at the basic structure.

The tonality frame discussed in Chapter 2 is one kind of drastic melodic pitch reduction, representing the pitch order around which a melody is organized. In this sense, many melodies could have the same tonality frames; it is the varied "elaborations" of the frames that create the uniqueness and the charm of particular melodies.

The Mozart and Beethoven melodies in Ex. 7-1 not only share the same tonality frame types; they also resemble one another in the way this common pitch nucleus has been elaborated.

Ex. 7-1a. Beethoven: Sonata in F Minor, Op. 2, No. 1, I.

Ex. 7-1b. Mozart: Symphony in G Minor, K. 550, IV.

The tonality frame is, then, a basic level of pitch organization, serving as the tonal outline within which melodic activity takes place.

Moving on to the second higher level of organization, the pitches that determine total melodic shape constitute *basic melody*. By shape is meant the general sweep of melody, its important high and low points, its beginning and ending, and the important junctional pitches in between.

Any analysis of melody for discovering "tones of greater importance" is to a certain degree subjective. See if you would not agree, however, with the reductions shown below.

Ex. 7-2a. Beethoven: Basic melody of Ex. 7-1a.

Ex. 7-2b. Mozart: Basic melody of Ex. 7-1b.

Perhaps we could be even more drastic in our reduction analysis by further simplifying the above schemes to the more basic patterns shown next. This suggests that there can be more than one accurate basic melody for a single full melody, although any such representations should have a great deal in common.

Ex. 7-2c. Beethoven.

Ex. 7-2d. Mozart.

The third (and most complicated) level of melodic organization is the full-blown pattern, complete with the rhythmic life that creates the wonderful illusion of *moving tones,* the experience of music. Here the basic melody has been fleshed out with the patterns that link basic pitches and form the interesting relationships that make true melody. Look back to Ex. 7-1 and compare the whole melodic patterns there with the reduced forms of Ex. 7-2. These latter abstractions are mere skeletal outlines of their parent melodies.

For the present we shall view with greater interest the melodic skeleton, shifting our attention in Chapter 8 to the vital elaborations which form the final product.

Terminal Pitches in Tonal Melody

From the standpoint of basic melody, the most important tones are the first and the last. As end-points of what is heard, these tones are the structural time boundaries of melody. The last pitch is particularly important because, as the last sound heard, it offers an ultimate point to which all preceding pitches can be referred. Thus the final pitch in most tonal melodies is the *tonic* (I). When it is not, the pitch is usually a member of the tonic chord, the *dominant* (V), or the *mediant* (III).

The *first* pitch is the beginning of melodic pattern. As we observed in Chapter 2, it helps to lead the listener's attention into the rhythm and pitch frames within which the whole melody operates. The first pitch of melodies beginning on a metric accent is generally *tonic,* with the *dominant* and the *mediant* as lesser possibilities. Whatever the first pitch of the downbeat beginning, it usually is linked immediately with another member of the tonality frame, thereby leaving no doubt as to pitch orientation. (If this does not occur, a tonally ambiguous melody may be the result.)

Ex. 7-3a. Dufay: *Mon chier amy.*

Tonic beginnings

Ex. 7-3b. Mozart: Sonata in C Major, K. 545, I.

Ex. 7-3c. Schubert: Symphony in B Minor, I.

b:

Ex. 7-3d. Hindemith: Third Piano Sonata, I. (C) 1936 by B. Schott's Soehne, Mainz. Renewed 1963.

Mediant beginnings

A:

Ex. 7-3e. Mozart: Sonata in A Major, K. 331, I.

A:

Ex. 7-3f. Dvořák: Symphony In E Minor, II.

Db:

Ex. 7-3g. de Lantins: *Puisque je voy.*

Dominant beginnings

F:

Ex. 7-3h. Schubert: Symphony in B Minor, I.

b:

Melodies with weak metric beginnings—the *anacrusis* or *upbeat* pattern—do not often start with *tonic.* Rather, their first sound is usually the *dominant,* the *mediant,* or, in rare instances, the *leading tone.* This first pitch is then followed on the first strong beat by the *tonic* or another member of the tonality frame. The excerpts of Ex. 7-4 show various ways in which the anacrusis melody initiates its tonal pattern.

Ex. 7-4a. Liszt: Hungarian Rhapsody No. 9.

Ex. 7-4b. Telemann: Fantasia for Harpsichord No. 1.

Ex. 7-4c. Shostakovitch: Symphony No. 7, I. (C) Copyright by Leeds Music Corporation, New York, N.Y. Used by permission. All rights reserved.

Ex. 7-4d. Haydn: Sonata No. 6, II.

In still other melodies the first tone's relation to the tonality is not made clear immediately. In association with other parts of a texture the relation might be made clear by accompanying chords (as in Ex. 7-5a). But in terms of solely melodic pattern, the delayed appearance of the tonic pitch can create a degree of tonal suspense. This is particularly evident in melodies like 7-5c; here the tonic (*B*) occurs as early as measure 3, but its function in its early appearances is so decorative that it seems to arrive *as tonic* only at the end.

Ex. 7-5a. Copland: Concerto for Clarinet, I. Copyright 1949, 1950, 1952 by Aaron Copland. Reprinted by permission of Aaron Copland, Copyright Owner, and Boosey & Hawkes Inc., Sole Licensees.

Ex. 7-5b. Chopin: Etude, Op. 25.

Ex. 7-5c. Bartók: Concerto for Orchestra, IV. Copyright 1946 by Hawkes & Son (London) Ltd. Reprinted by permission of Boosey & Hawkes Inc.

The interior cadence pitches at phrase endings are also emphasized links in the tonal chain. It is not an exaggeration to think of the cadence as a point of respite at which the listener can take stock of what has preceded, instantly forming an impression of the important tonal events that have led to this point in the melody. The role performed by cadence pitches is basic, then, to the total organization of the melody.

At this point we can make a rudimentary analysis of melody by abstracting the first and last pitches and all cadence pitches to reveal a good deal more than what is provided by the tonality frame.

Ex. 7-6a. Brahms: Intermezzo in E-flat Major, No. I.

Ex. 7-6b. Barber: *School for Scandal,* Overture. Reprinted by permission of copyright owner, G. Schirmer, Inc.

Ex. 7-6c. Vivaldi: Violin Concerto in C Minor, III.

To make our search for basic pitches more penetrating we must study units smaller than the phrase. In addition to the terminal pitches, others can be basic because of: (1) their positions as parts of the overall melodic contour, (2) their relatively great duration, and (3) their favored metric position.

Melodic Contour and Step-Progression

If we regard a melody as a line that weaves through points on the musical staff, we see that the resultant wave usually possesses height and depth. Like the first and last pitches, the highs and lows of melodic motion are impressive parts of melodic shape.

The basic structure of Ex. 7-7 becomes clearer when these tops and bottoms of emphasis are incorporated into the reduction that first was attempted in Ex. 7-6.

Ex. 7-7. Barber: *School for Scandal,* Overture. Reprinted by permission of copyright owner, G. Schirmer, Inc.

(Partial reduction)

The *g* of measure 6 is not a low point of the immediate pattern, for the *e* that follows is still lower. The *g* is structurally important, however, because it is part of a *step-progression* formed between the low pitch of measure 5 (*a*) and the final *f*. As one level in this brief descending stair-step, its basic role in the melodic shape is established.

This does not mean that every step relation in a melody automatically forms a *step-progression*. On the contrary, step-progression refers to delayed ascending or descending steps *which outline the contour of the melody over the whole or a large segment of the phrase.*

Almost any melody contains a step relation of some kind between some two or more pitches, but this alone does not warrant recognition as a step-progression. To achieve this status such a pattern must create a recognizable uniformity within the pitch design, an obvious linking of highs and lows that controls the melodic progress from one melodic segment to another. Exx. 7-8 through 7-12 clarify the function of a step-progression within a melodic form.

The circled notes of Ex. 7-8 establish a clear line of ascent by step for a sizable portion of the pattern. The successive steps in other parts are mere decorative motions, activities which lead from one basic pitch to another. Bach did not allow this rather strict and obvious ladder of steps to dominate his line altogether, for the *e* of measure 3 overshoots the conclusion of the ascending pattern, thus avoiding monotony and stressing the pitch *d* as the beginning of the following part of the melodic shape.

Ex. 7-8. J.S. Bach: Fugue in G Major (*Well-tempered Clavier*, Book I).

Step-progression

These tracings of pitch by delayed steps sometimes form the backbone for whole melodies, sometimes for only isolated parts, and then in some melodies it is impossible to find a genuine step-series that seems to provide this organizing function. When they do occur, they can lead the listener to expect melodic contours of a particular shape and to anticipate climactic points. In the latter case, the pitch of "arrival" usually will be a part of the tonality framework or a pitch that rhythmically "leans" on a member of this group.

In some melodies the step-progression forms a periodic ascent or descent clearly allied with metric accent, as in the Bach melody of Ex. 7-8. In others its contour is more subtly imbedded in the pitch motion, as in (b) of Ex. 7-9.

Ex. 7-9a. Lully: Overture to *Alceste.*

Step
pro-
gression

Ex. 7-9b. Palestrina: *Missa Vestiva i Colli,* Kyrie.

Ex. 7-9c. J. Strauss: *Emperor* Waltz.

Still other melodies display partial ascent or descent by delayed step relations without really forming a step-progression. The patterns marked with brackets in Ex. 7-10 are fragmentary; none adds up to a pattern that controls the ascent or descent of the whole line.

Ex. 7-10. Glazunov: *Carnival* Overture.

The highest pitches of the smaller groupings in measures 2 and 4 do not lead in a *regular* way to the apex of the line, the *a* of measure 5. Even if *g* is heard as the most important high pitch (because of its repetition in measure 6), it too is not reached by delayed steps.

The ascending step-progression is probably a structural feature in more melodies than the descending, but the same organization can be found as a falling pattern in enough melodies to justify recognition. In many cases the low pitch of a line will return after intervening patterns, creating a mild form of pedal or "drone." This kind of repetition serves as a structural ground over which the melodic motion freely unwinds, as in Ex. 7-11b.

Ex. 7-11a. J.S. Bach: Fugue in F Major (*Well-tempered Clavier,* Book I).

Ex. 7-11b. J.S. Bach: Three-voice Invention in B Minor.

Ex. 7-11c. Handel: Organ Concerto, Op. 4, No. 4.

The pitch basis of the melody in Ex. 7-11c is clearly a double step-progression, the upper pattern moving in contrary motion to the lower. The combination of two such distinct step-lines can create the illusion of two separate parts if the lines have a distinct separation of range. The Bach melody in Ex. 7-12 is typical of such "one-line counterpoint." Its step-progressions descend.

Ex. 7-12. J.S. Bach: Three-voice Invention in D Major.

Like two wires suspended in space, the delayed steps formed by these two lines frame the pitch activity sandwiched in between, which in this excerpt is relatively negligible.

The pitches that constitute a clear step-progression are significant parts of the melodic shape and are, therefore, parts of the *basic melody*. When no step-progression is evident only the peaks of melodic motion can be regarded as basic pitches, and then only when their metric location and duration favor them over their neighbors.

Duration and Metric Locations

If other elements are equal, a tone that sounds longer than those around it will attract more attention. Even when metric accent coincides with one pitch, another close by will be regarded as more important if its duration is considerably greater or if it acts as the cadence point for the phrase.

Ex. 7-13. Tchaikovsky: Symphony No. 5, II.

Basic
melody

When greater duration *and* metric accent are embodied in the same pitch, that pitch is thereby all the more impressive. Such couplings of organizational functions produce a simplicity of structure that reduces the listener's problem of understanding, because rhythmic stress coincides with metric stress.

Ex. 7-14a. J.S. Bach: Passacaglia in C Minor.

Basic
melody

Ex. 7-14b. Brahms: Symphony No. 2, I.

The third measure of the Brahms melody of Ex. 7-14b shows how repetition within the measure can confirm a pitch's basic role. Obviously, repetition without intervening pitches is a simple extension of duration, for no other pitch competes for attention. But repetition within the immediate pattern (of approximately one measure), even after intervening tones, also emphasizes the returning pitch.

The Beethoven melody in Ex. 7-15 shows arabesques of eighth notes moving around the repetition of the pitches that fall on metrical accents in measures 1 and 2. Because of their subsequent return these pitches are confirmed as basic. Note the dual step-progression formed in the final three measures.

Ex. 7-15. Beethoven: Symphony No. 5, III.

Basic
melody

In highly ornamented music, consisting of a broad range of rhythmic values, some pitches act as pivots around which others skitter as orbitings around a mother planet. Repeated returns to a single pitch as the rallying point substantiate it as basic for the pattern. The melodies in Ex. 7-16 contain some pitches that are basic because of their extended durations; others are fundamental because of this concentration of neighbors around the one pitch.

Ex. 7-16a. J.S. Bach: Prelude in E Minor (*Well-tempered Clavier*, Book I).

Basic melody

Ex. 7-16b. Corelli: Concerto Grosso.

As dual representatives of basic structure, the *basic melody* and the *tonality frame* reveal the organization of pitches within a particular melody in its barest form. As we have seen, the two are similar, the tonality frame itself a maximum reduction of melody to the tonal nucleus of overall structure.

Melodies which lack the tonal orientation typical of the kinds of traditional patterns we have been discussing still usually exhibit some pitches that function as reference points for their less basic associates. For this reason the concept of basic melody is relevant to a greater body of music than the concept of the tonality frame.

In the following chapter we shall examine the various ways basic pitches are linked to create the logical tonal flow that characterizes the successful melody. Naming these links *elaborations* or *decorative patterns* is no indication of lesser importance. Melody is as much the manifestation of its decorative overlay as of its basic structure. The separation of *basic* from *decorative* is made for purposes of understanding rather than as a standard of musical values.

The pattern (a) in Ex. 7-17 by itself would interest no listener for long. But when used as the basis for the pattern shown at (b), it is transformed into a dynamic melodic statement that seizes a listener's attention and begs of continuation.

Ex. 7-17. Beethoven: Quartet in F Major, Op. 18, No. 1, I.

Any melody is to a certain degree unique; it therefore draws attention to those aspects of its structure that are different from those of another melody. Because of this singularity, each melody demands recognition of its peculiar arrangement of tones. We can nonetheless establish a guide to analysis that will serve efficiently for any attempt to determine basic pitches within the whole melody. One should attend to the following:

1. *Terminal pitches*, both first and last (within phrases) and highest and lowest;
2. *Stressed pitches*, because of agogic, dynamic, or metric accent;
3. *Repeated pitches*, both immediate or delayed within the phrase; and
4. Pitches which help to form a notable *step-progression*.

Exercises

For more detailed assignments see *Materials and Structure of Music I, Workbook*, Chapter 7.

1. Select a number of melodies six to eight measures long (from a collection of sight singing melodies, violin sonatas, songs, etc.). Copy each melody on manuscript paper, leaving one blank staff beneath each line of melody. On the blank staff plot the basic pitches for the accompanying melody, using whole note heads for basic pitches and black note heads for any less basic pitches which seem too important to exclude. Keep in mind the four points made at the end of this chapter in determining which pitches are basic.
2. Make up several basic melodies, assigning one pitch to each measure of any meter. Using this framework as a basic guide, add other pitches in a variety of rhythms which make a full and logical melody that you can sing or play. Be sure that the basic pitches are preserved as the dominating elements in each measure.
3. Follow the same procedure as in 2, but improvise (by singing or playing) the patterns around the selected basic pitches. Be sure to keep a steady tempo in your performances.
4. Abstract basic pitches from any melody or use basic pitches from melodies shown in this chapter and create new melodies which use these as a basis.
5. Write a melody that corresponds to each of the following basic contours. Use any key, meter, and scale desired.

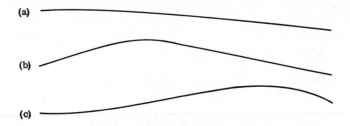

(a)

(b)

(c)

Make up other contour patterns to be used as guides for melodies, and analyze the contours of melodies found in literature.

6. Find several melodies which clearly incorporate a step-progression (or step-progressions) as a main feature of organization.

7. Have a friend play a melody for you. Measure off the number of bars contained in the melody and plot the basic pitches of the whole pattern. Don't try to get every pitch at first; begin with the first and the last pitches, proceed to the highest and lowest, and then fill in other pitches as they become known.

8

MELODIC ELABORATION

Reduction to basic melody reveals pitch organization in its simplest form. Few melodies exist in such bare outline. In most melodies the skeletal structure is a support for the distinguishing pitch activity by which we recognize melodic individuality. The pitches that are the overlay of the melodic skeleton are elaborative; they decorate and link the basic pitches. Distinct melodic patterns are created by the linking activity of these decorative pitches, and various types are identifiable by their particular relationship to the basic melody.

The simplest form of melodic elaboration is created by repeating a note. In Ex. 8-1 the repetition of *g-flat* emphasizes that note; however, its relative duration is not changed by the rearticulation.

Ex. 8-1. Bartók: "Fourths" (*Mikrokosmos,* Vol. V). Copyright 1940 by Hawkes & Son (London) Ltd., Renewed 1967. Reprinted by permission of Boosey & Hawkes Inc.

The basic pitches of many melodies (particularly those of the Classical period) are elaborated by disjunct tonal activity, often involving chord outlining. In Ex. 8-2 *e-flat* and *b-flat* are the basic pitches by virtue of their metric position and duration. Because of their unaccented positions and lesser durations, the notes marked * have a lesser structural significance.

Ex. 8-2. Beethoven: Symphony No. 3, I.

These less important pitches will be called *secondary* pitches. Secondary pitches are joined to basic pitches by leap and generally occur in unaccented rhythmic positions within the phrase. There are essentially two types of secondary pitches, those with clear chordal associations (as in Ex. 8-2) or those with only intervallic associations with adjacent basic pitches, as in Ex. 8-1 and measure 2 of Ex. 8-3.

Ex. 8-3. Schoenberg: Piano Piece, Op. 11, No. 2. Used by Permission of Belmont Music Publishers, Los Angeles, California.

The secondary and repeated pitches are important aspects of melodic organization, but they represent only two types of melodic elaboration. Other, less obvious, decorative patterns are also significant.

The sequential phrase shown in Ex. 8-4 uses two different types of melodic elaboration.

Ex. 8-4. Stravinsky: Octet, Sinfonia. Copyright 1924 by Edition Russe de Musique; Renewed 1952. Copyright & renewal assigned to Boosey & Hawkes Inc. Revised version Copyright 1952 by Boosey & Hawkes Inc. Reprinted by permission.

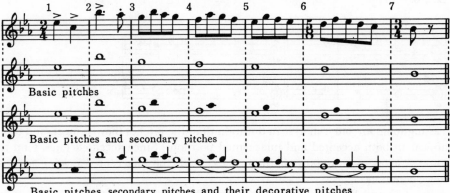

In measures 3–6 the first note of each measure is a basic pitch because of its metric position. The predominant pitch activity is a sequence of thirds. The upper note of each third has a subsidiary structural significance, hence a secondary pitch. In the descending motion to the last note of each pattern the third is filled in. This filler tone smooths out the disjunct motion of the sequential pattern and at the same time embellishes each basic pitch. The decorative notes (shown as ♩ in the sketch) participate in a step-progression that links a secondary pitch to a basic pitch.

Decorative pitches can embellish a basic melody with either of two different types of tonal activity: (1) the decorative pitch *exceeds* the range of two basic pitches or a basic pitch and a secondary pitch (as in Ex. 8-5a and Ex. 8-5b); or (2) the decorative pitch remains *within* the range of two basic pitches or a basic pitch and a secondary pitch (as in Ex. 8-5c). In Ex. 8-5, and in all subsequent examples the basic pitches are represented by o, the secondary pitches by •, and the decorative pitches by ♩. The tie, ⌣, denotes that the same basic pitch is being decorated over a period of time.

Ex. 8-5.

Decorative pitches often have names that describe clearly the role they play. For example, since most melodies use a preponderance of steps, decorative pitches called *passing tones* appear frequently. This is an apt description, because passing tones connect two different basic pitches (or a basic pitch and its secondary pitch), as in Ex. 8-6.

Ex. 8-6.

Passing tones are often shorter in duration than the pitches they connect, and they appear in both accented and unaccented positions. Since accented tones tend to impress us as more important than unaccented, the unaccented passing tone is more common.

Ex. 8-7a and Ex. 8-7b show both types. The *d-natural* in measure 4 of Ex. 8-7c is a chromatic passing tone. Note that the diatonic passing tones (notes belonging to one diatonic scale) link two notes a third apart; chromatic passing tones generally link two notes a major second apart.

Ex. 8-7a. Beethoven: Quartet in E-flat Major, Op. 74, IV.

Ex. 8-7b.

Ex. 8-7c. Beethoven: Sonata in A-flat Major, Op. 110, I.

In highly ornamental melodies several tones sometimes link structural pitches that are more than a third apart. Generally these linking notes are of short duration, playing the same decorative role as a single passing tone. For this reason they also are referred to as passing tones (bracketed in Ex. 8-8).

Ex. 8-8. Bach: Gigue (*Little Notebook of Anna Magdalena Bach*).

Another decorative pitch that appears frequently is the *neighbor tone*.[1] Like the passing tone, this type of embellishment can be found in both accented and unaccented positions. Step motion is again involved, the neighbor moving away (either up or down) from a basic pitch and returning to it. Neighbor tones also may be diatonic or chromatic. Since neighbor tones embellish a single tone, delayed repetition is involved. This emphasizes the repeated tone, creating a more interesting pattern than simple rearticulation.

In Ex. 8-9 the neighbor tones are indicated by N.T. The neighbors (*b-sharp* in measure 9, *a-sharp* in measure 11) in Ex. 8-9b are chromatic.

---

[1] Sometimes called *auxiliary tone* or *returning note*.

Ex. 8-9a. Mozart: Sonata in D Major, K. 576, III.

Ex. 8-9b. Beethoven: Sonata in E Minor, Op. 90, II.

Chromatic passing tones and neighbor tones do not affect tonality. Even if a note has the appearance of a new leading tone, duration will determine the amount of influence it can exert and helps to distinguish a chromatic *decorative pitch* from a chromatic *structural pitch*.

The frequent use of passing tones and neighbor tones does not make them more significant than other kinds of decorative pitches. As a matter of fact, their repeated occurrence indicates that the conditions for their particular decorative role are often present. Thus, in those melodies containing structural pitches that are a third apart, passing tones smooth the line by filling in melodic gaps, thereby bringing the structural pitches into closer relationship. Similarly, if repeated tones play an important part in the structure of a melody, the effect of such repetition is intensified by the incorporation of neighbor tones and secondary pitches.

Both the passing tone and the neighbor tone are approached and followed by step. Motion by step is a factor in most decorative patterns; some types do not use step-step pitch configuration. At times a decorative tone is given greater emphasis because it is either approached or left by skip. This added emphasis directs attention to the decorative tone; consequently, decorative patterns containing skips other than between a basic pitch and a secondary pitch appear infrequently. Two different decorative pitches can be classified in this way: the *appoggiatura*[2] and the *escape tone*.[3]

---

[2] Literally, *leaning tone*. A phrase that may be used instead of the Italian.
[3] Sometimes called an *échappée*.

Appoggiaturas are approached by skip and then move to a structural pitch by step. The appoggiatura directs attention to the note of arrival by delaying it momentarily. Furthermore, the motion by step to the embellished tone creates the impression of "leaning," which explains the use of this particular descriptive term.

Ex. 8-10.

Appoggiaturas appear in both accented and unaccented metric positions. They are usually shorter in duration than the notes they embellish, and the motion to the subsequent basic pitch is frequently in the opposite direction from the skip that introduces the appoggiatura. In all cases it follows the pattern of skip (either up or down) step.

In Ex. 8-11 the appoggiatura in measure 1 is easily recognized because its relative importance is clearly indicated by the notation. This literal representation of a leaning tone is common.

Ex. 8-11. Mozart: Sonata in D Major, K. 284, III (Variation 12).

If this type of notation is not used, the duration of the appoggiatura is designated the same way as the other notes. In Ex. 8-12 the appoggiaturas are not set apart by notation, but are notated as part of the total fabric of the phrase. In this example the basic pitches create an ascending step-progression.

Ex. 8-12. Beethoven: Sonata in C-sharp Minor, Op. 27, No. 2, III.

Sometimes the appoggiatura and the pitch it embellishes have the same duration. When this occurs it can be difficult to differentiate between decorative and structural notes. However, in Ex. 8-13 the appoggiatura is also the leading tone of the key, and it embellishes the tonic note.

Ex. 8-13. Mendelssohn: *A Midsummer Night's Dream,* Intermezzo.

In Ex. 8-14 the chromatic appoggiaturas emphasize the second and third scale steps, while the diatonic appoggiaturas emphasize the tonic and the subdominant. Notice that the duration of the structural pitches varies, and the half-step relations create a strong motion to the structural tones.

Ex. 8-14. Beethoven: Sonata in G Major, Op. 14, No. 2, I.

A more complex situation is illustrated in Ex. 8-15. Here the duration of the appoggiatura is greater than that of the embellished note. In measure 3, *a* is a secondary pitch to *f-sharp*; therefore, even though *g-sharp* receives greater stress because of its duration, its melodic role is decorative.

Ex. 8-15. Carter: Woodwind Quintet, I. (C) 1952 by Associated Music Publishers, Inc., New York. Reprinted by permission.

The melodic opposite of the appoggiatura, the *escape tone*, moves to a basic pitch or a secondary pitch by skip, while the motion preceding it is by step. Although it can be found in both accented and unaccented positions, it is usually an unaccented elaboration.

Ex. 8-16.

Like the appoggiatura, the motion away from an escape tone usually involves a change of direction, as shown below. In both examples the decorative note "escapes" from one important tone before moving to the next.

Ex. 8-17a. Chopin: Sonata in B Minor, Op. 58, I.

Ex. 8-17b. Bach: *St. John Passion,* "Wäre dieser nicht ein Übeltäter?"

Sometimes, however, the motion continues in the same direction, as in Ex. 8-17. We can still recognize this as a variation of the more common pattern which changes direction.

Ex. 8-18. Beethoven: Sonata in A Major, Op. 101, I.

Whichever direction it moves, the escape tone is usually of shorter duration than the tones surrounding it. If not, it normally appears in a less prominent metric position.

The decorative patterns discussed in the preceding sections involve only one embellishing tone, with the exception of a group of passing tones used to fill in an interval larger than a third, or a third with chromatic activity. The figure called a *neighbor group* always involves two decorative tones that embellish a single basic pitch. Both decorative notes are neighbors to the basic tone, one located a step above, the other a step below; a skip occurs between the two neighbor tones, the resulting pitch pattern forming a step-skip-step sequence. Often one of these decorative tones is unaccented, the other accented.

The neighbor groups in Ex. 8-19 embellish the cadence pitch. Since the repeated cadence tone is in evidence for a relatively long period of time, the neighbor groups in this excerpt create greater tonal activity and variety.

Ex. 8-19. Haydn: Quartet in F Major, Op. 74, No. 2, I.

In Ex. 8-20 the neighbor groups extend the duration of the basic pitches. Notice how closely the decorative activity of this figure resembles the neighbor tone figure.

Ex. 8-20. Mozart: Quartet in A Major, K. 464, I.

Another type of decorative pitch, the *anticipation*, prepares for the appearance of a basic pitch. It is by nature an unaccented pattern, almost always of lesser duration than the pitches surrounding it. The pitch motion is generally step-rearticulation, as in Ex. 8-21.

Ex. 8-21. J. S. Bach: Two-voice Invention in C Minor.

Sometimes the motion preceding the anticipation is by skip, resulting in a skip-rearticulation pattern. Generally when this variation of the more common pattern occurs, disjunct secondary pitches are also present. Therefore, the anticipation announces one of the notes that is contained in the disjunct line, as can be seen in the opening of Ex. 8-22. As is apparent, the anticipation is primarily a rhythmic elaboration.

Ex. 8-22. Beethoven: Sonata in E-flat Major, Op. 31, No. 3, III.

Melodic *suspension* is another form of rhythmic elaboration. Very often the suspension involves a basic pitch that moves to another basic pitch or to a secondary pitch by step, usually down. In this process the first basic pitch extends beyond a metric or rhythmic accent by means of a tie or rearticulation. This delays the appearance of the second basic pitch and makes the middle note of the pattern fall in an unaccented position.

Ex. 8-23.

The suspension figure is characterized by the following: (1) a basic pitch is prolonged by means of a tie or rearticulation; (2) this basic pitch extends past a metric or rhythmic accent; and (3) this suspended basic pitch moves to an unaccented basic pitch or secondary pitch by step.

In Ex. 8-24 a suspension appears on the first beat of measure 3. Here the suspension is created by the tied basic *f*. The result is an elaboration of the phrase rhythm. In addition, the entire process emphasizes the basic pitch more than if the suspension had not occurred.

Ex. 8-24. Hindemith: *Mathis der Maler,* I. Copyright 1934 by B. Schott's Soehne-Mainz. Copyright renewed 1962 by B. Schotts Soehne-Mainz.

In Ex. 8-25 the duration of the basic *g* is extended by its rearticulation on the first beat of measure 4. This delays the anticipated appearance of a different pitch on an accented first beat. The rearticulated suspension creates an effect similar to that of the tied suspension.

Ex. 8-25. Tchaikovsky: Symphony No. 5, II.

Sometimes the motion of the suspended basic pitch to the second note of the pattern is "interrupted" by the interpolation of a decorative pitch, as in Ex. 8-26. Here the two tones of the suspension figure are separated by the interpolated appoggiaturas.

Ex. 8-26. Bach: *Art of the Fugue.*

If melody alone is considered, the distinction between basic pitches, secondary pitches, and decorative pitches may not always be readily apparent. Most melodies occur in association with other melodies or chords and in specified tempos. When all factors are weighed, including tempo, the distinctions will become more apparent; similarly, some interpretations based purely on linear premises may have to be changed in a contrapuntal or chordal surrounding.

Outline of Decorative Pitches

Type	Pitch Motion	Rhythmic Characteristics
Passing Tone	Step-step	Accented or unaccented
Neighbor Tone	Step-step	Accented or unaccented
Appoggiatura	Skip-step	Accented or unaccented
Escape Tone	Step-skip	Usually unaccented
Neighbor Group	Step-skip-step	Accented or unaccented
Anticipation	Step-rearticulation; or skip-rearticulation	Unaccented
Suspension	Step	Accented

Exercises

For more detailed assignments see *Materials and Structure of Music I, Workbook*, Chapter 8.

1. Determine the basic pitches of familiar melodies. Then use these basic melodies as the pitch framework for melodies that you write.
2. Use the phrase patterns from any example as the rhythmic basis for melodies that you write. Before writing, sketch in a pitch framework.
3. Create "new" melodies by elaborating the basic melodies of any of the examples in this chapter.
4. Create an original basic melody. Then elaborate this framework, using the same basic melody for melodies in simple and compound meters.
5. Describe all of the decorative pitches not identified in the analyses given in this chapter.
6. Analyze melodies selected from the following: Bartók, *Mikrokosmos*, Volumes I and II; Bach, *English Suites;* Mozart, *Piano Sonatas;* Beethoven, *Piano Sonatas;* Stravinsky, *Sonata for Two Pianos;* etc. Reduce each of the melodies selected to its basic pitches; then identify the role of each of the decorative pitches.

9

TWO-VOICE
COMBINATIONS

Our study so far has dealt with melody. Although we usually associate melody with a single prominent voice or instrument (as it is quite natural to do), it is essential that we see how melody exists in one way or another in each voice or part of a composition, and how features of melodic organization are present in varying degrees in different styles, forms, and textures of music.

Texture

Texture is a word that, as used by musicians, has taken on several different meanings. It refers to the number of voices or parts in a composition or section, but it also denotes the relationships of parts to each other. For instance, our next area of study will deal with two-voice textures, i.e., two-part music. But in addition, the texture of two-part compositions is often contrapuntal. Contrapuntal texture, that is, *counterpoint*, results from the simultaneous occurrence of two or more melodies, both of which maintain some degree of independence.

A more general distinction can be made among three basic kinds of textures; *monophonic*, comprising a single voice; *homophonic*, in which a predominant melody is supported by an essentially chordal accompaniment; and *polyphonic*, which literally means "many voices." [1]

Rhythmic Association

The possibilities of rhythmically combining two or more voices are enormous, but several basic observations can be made. A study of the examples in this section will reveal several different kinds of rhythmic combinations, each of which represents a common treatment of two relatively independent parts.

---

[1] *Polyphonic*, in the commonly used sense, refers to contrapuntal music consisting of rhythmically independent voices. However, this does not exclude many-voiced music that is essentially homorhythmic.

Ex. 9-1. Leonin: Organum.

Ex. 9-1 contains two voices of contrasting rhythms organized in $\frac{6}{8}$ meter. The upper part clearly predominates because of its greater activity. Both parts are unified through the use of recurrent patterns. This is a rudimentary kind of rhythmic association.

A relationship of 2 to 1 (![figure]) is established in Ex. 9-2.

Ex. 9-2. Handel: Suite No. 7, Allegro.

A more active and more interesting upper line is accompanied by a slower paced lower voice, which by itself is somewhat dull, since it consists mainly of continuous eighth notes, outlining broken chords. However, it is a logical foil for the more active part, providing a solid tonal-rhythmic basis for the upper voice. In the second measure the lower voice momentarily assumes a leading role.

A more smoothly fashioned supporting part is seen in Ex. 9-3. Here the two voices are completely independent rhythmically, and each makes a perfectly acceptable melody.

Ex. 9-3. Marini: Sonata for Violin and Organ (two outer parts).

Ex. 9-3 continued.

More equality of movement occurs in Ex. 9-4, and the distinction between main voice and accompaniment is less obvious than in Ex. 9-1 and Ex. 9-2.

Ex. 9-4. Haydn: Sonata in E-flat Major, III.

Both phrases are begun by the upper part alone, and its rhythmic diversity establishes it as the more interesting. In the second phrase, however, the voices enter imitatively, and the lower part matches the upper in activity and design for two measures. The close of the second phrase restores the original relationship of leader and subordinate associate.

Two equally active parts compete for attention in Ex. 9-5. Such competition is not infrequent in two-voice textures, although the capabilities of our own hearing almost rule out the clear perception of two equally active voices. However, we can shift attention from one voice to another to understand essentially what is going on, particularly if such activity is maintained for very long.

Ex. 9-5. Ockeghem: *Agnus Dei.*

In contrast to Ex. 9-5 by Ockeghem, a clear rhythmic distinction between two interesting independent voices can be noted in Ex. 9-6. Both parts reveal individual contours and remain rhythmically independent. Although the lower (piano) voice clearly provides a strong tonal framework (*a* minor) for the upper, its rhythmic individuality makes it equally important.

Ex. 9-6. Piston: Sonata for Violin and Piano, III. (C) 1940 by Associated Music Publishers, Inc., New York. Reprinted by permission.

In Ex. 9-6 the rhythmic separation of parts ( ) enables the listener to grasp more readily the activity of both voices. The recognition of equally important, simultaneously heard melodies is most clear when the voices have contrasting durations. When identical rhythms occur simultaneously, independence is minimized, and other factors, particularly pitch association, direction, and contour produce independence of parts.

Ex. 9-7 contains the same kinds of activity between parts. The listener is drawn from voice to voice, so to speak, by the give and take relationship which establishes the lower part as an imitator, derivative, or "borrower" from the upper. The lower voice systematically echoes the opening motive of the top voice and punctuates the movement of the continuous upper voice with octave leaps in eighth notes, followed by rests.

Ex. 9-7. Bach: Two-voice Invention in E Minor.

The opening of Bartók's First String Quartet, shown in Ex. 9-8, contains a rhythmic association somewhat comparable to the Bach excerpt discussed previously. It affords an excellent study of two-voice association in contemporary music and illustrates several of the basic principles noted in this chapter.

Ex. 9-8. Bartók: String Quartet No. 1 (opening). Reprinted by permission of Boosey & Hawkes Inc. Sole agents for "Kultura" (Hungarian Trading Company) in the U.S.A.

We have surveyed three basic rhythmic associations thus far: (1) a predominant melody, supported by a much less engaging associate; (2) a combination of two rhythmically independent parts, each of which makes acceptable melody with one understood as a leading voice, creating a give and take relationship; and (3), two equally active parts which move in different durations. When two voices employ identical durations (note against note style), the upper part usually prevails, and independence results from factors such as melodic direction, registration, and other aspects of pitch usage.

Pitch Association

Vocal Ranges and Spacing

Throughout the first sixteen hundred years of Western music the organization of melody depended most upon the vocal forms that dominated that broad time span. In these early forms, e.g., Gregorian chant, secular song, motets, chansons, and masses, our predecessors established and developed techniques of melodic composition that exploited the capabilities of the human voice. Instrumental melody had its origin in vocal music of the fifteenth and sixteenth centuries. During these years vocal works were often transcribed for small instrumental groups, or vocal parts were sometimes doubled by instruments. Many of the melodic patterns we have come to know through instrumental performance are of vocal origin.

In our beginning two-voice studies we shall limit our writing to the human voice, later expanding our study to include instrumental combinations. The necessity of performing all musical exercises and illustrations cannot be overstressed.

Consistent with most vocal compositions, we shall employ the following as practical voice ranges:

Each voice is granted a potential range of a twelfth. Needless to say, considerable care should be taken in approaching the extremities of any voice range. The effectiveness of the high or low areas of any voice is lost when overused, and average singers are not "at home" with melodies that remain in extreme lows or highs for long periods. Low tones in the bass, like high notes in the soprano, are often thin and lack definition.

The distances between two parts will depend partially on the particular voices used. For example, the widest gap that might occur between alto and soprano (in two-voice writing) would be a perfect fifteenth, considering the given ranges of both voices. Although possibly effective in isolated cases, such a wide space between two adjacent, unsupported voices would be rare indeed. On the other hand, unisons represent the smallest distance (or relationship) and are quite common cadentially. The usual limit for two adjacent voices is the octave, with tenths and even twelfths as rare possibilities.

Less common two-voice combinations such as tenor and soprano, or alto and bass, may exploit wider spacings because of the natural separation of the individual registers. In these cases the interval of a twelfth should be regarded as normal, with two octaves as a usual limit of separation. Common two-voice spacings are shown in the following excerpts.

Ex. 9-9. Palestrina: *Sicut cervus.*

Ex. 9-10. Josquin des Près: *Tu pauperum refugium.*

Ex. 9-11. J.S. Bach: B minor Mass, "Cum sancto spiritu."

The principles for two-voice spacing that have been outlined here can be summarized as follows: adjacent voices seldom exceed the octave, while non-adjacent pairs (such as soprano and tenor, or alto and bass) may move as far apart as two octaves. These principles will generally apply even when more than two parts are present; they will be modified when applied to instrumental deployment, as we shall see in Chapter 15.

Vertical Considerations in Two Voices; Consonance and Dissonance

We have been concerned up to now with horizontal aspects of pitch. But if we are to combine melodies, there must exist a basis for the selection of the harmonic intervals that they will create. A glance at any two-voice composition will show a variety of vertical combinations, and further study will reveal that composers employ systematic techniques for organizing harmonic intervals and successions of interval roots.

In Chapter 2 interval roots were discussed, and their relationship to the harmonic series was established. It is entirely logical that those intervals which are most stable, octaves, fifths and thirds, are most often found as the beginning and cadential harmonic intervals in two-voice textures. These intervals are essentially stable, or consonant, and because of the role that they have played in music are described as *cadential* or *basic consonances*. It is only in recent times that composers have accepted the possibility of beginning or closing on less stable intervals.

The perfect fourth and major and minor sixths seldom occur as cadential intervals *in two voices*. Because of their role in musical practice, these intervals are regarded as *decorative consonances*,[2] and their use in two-voice textures is subject to considerations of contrapuntal technique. The perfect fourth in particular is generally afforded a special kind of preparation and resolution.

You should note in Ex. 9-12 that most on-the-beat intervals are consonances; all phrase beginnings and endings involve stable intervals. Dissonances arise logically and unobtrusively from passing melodic activity as seen in measure 1, beat 4, measure 4, beat 2, measure 5, beat 4, and numerous other similar occurrences in the piece. The importance of such briefly heard activity is usually minimized by its incorporation into *step* motion in one or both parts. Verify the preceding remarks by a careful study of the harmonic materials of this example.

Ex. 9-12. Bach: Overture in F Major for Harpsichord, Bourrée.

---

[2] This applies, in the main, to tonal music.

Ex. 9-12 continued.

Ex. 9-13 can serve as an adequate reminder, for the time being, that more tense harmonic materials than those of Ex. 9-12 constitute the staples of much recent music; even many compositions of periods earlier than ours unfold a harmonic palette considerably more varied and dissonant than that of the Bach Bourrée cited above, as we shall find in future study. For the time being we shall center on two-voice compositions revealing a ready allegiance to tonality and essentially simple harmonic materials.

Ex. 9-13. Lukas Foss: Invention (for piano). Copyright © 1938 by Carl Fischer, Inc., New York. Copyright Renewed. International Copyright Secured.

Contrapuntal Motion Between Parts and Approaches to Structural Intervals

An important consideration in counterpoint is the directional relationship formed by the moving voices. When the parts proceed in opposite directions they produce *contrary motion,* and thus they assume an independence that is denied when they move in tandem, up or down. Contrary motion is an important feature of the cadence in two-voice textures, and it is often found in the interior areas of a phrase as well.

Contrary motion is generally balanced by other types of relations: *similar, parallel,* and *oblique* motion. Any two-voice work will reveal a variety of motion types. Those obtainable are illustrated in the examples below.

Ex. 9-14a. Illustration of contrary motion.

Parallel motion occurs when both voices move in the same direction while maintaining the same generic intervallic distance.

Ex. 9-14b. Illustration of parallel motion.

Similar motion results from movements in the same direction but which involve changing interval combinations.

Ex. 9-14c. Illustration of similar motion.

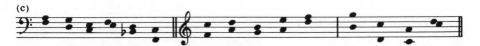

Oblique motion is produced by movement in one voice combined with a stationary second voice. (Repetition of the same tone is considered to be stationary movement as well as uninterrupted sound.)

Ex. 9-14d. Illustration of oblique motion.

Study the counterpoint in Ex. 9-15 having first performed the music. Note the various types of motion that are employed.

Ex. 9-15. J.C. Bach: *In dich hab ich gehoffet, Herr.*

A further consideration of contrapuntal motion concerns the *approach* or movement to cadential consonances, particularly the octave, fifth, and unison. Since these intervals produce stability and relative repose, it is logical that they have been used as the basis for achieving tonal stability. However, when these intervals are used in uninterrupted succession, they produce an effect of mutual dependence and inactivity that opposes the very nature of counterpoint, melodic independence. For these reasons (coupled with the desire to avoid monotonous repetition) composers have generally avoided consecutive fifths, octaves, and unisons in contrapuntal writing.

Furthermore, the movement to these intervals is often by *contrary motion*, with at least one voice (or both) moving by step. This principle is evident in measures 4, 5, and 10 of Ex. 9-16. Movement in contrary motion to basic intervals is more often found where these intervals fall on strong beats, or strong parts of the beat, as in Ex. 9-16.

Ex. 9-16. Zachau: *Vom Himmel hoch, da komm ich her.*

In Ex. 9-16 the composer has used a wide variety of consonances as basic intervals, and unstable intervals, which further contribute to variety, are the result of decorative patterns. The choice of intervals used and, to a large degree, the way in which they are treated, differ somewhat in individual musical styles. However, the proportion of thirds and sixths usually outweighs fifths, octaves, unisons, and fourths.

A comparison of Ex. 9-17 with Ex. 9-18 will suggest the intervallic variety possible in two-voice writing.

Ex. 9-17. Bach: Two-voice Invention in D Minor.

Ex. 9-18. Hindemith: *Marienleben.* (C) 1924 by B. Schott's Soehne-Mainz. Renewed 1951. Reprinted by permission.

In Ex. 9-17 Bach has relied upon thirds and sixths, primarily, as on-the-beat sonorities. Not until the cadence to *A* is a prominent octave heard. It is approached by contrary motion. The excerpt by Hindemith, Ex. 9-18 reveals considerably more intervallic variety, but it shows a kinship in the way fifths and octaves are approached by contrary motion.

Rhythm also affects vertical relationships. Fifths and octaves that fall on strong beats naturally attract more attention than those occurring on weak beats, and so the approach to these cadential intervals should be viewed in relation to metric position. Again, contrary and oblique motion are usually found in the approach to fifths, octaves, or unisons on strong beats. Similar motion, on the other hand, is not uncommon at cadences to the octave. In such cases the upper voice most often moves by step, while the lower voice skips up or down. As in Ex. 9-19a and Ex. 9-19b, cadential finality can be emphasized by directional agreement. Final cadences to a perfect fifth (which are quite rare) are almost never approached by similar motion (direct fifth).

Ex. 9-19a. Bach: Two-voice Invention in G Major.

Ex. 9-19b. Bach: Two-voice Invention in D Minor.

Contrapuntal Treatments of Other Consonances

Two-voice cadences to the fourth are uncommon, nor is the fourth often formed by the two basic pitches which approach a cadence. Its use is confined primarily to the interior areas of the phrase. Typical appearances of the fourth in two-voice writing occur in the next excerpt.

Ex. 9-20. Bach: Suite in B Minor, Allemande.

The fourths found in this example involve either a step approach, step resolution, or both. Like fifths, most accented fourths are reached by contrary motion, seldom by parallel or similar motion in two-voice textures; and examples of both voices moving in similar motion by skips to a fourth are rare. As we shall see, fourths, especially when accented, usually resolve to thirds.

When parallel fourths do occur, they generally involve durations of less than the prevailing basic duration. An example of movement in parallel fourths occurs in measure 1 of the excerpt in *d* minor by Bach (Ex. 9-19b.) Here the parallel motion in consecutive fourths is the result of movement around the basic pitch *A*. *D''*, the upper member of the first fourth moves to a lower neighbor, *c''-sharp*, while a passing tone *g* connects the lower *a* with *f*. The prominence of these fourths is negligible, since they fall on a weak beat.

Thirds and sixths are used more freely than eighths, fifths, and fourths in two-voice writing. Thirds, of course, occur cadentially, while sixths are seldom found as cadential intervals. Like other intervals, thirds and sixths represent only a part of a well-balanced contrapuntal formula. In contrast with other consonances, these intervals are often approached by similar and parallel motion, as well as by contrary and oblique motion. As a rule, composers avoid more than three parallel thirds or sixths moving consecutively. When these do occur, they are generally a mixture of major and minor thirds, rather than three major or three minor thirds. Parallel motion in any *identical* intervals destroys melodic independence and undermines tonality.

The degree to which intervallic variety and treatment contribute to interesting counterpoint is apparent in the following Mozart illustration.

Ex. 9-21. Mozart: Quartet in D Major, K 575, IV.

While subject to exceptions, the following principles of intervallic succession and melodic movement are upheld in most two-voice writing. Their application to our study of two-voice counterpoint should be adopted and applied in written assignments.

Summation of Principles of Melodic Movement and Intervallic Succession in Tonal Music

1. Metrically strong (stressed) open consonances (octaves, fifths, fourths and unisons) are usually approached in contrary motion.
2. Successive fifths, octaves and unisons are generally avoided.
3. Any succession of parallel thirds or sixths should include a mixture of both major and minor thirds or sixths. For example, a major third will most often be followed by a minor third, or a minor sixth will generally follow a major sixth.
4. Skips in either voice are generally balanced by steps in the other.
5. Simultaneous leaps in both voices are rare, and when they occur, they will generally be in contrary motion.
6. Leaps are usually followed by step motion or opposite leaps.
7. Melodic or harmonic tritones, like most augmented or diminished intervals, are generally resolved by step.

Perform and analyze the illustrations shown below.

Ex. 9-22a. Approaching open consonances.

Ex. 9-22b. Parallel fifths (avoid).

Ex. 9-22c. Parallel octaves (avoid).

Ex. 9-22d. Consecutive fifths (avoid).

Ex. 9-22e. Consecutive octaves (avoid).

Ex. 9-22f. Parallel thirds or sixths (common).

Ex. 9-22g. Skips balanced by steps.

Ex. 9-22h. Leaps resolved.

Basic Contrapuntal Treatments of Unstable Intervals

We are familiar with the unstable and ambiguous quality of the melodic tritone, and the problems it poses to vocal performance. It is this same unstable characteristic that, on the other hand, gives the tritone its special quality of expressiveness which many composers have favored as in Ex. 9-23a.

Ex. 9-23a. Wagner: *Tristan und Isolde,* Act. II.

Ex. 9-23b. Tritones in major-minor scales.

The tritone is perhaps most prominent where it occurs between the subdominant and the leading tone (4–7) of the major or minor scale. This relationship occurs both melodically and harmonically in two-voice counterpoint, and is quite effective in developing melodic or harmonic tension and in building strong "resolution tendencies." We shall see in subsequent study that the tritone figures significantly in two-voice cadences, especially in connection with dominant-seventh-to-tonic cadence.

There are predictable treatments of melodic and harmonic tritones which are basic to much music, and which can easily be related to our notational practices. Some of their more common treatments are shown in Ex. 24.

1. Skips up or down an augmented fourth are usually followed by stepwise motion in the same direction as the leap. This is true with *all* augmented intervals.
2. Like skips of an augmented fourth, skips of an ascending or descending diminished fifth are normally succeeded by stepwise motion, but generally in the *opposite* direction from the leap. This is true with all diminished intervals.
3. Tritone leaps occur more often as *unaccented* leaps, often in the course of repetitive patterns whose main feature is rhythm. Stepwise resolutions are usually found here too.

4. Tritone skips, *like most leaps*, are most often approached by step, generally in the opposite direction from the leap.
5. Leaps that follow melodic tritones usually take the opposite direction and frequently resolve to pitches that form step progressions with members of the tritone.
6. Harmonic tritones formed by the movement of two contrapuntal voices usually resolve by the same kinds of stepwise movement associated with melodic tritones. Augumented fourths will "expand" by step, while diminished fifths will contract.

Locate all melodic and harmonic tritones in Ex. 9-24a and Ex. 9-24b. Then compare the appearance of each with the various principles described above.

Ex. 9-24a. Bach: Suite in A Major, Courante.

Ex. 9-24b. Haydn: Sonata in E flat Major, Menuet.

Ex. 9-23c. Bach: Minuet (*Little Notebook of Anna Magdalena Bach*).

Most of the tritones in Ex. 9-23 are the result of decorative patterns. *Both* members of a harmonic tritone are seldom basic pitches. Furthermore, the tritones illustrated in Ex. 9-23a and 9-23b involve the 4–7 scale degree relationship as is most often the case in major-minor music, while the tritones in Ex. 9-23c occur in a modulatory passage which closes with a progressive cadence in *g* minor. In later study we shall deal with the treatment of tritones as structural pitches, particularly as members of harmonic progressions.

Other Unstable Intervals

The treatment of other unstable intervals, such as seconds, sevenths, and augmented and diminished intervals, is similar to that of the tritone; they are generally decorative, and they move by step. (Important exceptions to this will be dealt with in Chapter 12 in connection with other forms of decorative activity.)

Step motion in the upper voice creates a variety of dissonances in Ex. 9-24. Such activity decorates basic pitches.

Ex. 9-24. Sweelinck: Fantasia (for organ).

Considerable tonal movement and much decorative activity can be found in Ex. 9-25. Virtually all of the unstable pitches, producing a great variety of melodic and harmonic intervals, are treated in step motion.

Ex. 9-25. Bach: Prelude in A-flat Major (*Well-tempered Clavier,* Book II).

Organization of Two-Voice Phrases

The contour relationship of both voices is a basic consideration in organizing a two-voice phrase. If one voice is a mere follower, reaching high and low peaks simultaneously with the other, its interest is diminished in the same way that rhythmic duplication minimizes the independence of parts.

In Ex. 9-26 the lower voice is essentially accompanimental. Its contour, like the upper part, is primarily descending, so its importance as an independent voice is minimized.

Ex. 9-26. Haydn: Sonata in D Major, II.

Two voices of more equal rhythmic interest are shown in Ex. 9-27. Again, however, both voices outline similar contours, and the low and high points of both occur at about the same points in the phrase, although not simultaneously. The accompanying reduction to basic pitches shows the similarity of contour in a skeletal form.

Ex. 9-27.

In contrast to Ex. 9-26 and Ex. 9-27, the voices in Ex. 9-28 have more independent melodic curves. Here the voices *take turns* as predominant parts, but even so, they outline basic pitches in essentially contrary motion, and the high and low points of succeeding motives occur one after the other, rather than simultaneously.

Ex. 9-28. Bach: Two-voice Invention in D Major.

Ex. 9-28 continued.

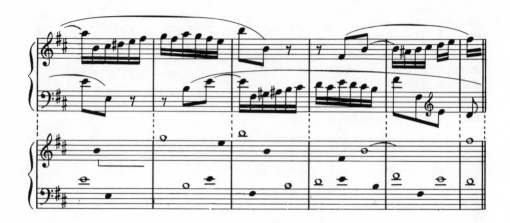

Two equal voices compete imitatively in Ex. 9-29. Although they use identical melodic materials, successively, the two voices are delineated effectively by two simple processes: Each successive basic interval is approached through contrary motion, which is continued right up to the last interval. The highest note of the upper line occurs with the lowest note in the bottom part. Furthermore, each basic pitch, as shown in the reduction, is approached in contrary motion. The effectiveness of the example illustrates the degree to which contrasting contours can contribute to melodic interest and independence, even when other factors are virtually equal.

Ex 9-29. C.P.E. Bach: Keyboard Sonata.

Pitch Material in Tonal Music

A glance at any of the preceding musical examples will confirm the fact that most two-voice textures employ the same key or mode in both voices. We have also seen that the addition of a second part often clarifies the tonic in a melody whose key or tonic is ambiguous. Comparing Ex. 9-30 and Ex. 9-31, we find that the tonic (*A-flat*) is strongly asserted by *both* voices in Ex. 9-30, but only by the lower part in Ex. 9-31. The upper voice of the latter example is *apparently* in *E-flat* (considered as a separate line), while the lower clearly establishes *A-flat* (the actual tonic of the combined parts).

Ex. 9-30. Bach: Fugue in A-flat Major (*Well-tempered Clavier* Book I).

Ex. 9-31. J.S. Bach: Prelude in A-flat Major (*Well-tempered Clavier,* Book I).

Although *both* parts must be considered in any discussion of tonic, key or mode, the lower voice, because it is the tonal foundation for most two-voice works, often exerts more *tonal force* than the upper. This is well illustrated in Ex. 9-31, which is heard in *A-flat* primarily because of the pull towards *A-flat* created by the lower voice.

Two voices which possess the same tonic may use conflicting variants of the same note. This is particularly true in the minor mode with its different scale patterns. In Ex. 9-32, *D-flat* in the upper part conflicts with the lower part's *D-natural*.

Ex. 9-32. Bach: Two-voice Invention in F Minor.

D-natural in the lower voice is explained by the ascent of the line and the avoidance of the augmented second which would result if *D-flat* were not altered.

Considerable variety of pitch resources has been used in two melodically independent parts in Ex. 9-32. The tonality is *D*, but it incorporates all twelve tones of a chromatic scale, rather than a seven-tone mode.

Ex. 9-33. Hindemith: *Ludus Tonalis,* Fugue in E. (C) 1943 by Schott & Co., Ltd., London. Reprinted by permission.

Cross Relation

Cross relation (sometimes called *false relation*) results when variants of the same note occur on successive beats (or beat divisions) between *different* voices. In Ex. 9-34a, *f-natural* in the lower part is followed by an *f-sharp* in the upper. A cross relation results, although the melodic effect of each voice is perfectly satisfactory. In the approach to the cadence of the same passage, *b-natural* and *b-flat* are cross related, producing the effect of a change of mode. Ex. 9-34b contains three cross relations, and creates an inconsistency of mode (modal conflict), by pitting *A* major in the upper voice against *a* minor in the lower. Simultaneous cross relation occurs when different note variants occur at the same time, rather than successively, as in Ex. 9-34c.

Ex. 9-34. Cross relations.

Ex. 9-35 and Ex. 9-36 illustrate numerous cross relations.

Ex. 9-35. Bach: Fugue in E Minor (*Well-tempered Clavier,* Book I).

Ex. 9-36. Stravinsky: Symphony in Three Movements, I (piano part). (C) 1946 by Schott & Co., Ltd., London. Reprinted by permission.

Several generalizations pertinent to the use of cross relations can be made:

1. Ascending movement in one part in contrast with descending movement in the other frequently creates acceptable cross relations, as in Ex. 9-37, which involves the ascending and descending forms of a melodic minor scale.

Ex. 9-37. Treatments of cross relation in two voices.

2. Cross relations occur naturally from combinations of essentially diatonic movement in one part with chromatic alterations in another. Chromatic alterations, such as those in Ex. 9-38 are essentially decorative.

Ex. 9-38. Cross relation.

3. Mutation (a change of mode) as found in Ex. 9-39 with a clear change of mode from minor to major, frequently results in cross relation.

Ex. 9-39. Cross relation.

Some composers of the twentieth century have created further independence of lines by employing two tonalities or keys simultaneously.

Ex. 9-40. Bi-tonality.

Ex. 9-41 contains a section of a canon by Josquin des Près, a fifteenth-century composer. The most significant feature of this example, from the standpoint of pitch organization, is that the two canonic voices consistently cadence on different tonics. The result is that, although the two parts are highly unified through the use of identical melodic material, they are delineated tonally through their adherence to different tonics, *D* and *G*.

Ex. 9-41. Josquin des Près: Chanson.

Exercises

For more detailed assignments see *Materials and Structure of Music I, Workbook*, Chapter 9.

1. Invent two-voice rhythmic phrases of eight measures, choosing rhythm patterns from examples in the beginning of the chapter as a basis for repetition.
2. Identify the kinds of rhythmic associations of several examples in this chapter.
3. Write out the normal ranges of soprano, alto, tenor, and bass voices.
4. Construct all the diatonic intervals within an octave span and label their precise size; then identify each as a basic or decorative consonance or dissonance.
5. Discuss Ex. 9-12 from the standpoint of types of motion, rhythmic association, treatments of consonant and dissonant intervals, and dual contours. What factors tend most to unify the composition?
6. Consider Ex. 9-13 from the same standpoints as Ex. 9-12.
7. Transpose the upper voice of Ex. 9-12 down a perfect fifth and add a new bass, employing an accompanimental rhythmic association and emphasizing basic and decorative consonances.
8. Invent three phrases, each illustrating a different rhythmic association. Use any pitch materials and vertical combinations that interest you. Vary the length, tempo, meter, and mood of each phrase.

10

CONTINUATION OF TWO-VOICE COMBINATIONS

One of the most significant areas of a musical work, regardless of its texture or form, is the cadence. It is here that both tonal and rhythmic elements must be drawn to a convincing and satisfying conclusion.

Three principles of cadence construction are basic to tonal music in general: (1) a slackening of motion, usually evidenced by longer note values; (2) the confirmation of a tonal center; and (3) consonant intervallic relations between the parts.

The illustration of cadences in Ex. 10-1, Ex. 10-2, and Ex. 10-3, although products of musical styles separated by hundreds of years, clearly adhere to the principles described above.

Ex. 10-1. Josquin des Près: Chanson.

Ex. 10-2. Bach: Two-voice Invention in D Minor.

Ex. 10-3. Bartók: *Mikrokosmos*. Copyright 1940 by Hawkes & Son (London) Ltd., Renewed 1967. Reprinted by permission of Boosey & Hawkes Inc.

In each case (Ex. 10-1, Ex. 10-2, and Ex. 10-3), cadential tones occur on strong beats. Cadences that fall on weak beats or weak parts of the beat (sometimes called "feminine endings") are exceptions. A certain prominence is assured cadential tones because of their duration (usually more than one beat), by their strong metric location, and through their obvious importance as the last tones of a melodic pattern. Furthermore, this prominence is often signalled by slowing the melodic pace with longer note values introduced in the approach to the cadence. Such is the case in each of the excerpts just seen.

Composers sometimes prolong activity in one voice after the cadential tone has been reached. Through such an extension, each voice maintains its individuality and independence into the cadence proper. In Ex. 10-4, the lower voice asserts the tonic *A*, while the upper voice, having touched upon *a′*, continues down by a series of leaps to the octave *a*.

Ex. 10-4. Bach: Two-voice Invention in A Minor.

A *codetta* is an extension of musical activity that prolongs the cadence area.

Ex. 10-5. Sweelinck: Organ Toccata (cadence).

Ex. 10-5 continued.

Cadential Intervals Formed in Two-Voice Textures

Any cadential consonance (unison, octave, fifth, third) may occur as the final sonority of a two-voice work. The same applies generally to internal cadences. Regardless of the interval, the tonic pitch is always the lower tone at a final cadence. (It may also be in the upper part if the cadential interval is an octave or unison.) Final cadences to intervals other than cadential consonances, are exceptional.

The particular choice of cadential interval is determined by the prevailing tonality, the kind of melodic activity that reaches its fulfillment in the cadence, and the composer's choice of sonority. The octave is common as a closing sonority, and with the unison it represents the strongest, in terms of stability. It is perhaps less interesting as a sonority than the third or fifth. The perfect fifth, though a strong tonal relationship, is not found as often in two-voice cadences as octaves, unisons, or thirds. Both major and minor thirds, the choice of which is determined primarily by the mode of the work, occur frequently. Any cadential consonance that confirms the tonality of the piece or its closing section may be employed.

The cadential interval is often called the *ultimate interval,* and the interval that immediately precedes it is called the *approach interval.* Cadence patterns are formed by the movement from an approach to an ultimate (or final) interval. Some of the most common two-voice cadence patterns are shown in Ex. 10-6.

Ex. 10-6. Basic cadences in two-voices (approach and ultimate intervals).

(a) Stepwise contrary motion.

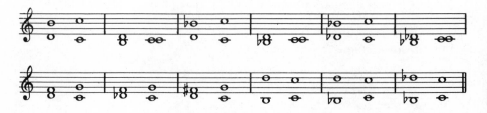

(b) Contrary motion, one voice moving by step.

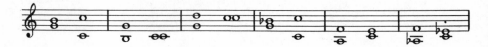

(c) Similar or parallel motion.

(d) Skips in contrary motion.

Various forms of scales are implicit in the different patterns. These patterns are often labelled according to the melodic movement of the voices in their relation to tonic. For instance, the first pattern in Ex. 10-6a would be indicated as 2–1, and the first pattern under Ex. 10-6b would be written as 5–1. The numbers 7–8 indicate step-movement from the leading tone (or subtonic) to tonic, whereas 2–1 indicates a step descent from supertonic to tonic. These patterns represent an intervallic framework that results from melodic movement at the cadence. However, any of these basic pitches could be decorated with a variety of embellishment involving passing tones, neighbors, or other elaborative pitches.

Two voices moving in similar motion to a perfect fifth or octave produce the *direct fifth* or direct octave. This effect has been generally avoided in two-voice cadential practice. *Direct octaves*, on the other hand, are quite common, if the upper voice moves by ascending or descending step.

It is significant that the approach intervals of the basic patterns shown in Ex. 10-6 are all comprised of cadential and decorative consonances. Perfect fourths do not occur frequently as approach intervals in two-voice writing, nor do tritones.

Modal Cadences in Two Voices

We are familiar with some of the characteristics associated with modal melodies, and the group of scales known as modes:

Ex. 10-7.

Just as modal melodies exploit certain characteristic interval relationships, so two-voice combinations often adhere to a group of basic cadence patterns that incorporate modal patterns. It is significant also that many of these patterns, some of which are shown in Ex. 10-8, are by no means limited in use to modal melodies; they can also be found in compositions oriented around major-minor scales and more chromatic works. All of these patterns, associated with two-voice textures, involve the basic pattern $\frac{7-8}{2-1}$ or its inversion, $\frac{2-1}{7-8}$.

Ex. 10-8. $\frac{7\text{-}8}{2\text{-}1}$ Two-voice modal cadences.

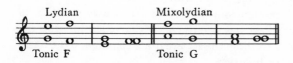

Ex. 10-8a. Willaert (Aeolian Mode).

Ex. 10-8b. Giovanni da Florentia (Phrygian Mode).

Ex. 10-8c. Josquin des Près (Dorian Mode).

Dorian and Aeolian mode compositions, as shown in Ex. 10-8, usually employ cadences that approach tonic from the whole step below and the whole step above, while Phrygian cadences approach tonic from the whole step below and the half-step above. Cadences in the Lydian mode, as in major and minor, involve a leading tone to tonic ascent while the other voice (usually the lower) moves by a descending whole step from 2–1. Mixolydian cadences, like Dorian and Aeolian, contain no half-step, and tonic is approached from the whole step below and above tonic. All of these are cadences to the octave or unison, reached by contrary motion. Other patterns can be found in two-voice textures employing modal melodies. However, those which employ the octave or unison as an ultimate interval are most common.

Two-Voice Cadences in Major and Minor Keys

In Ex. 10-9, a cadential *f-sharp* has been introduced to create a leading tone to tonic, thereby emphasizing *G* as a tonic. The scale structure of the whole example is a mixture of *G* Mixolydian and *G* major.

Ex. 10-9. Obrecht: Agnus Dei, *Missa Sine Nomine.*

With the gradual incorporation of leading tones, first cadentially only, then into melody as a whole, the major-minor scales became established, and a group of cadences reflecting the use of leading tones developed. As we shall see, some of these cadential patterns still embody features of modal cadences.

Terminal Cadences

The most common final cadential pattern of music written during the past five hundred years is described as the V-I cadence. It is comprised, usually, of the following features: melodic movement in the lower (less often upper) part up a perfect fourth or down a perfect fifth, motion from leading tone to tonic in the upper voice, and a succession of two consonant intervals whose roots are a perfect fourth or perfect fifth apart; that is, *G* to *C*, *F* to *B-flat*, *A* to *D*, or *D-flat* to *G-flat*. The roots of the intervals that form the V-I pattern correspond to the dominant and tonic degrees of the prevailing tonality. Several illustrations of the V-I pattern are shown in Ex. 10-10.

Ex. 10-10a. Bach.

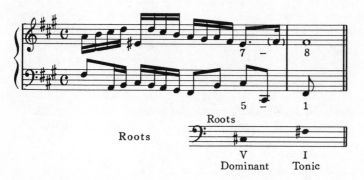

Ex. 10-10b. Handel.

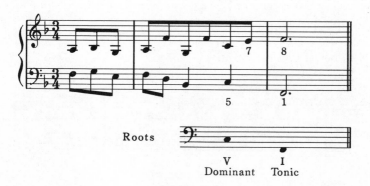

In contrast with the ascending leap of a fourth (or descending fifth) that is found most often in the lower part, the upper voice usually moves by step from 7–8 (leading tone to tonic), or from 2–1 (supertonic to tonic).

B♭: 7 — 8   2 — 1
     5 — 1   5 — 1

As shown in Ex. 10-10a and Ex. 10-10b, the melodic movement of both voices can be indicated by numbers which represent the horizontal movement of the voices. Several basic V-I patterns are shown in Ex. 10-11.

Ex. 10-11. V-I cadences.

The following principles apply to the handling of V-I cadences in two-voice textures:

1. The lower voice usually moves by ascending perfect fourth or descending perfect fifth, while the upper part moves from 2–1 or 7–8, generally in contrary motion with the lower.

Ex. 10-12.

2. The inversion of the above, with 7–8 movement in the lower voice and a leap up a fourth or down a fifth, although possible, is an unusual exception in final two-voice cadences. 2–1 movement in the lower part is virtually never found when the upper part moves by a leap.

Ex. 10-13.

3. Contrary motion prevails, although direct octaves may be found when the upper voice moves by step.

Ex. 10-14.

4. 7–8 movement most often involves the leading tone to tonic, but 7–8 motion by a whole step (subtonic to tonic) may be found. (Leading tones in minor keys must be indicated by accidentals.)

Ex. 10-15.

5. V-I cadences create root relations up a perfect fourth (or down a perfect fifth). The roots of these two intervals always correspond with dominant and tonic at final cadences.

Ex. 10-16.

6. The cadential interval frequently falls in a strong metric position.

Ex. 10-17.

7. V-I cadences are often embellished by decorative pitches. Codettas frequently occur as extensions of these basic patterns.

Ex. 10-18.

Progressive Cadences

Composers have employed a great variety of patterns to terminate phrases and larger sections of two-voice compositions. The types fall into two principal groups: progressive and transient-terminal cadences.

The possibilities for creating progressive cadences are enormous. Several basic observations can be made: (1) tonic will not be the *root* of the cadential interval, (although there are some progressive cadences which do include tonic); (2) active pitches, such as the leading tone or subdominant, usually will form part of the cadential interval; (3) decorative consonances as well as cadential consonances may be found, and even dissonances may occur as cadential intervals of progressive cadences; and (4) rhythmic activity may be maintained in one or even both voices, thus weakening the cadential effect.

In Ex. 10-19, a progressive cadence in the key of *b* minor occurs in measure 6.

Ex. 10-19. Handel: Fughetta.

The cadential major third is formed by the leading tone *A-sharp* and *F-sharp*. The *root* of this interval, *F-sharp*, is the dominant of *b* minor; "more to follow" is strongly implied by the absence of tonic, and by the presence of the leading tone. Progressive cadences to intervals whose *roots* are the dominant are traditionally called *half cadences*.

Another form of progressive cadence involves root movement from the dominant to the submediant (V to VI). This pattern, often used to avoid the sense of finality associated with movement to a tonic root, is generally introduced by ascending step motion in the lower voice, accompanied in the upper part by parallel or contrary motion to tonic, or contrary motion to the mediant. The resulting effect is called *deceptive*, (deceptive cadence), because anticipated movement to a tonic root is evaded. Bach has employed a deceptive cadence in measure 4 of Ex. 10-20.

Ex. 10-20. Bach: Two-voice Invention in D Major.

Anticipated movement to *d*, in the lower part, is replaced by movement to *b*, the submediant. The root progression is up a major second. The root of the approach interval in the deceptive cadence is usually the dominant (V), producing the root progression V-VI. (Deceptive cadences involving other root progressions are a possibility, as we shall see in later study.)

Several other types of progressive cadences are shown in Ex. 10-21.

Ex. 10-21. Progressive cadence patterns.

Although modal cadence types are not indigenous to major-minor music, they do occur frequently at interior cadences—particularly progressive cadences—as a comparison of Ex. 10-6 and Ex. 10-21 will show. The tritone, although not used often as a basic harmonic interval in final cadences, can be found as the approach interval in both progressive and transient-terminal cadences. Cadential uses of tritones are usually the product of decorative activity in one or both voices.

A study of the cadences discussed in this chapter will show that most cadences involve root movement in ascending or descending perfect fourths, or ascending or descending major or minor seconds. Root movement in thirds is infrequent.

Other Interior Cadence Patterns

Cadences which confirm or imply changes of tonal center are an important means of creating tonal variety, and help to delineate melodic form. *These cadences, occurring at phrase or sectional closes*, are often of the V-I group, although $\frac{7-8}{2-1}$ cadences and any cadences which are *terminal in effect* may be found. As in final cadences, the *root* of the cadential interval is generally in the lower voice.

The opening eleven measures of Bach's G Minor Invention contain a terminal cadence to *G*, a transient-terminal cadence to *B-flat*, and a modulation to *d* minor. All of the cadences are basic V-I patterns, elaborated. Each cadence marks the close of a phrase and is signaled by the introduction of longer durations in one of the voices. Melodic activity continues in the other voice, however, thus diminishing the rhythmic effect of cadence. The cadential pitches inevitably occur on strong beats.

Ex. 10-22. Bach: Two-voice Invention in G Minor.

Measures 5 and 6 contain a modulatory sequence, which represents a patterned means of effecting a change of key from *g* minor, through its relative major, *B-flat*, to *d* minor. Two shifts of tonality, each up a third and each punctuated by a cadence, bring about the change.

Dominant-tonic cadences to *F* are heard in bars 3 and 5 of Ex. 10-23. The first is transient-terminal, since *B-flat* has been established as tonic in the music preceding the cadence. *F* is momentarily emphasized, by the leading tone *e″*-natural, which with *c‴* forms a V-I pattern. We anticipate a return to the *B-flat* tonic. This is denied, however, and *F* remains the tonic. The cadence in bar 5 further confirms *F*. As in the example by Bach quoted in Ex. 10-22, the change of key represents a modulation to the *dominant key*. The interplay of tonic and dominant keys is a most common tonal relationship in Western music.

Ex. 10-23. Handel: Suite, Allemande.

Tonal Function Within the Phrase; Root Relations in the Two-Voice Frame

The melodic and harmonic action of the cadence has been described in terms of the root relations of cadential patterns such as V-I, V-VI, I-V, and so forth. Any cadential pattern can be described with roman numerals representing the roots of basic intervals. This procedure is equally applicable to an entire phrase or composition. In other words, having discovered the basic harmonic intervals and their roots, one can represent their relationship to *tonic* by using a roman numeral for each scale degree, regardless of the type of key or mode dealt with.

The passage of Ex. 10-24 consists of *basic* harmonic movement I-VI-II-V-I, as an analysis of the accompanying reduction will show.

Ex. 10-24.

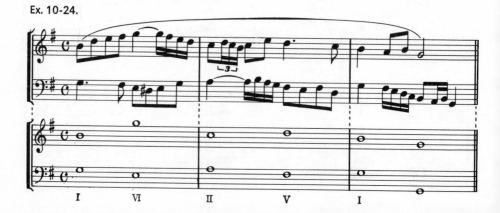

I   VI   II   V   I

When a change of tonality occurs, the same procedure can be adapted to the different degrees of the new key, as shown in Ex. 10-25. This analytical set of symbols will be discussed extensively in subsequent chapters. It is a convenient method for both planning and analyzing the harmonic basis of two-voice writing.

Ex. 10-25. Handel: Suite, Allemande.

Implied Triads

The harmonic organization of two-voice combinations is readily understood as a product of intervallic combinations. However, the harmonic intervals that occur in two-voice music often imply the use of a harmonic unit larger than the interval, the chord. The most common chordal unit in tonal music is the triad; two voices often *imply* triadic chords and chord progressions even though they obviously cannot produce vertical statements of complete triads, since triads are composed of three different pitches arranged in stacked or superposed thirds.

A Major   A Minor
Triad on F   Triad on F

We have already observed examples of linear triads in this book; it should be obvious that triadic outlining can occur as well when *two* parts are combined. An emphasis upon triadic members in one voice is quite often reinforced by a similar emphasis in the other; that is to say that harmonic agreement between voices is often achieved through the selection of basic and secondary pitches that are part of the same chord. In two-voice textures such relations are often produced by combined melodic motion, as in the example that follows. An analysis of the implied triads is given below the music.

Ex. 10-26. Mozart: Sonata for Piano in C Major, I, K. 545.

As we shall learn in later study,[1] the triad represents an amplification of the notion of root, since all three of its tones are understood to be governed by the same root. It is important to note, therefore, that our perception of roots and root relations in two-voice music is often enhanced and reinforced by the patterning of implied chords through essentially horizontal motion, counterpoint; this is obviously the case in the excerpt that follows.

---

[1] We shall deal extensively with chords in Chapters 14 to 25.

Ex. 10-27a. Bach: *Twelve Little Preludes,* Prelude No. I.

Counterpoint in the preceding passage is minimal, having been achieved primarily by distributing triadic tones between two rhythmically contrasted voices. Directional contrasts and suspension figures produce further independence of parts. Such a passage might well be regarded as four-part homophony realized by two voices.

Example 10-27b shows the chordal basis implied by the passage in 10-27a, distributed among four implied voices. Examples such as the preceding are obvious manifestations of the degree to which chords may influence melodic combinations. Although our concern in this unit of study is primarily with linear matters, a study of tonal counterpoint must take into account the fact that the relation between melody and harmony is an interaction. Although melody and harmony always interact to some degree in effecting a contrapuntal texture, it is in the emphasis on combined lines that counterpoint is found. Compare the chordal reduction of Ex. 10-27a, shown below, with the original shown above.

Ex. 10-27b. Chordal realization of Ex. 10-27a.

Ex. 10-27b continued.

The Two-Voice Framework

It should be recalled that most melodies reveal an underlying structure whose pitches constitute the basic melody, determined by such factors as duration, contour, step progression, and cadence. The structural pitches of two combined voices form a two-voice framework. All of the factors that determine the basic pitch structure of a single line may contribute to the determination of the two-voice framework, but the two-voice frame is also predicated on the basic harmonic relations formed by two coinciding parts; the latter is especially true in tonal music. The degree to which this is true may be observed by studying the example and analysis shown below. An analysis of the combined basic melodies, the two-voice frame, is shown below the music. On the third stave the triads implied by the example's two parts are shown, with an analysis of their roots. The functional relation of each root to the tonic, *F*, is indicated in roman numerals below the root pitch.

Ex. 10-28. Bach: Overture in F for Harpsichord, Bourrée.

The example that follows yields a two-voice framework that includes both consonances and dissonances. Note also that although a discernible root progression in the form of V to I clearly underscores the counterpoint, no triadic chord progression is implied. Basic and secondary pitches are a result of duration and placement, not implied triads. Such compositions, which are clearly written in a tonality (in this case *C*), suggest the importance of the two-voice framework to tonal music of a wide and diversified stylistic palette.

Ex. 10-29. Bartók: *Mikrokosmos*. Copyright 1940 by Hawkes & Son (London) Ltd., Renewed 1967. Reprinted by permission of Boosey & Hawkes Inc.

Ex. 10-29 continued.

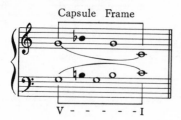

Rhythmic displacement of the upper voice is the main means for differentiating the two voices of Ex. 10-30. The harmonic materials are essentially consonances that imply triads. Basic melodic pitches, as determined by duration, placement, contour, and step progressions coincide with stable harmonic intervals to produce a structural basis that is typical of a great deal of tonal music. The tonal and contrapuntal organization of the passage is clear and convincing.

Ex. 10-30. Haydn: Piano Sonata in E-flat, Finale.

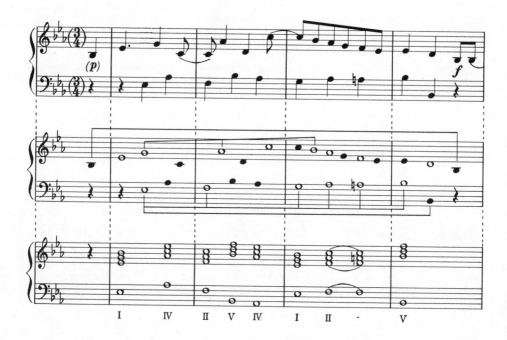

Two-voice frameworks from two contrasted styles of composition appear in Ex. 10-31a and b immediately below the pieces from which they have been realized. The examples have in common the use of two parts in a contrapuntal texture; they are contrasted in that *a* reveals a clear pattern of implied triadic harmonic materials, as shown in the analysis, whereas *b* reveals no such orientation. Both examples, however, are clearly fashioned elaborations of combined basic melodies and have in common essentially simple contrapuntal sub-structures. Most tonal music is composed in such a way as to unfold such structural bases.

Ex. 10-31a. Bach: Two-voice Invention in G Minor.

Ex. 10-31a continued.

Ex. 10-31b. Milhaud: Quartet No. 9, III. Reproduit avec l'autorisation des Editions "Le Chant du Monde," Paris.

Exercises

For more detailed assignments see *Materials and Structure of Music I, Workbook*, Chapter 10.

1. Invent ten two-voice cadences to the note *D*, using a variety of directional patterns. Then elaborate several of them by interpolating passing and neighboring tones.
2. Use the succession of roots shown in Ex. 10-24 as the basis for eight measures of two-voice counterpoint in $\frac{6}{8}$ meter. Adapt the root relations of the example to the key of *E♭* major. Employ a texture similar to that of Ex. 10-24.
3. Extract an analysis of the implied triads in Ex. 10-25.
4. Make up two-measure phrases in each of the following modes: Dorian, Phrygian, Mixolydian, and Aeolian. Employ cadences typical of such modal compositions.
5. Compose a singable melody in $\frac{5}{4}$ meter, *C* minor, that outlines the harmonic pattern: I—VI—IV—V—IV—II—V—I. Then add a supporting voice.
6. Treat the notes *F, A♭, E, C♯*, and *D* as root, third and fifth of major and minor triads.
7. Use the harmonic pattern given in No. 6 as the basis for improvising a two-voice phrase at the keyboard.
8. Write out a current modal popular tune and make a sketch of its implied harmonic basis; add a simple accompanying lower part. Sample: the theme song from *Romeo and Juliet*

11

TWO-VOICE COMBINATIONS; DECORATIVE PITCHES

Passing Tones

When a second voice is added to the texture, a new dimension is created in the form of harmonic intervals. Thus our perception of basic and decorative pitches in *two-voice* combinations is affected by both *melodic* and *harmonic* elements.

Usually the addition of a second part will confirm an appraisal of basic or decorative activity in a single line. This is exemplified by the following pattern in which decorative pitches in the melody (a),

are heard as unstable in association with the supporting voice in (b):

analysis of (a)

Ex. 11-1.

Some of the most typical uses of passing tones are shown in Ex. 11-2. They may occur in either voice and in some instances occur simultaneously in both parts. Both diatonic and chromatic forms occur, filling in spans as small as the major second and as large as perfect fourth (or more). Dissonance is a common by-product of the essentially rhythmic role of passing tones. Such is the case in several of the following illustrations.

164

Ex. 11-2. Illustrations of passing tones.

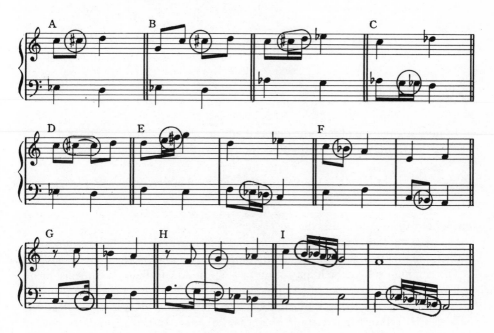

Play Ex. 11-3 and notice all passing tones. Consider both voices.

Ex. 11-3. Frescobaldi: *Canzona dopo l'Epistola.*

The e' after the first beat of measure 3, top voice, is obviously a passing tone. It is, however, consonant with the lower voice a, since it creates a perfect fifth with it. The e' connects two basic pitches, f' and d', as does the e' on the third beat of the same measure. The f' is a basic pitch both because of its metric position and because it forms a strong step progression with the preceding g' and the e' of the next measure. The importance of relating decorative pitches to basic pitches, rather than simply singling out dissonances, is illustrated in Ex. 11-3.

Neighbor Tones

Neighbor tones, together with passing tones, comprise another common type of melodic decoration. Like the passing tone, the neighbor represents the intermediary step of a three note figure. Thus, in the figure (a) ♩♪♪♩, e''

is a dissonant lower neighbor to f'', while in (b) , g'' embellishes the

f'' to which it returns, as an upper neighbor tone. Although neighbors appear most often as unaccented embellishments, they may be in an accented position.

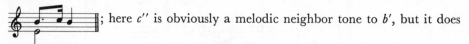

In fulfilling its role of melodic decoration, the upper or lower neighbor, like the passing tone, may occur without actually creating dissonance. For example:

; here c'' is obviously a melodic neighbor tone to b', but it does

not form a dissonance with the lower e'.

It is essential to understand, then, that passing and neighboring tones are embellishments that are determined by both melodic and harmonic relationships.

The neighbor tone, which may occur as a chromatic or diatonic embellishment, is a most useful figure for developing activity while focusing attention on one pitch. In two-part writing the neighbor, like the passing tone, is most effectively balanced by relative inactivity in the opposite voice. Just as melodic activity in two-part textures is generally divided between voices, so decorative activity is often distributed between parts, rather than centered in one. Some typical illustrations of neighbor tones are shown in Ex. 11-4. The figure formed by successive occurrences of both upper and lower neighbors is called a *neighbor group*. It is shown in the last two measures of Ex. 11-4.

Ex. 11-4. Illustration of neighbor tones.

Both neighbor and passing tones occur in Ex. 11-5.

Ex. 11-5. Bach: Two-voice Invention in F Minor.

Suspensions

In Chapter 8 we described the suspension, or syncope, as a decorative pattern involving a kind of melodic "delaying action," in which a basic pitch or basic associate is sustained through a subsequent strong beat, and resolved by step on the following weak beat to another basic pitch. Syncopation often results from suspension patterns, and the three elements which comprise the suspension figure

weak beat	strong beat	weak beat
preparation	*suspension* and	*resolution*
basic pitch	decoration	basic pitch

are shown in the following:

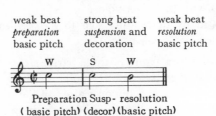

Preparation Susp- resolution
(basic pitch) (decor) (basic pitch)

The addition of a second voice generally involves the occurrence of a dissonance at the midpoint of the pattern.

The suspension pattern in two-voice textures, then, creates a tiny cycle of melodic-harmonic movement comprised of stability-instability-stability, and the addition of a second part simply reinforces an essentially melodic configuration.

Although the suspension figure is by no means limited to the cadence, we shall study first its use as a cadential embellishment.

Two versions of a $\frac{7-8}{2-1}$ cadence to *g* follow.

Ex. 11-6a. Basic cadence to *g*.

Ex. 11-6b. Elaborated with suspension.

In the second version the step movement in the upper part, from g^1 to f^1-*sharp*, has been delayed, or suspended, and g^1 forms a dissonance of a minor seventh with the *a* in the lower voice. Several observations pertinent to the approach and resolution of the suspended g^1 should be made:

1. *g'* was first heard as a consonant pitch, having been *prepared* as a consonance (upper member of a minor third), on the last beat of measure 1.
2. *g'* was sustained into the next strong beat so that it created a dissonance (minor seventh) with the lower voice.
3. *g'* resolved by descending step to *f'-sharp*—a consonance (major sixth)—on the subsequent weak beat.

The suspension is a figure of three parts: *preparation, suspension,* and *resolution.*

Preparation, then, refers to the point at which the suspended pitch (*g'*) is introduced. Syncopation, a common feature of the suspension figure, results when the preparation occurs on the weak beat, or the weak part of any beat preceding a tied suspension.

The preparation is usually as long as the suspension (dissonance) itself. In Ex. 11-7, the preparations are of differing lengths.

Ex. 11-7. Suspensions.

Ex. 11-8. Suspensions.

In Ex. 11-7 the preparations are at least as long as the basic duration, and they are no shorter than the dissonance itself. These are common preparations. Less typical preparations occur in Ex. 11-8 where the preparations are less than one beat's length and usually shorter than the displacement, or dissonance.

Articulated suspensions are shown in the first and last segments of Ex. 11-8. Although the suspended note is most often sustained, an articulation after the preparation is not uncommon.

Different Forms of Suspensions

In Exx. 11-7 and 11-8 the suspended (or displaced) note formed a minor seventh with the lower voice. Though it is common to refer to the suspension as a dissonance, all suspensions in two voices do not form dissonant intervals. However, they do create relative instability, and the interval of resolution will always be a cadential or decorative consonance. Furthermore, the resolution is usually to a basic pitch.

Suspensions are denoted by referring to the intervallic distance between the two voices at the point of instability (or dissonance), followed by the interval of resolution. For instance, in Ex. 11-9 a seventh is created by suspending f^2, which in turn forms a sixth when it resolves by step to e^2.

Ex. 11-9. Suspensions.

The resulting pattern is called a "7–6 suspension." The interval of preparation is not usually included in the analysis, although it is assumed to be consonant. The 7–6, then, describes one basic form of suspension. There are four other types: 4–3, 6–5, 9–8, and 2–3. All of these patterns, except the 2–3, have one important common feature: the suspension pitch is in the *upper voice*.

The instability of the perfect fourth is perhaps best illustrated by its frequent treatment in tonal music as a suspension, resolving to a stable major or minor third. We have already noted that fourths are usually approached and left by step in two-part writing. In Ex. 11-10 a V-I cadence has been written to incorporate a 4–3 suspension. By rewriting the passage in different keys we see how both augmented and diminished fourths may also be treated as 4–3 suspension figures.

Ex. 11-10. Suspensions.

Analyze the 4–3 suspensions in the excerpts shown in Ex. 11-11.

Ex. 11-11. 4-3 suspensions.

The suspension figure also occurs as 6–5, involving a decorative consonance resolving to a cadential consonance. The effect of this pattern in two-voice writing is mild.

Ex. 11-12. 6-5 suspensions.

The 6–5 suspensions occur frequently in approaches to V-I cadences, as seen in Ex. 11-13.

Ex. 11-13. 6-5 suspensions.

9-8 Suspensions

9–8 suspensions are rare in two-voice writing, especially at cadences. They are more common to three- and four-voice music. Although they occasionally occur, as shown below, they represent unusual exceptions in two-voice practice.

Ex. 11-14. 9-8 suspensions.

In two-voice music the 2–3 (or 9–10) suspension figure is in the *lower* part. This suspension, the 2–3 (or 9–10), is used both cadentially and within interior areas of the phrase like the others. It is not often found in *final* cadences, however, but more often in sectional or phrase endings.

Ex. 11-15. 2-3 suspensions.

Ornamental Resolutions

When one or more pitches are interpolated between the suspension and its note of resolution, the resolution is called *ornamental*. In most instances decorations of the suspension involve step movement. However, movement to secondary pitches may also occur as an embellishment of the suspended tone. The suspensions in Ex. 11-16a, measures 3 and 4, have been rewritten in Ex. 11-16b, ornamented. The d^2 in measure 3 is reached by step and creates an escape tone, while the a^1 in measure 4 is a secondary pitch.

Ex. 11-16a. Ornamental resolutions.

Ex. 11-16b. Ornamental resolutions.

As we know, suspensions usually resolve to basic pitches. This applies to ornamental resolutions as well. Furthermore, the note of resolution is usually equal to the duration of the dissonance, although exceptions to this principle showing resolutions of both more or less duration than the dissonance are not uncommon.

In measure 7 of Ex. 11-17 the basic pitch movement of the upper voice involves a^1—c^2—b^1. Although ornamented by the interpolation of two sixteenth notes (b^1 and a^1 which is a neighbor to b^1), the suspension resolution occurs with the arrival of the quarter note b^1 on the fourth beat of the measure.

Ex. 11-17. Praetorius: Chorale Prelude, *Ein' feste Burg ist unser Gott.*

The note of resolution of a suspension may be more pronounced because it forms part of a step progression than because it is the resolution of a dissonance. In Ex. 11-18 the g^2 of measure 4 is the resolution of the suspended a^2 heard on the first beat of measure 3. Five notes of an ascending pattern intervene between the suspension and its anticipated resolution. The step progression formed by the two basic pitches, a and g, is another factor that causes g to be heard as a natural point of arrival of a.

Ex. 11-18. Bach: Two-voice Invention in D Major.

A similar delayed resolution occurs in Ex. 11-19. Locate it and analyze the suspension.

Ex. 11-19. Bach: Two-voice Invention in D Major.

The Change of Bass Resolution

One of the most interesting techniques associated with the suspension is the so-called "change of bass."

Ex. 11-20. The change of bass resolution.

In some suspensions the lower voice, which normally remains stationary as the suspension in the upper part is resolved, moves to another pitch. The interval formed at the point of resolution of the suspended seventh is usually a third, and the resulting pattern is described in accordance with the intervals formed, as shown in Ex. 11-20, i.e., 7–3.

The change of bass, or change of soprano, may be found in any suspension figure. In general the bass may move to any pitch that is consonant with the resolution of the suspension. It usually moves in contrary motion with the top voice. The models in Ex. 11-21 represent change of bass patterns found in conjunction with all of the suspensions that we have studied to date.

Ex. 11-21. Suspensions with changes of bass (or soprano).

The name *retardation* is sometimes given to suspensions which resolve by *ascending* step. These patterns occur most often containing unstable intervals that resolve by expanding to a consonance. These include the augmented second, augmented fourth, augmented fifth, augmented sixth, and major seventh (particularly when the leading tone occurs in the upper voice).

Ex. 11-22. Retardations.

The various forms of the suspension clearly constitute an important facet of two-voice counterpoint. Like other contrapuntal and organizational techniques, the suspension figure is found in varying degrees in most musical styles, representing another type of patterned movement that establishes an interdependent relationship between basic pitches in two musical lines.

A summary of the foregoing study of the suspension should recall the following principles:

1. The suspension figure in a two-voice texture usually involves a dissonance or unstable tone, most often in the form of a syncopated pattern.
2. The three steps that comprise the figure are: Preparation (weak), Suspension (strong), and Resolution (weak).
3. Suspensions are usually, but not always, of the same duration as the prevailing basic duration.
4. The preparation is usually equal (or greater) in duration to the suspended tone. The duration of the resolution may be equal to or less than the suspended note.
5. Suspensions are denoted according to the vertical intervals formed at the suspension and its resolution; they include the 7–6, 4–3, 9–8 (rare in two parts) and 6–5 and 2–3.
6. Suspensions which resolve by ascending step motion are sometimes called *retardations*.
7. Series of suspensions which form a sequence are called *chain suspensions*.
8. Ornamental resolutions result from the interpolation of one or more pitches between the suspension and its resolution. Such interpolated pitches, usually no more than two, are often called *changing tones*.
9. The resolution of the suspension may coincide with the introduction into the other voice of a new tone. The change of bass generally occurs in contrary motion with the upper voice, and forms a consonance with the tone of resolution.

Despite the diversity of style reflected in these works, the principles of the suspension that we have discussed are incorporated in the excerpts that follow.

Ex. 11-23.

Ex. 11-24.

Ex. 11-25. Obrecht: Agnus Dei, *Missa Sine Nomine.*

In Ex. 11-26 the tonic, *E*, occurs as a rhythmically weak anticipation of the cadential basic pitch *E*. The anticipation, of course, involves note repetition and is effective as a patterned basis for creating rhythmic elaboration. The latter occurs in Ex. 11-27.

Ex. 11-26. Bach: Chorale, *Christ lag in Todesbanden* (outer voices).

Ex. 11-27. Bach: Fugue in D Minor (*Well-tempered Clavier*, Book I).

When anticipations occur at the beginning of or within the phrase, they generally form segments of characteristic motives, often treated sequentially, rather than mere pitch repetitions. A sequential treatment of anticipations can be seen in Ex. 11-27. Another example of a patterned use of anticipations is shown in Ex. 11-28.

Ex. 11-28. Haydn: Sonata in E-flat, I.

Tied anticipations create syncopations similar to those often found in suspensions. In the example by Stravinsky (Ex. 11-29), *f-sharp* in measures 2–3 is introduced as a tied anticipation.

Ex. 11-29. Stravinsky: Octet for Winds, III. Copyright 1924 by Edition Russe de Musique; Renewed 1952. Copyright & renewal assigned to Boosey & Hawkes, Inc. Revised version Copyright 1952 by Boosey & Hawkes, Inc. Reprinted by permission.

Appoggiaturas (Leaning Tones)

The use of the appoggiatura in two-voice writing is limited almost entirely to the upper part, as illustrated in Ex. 11-30.

Ex. 11-30. C.P.E. Bach: Prussian Sonata.

The appoggiatura has been regarded as a particularly expressive melodic element, and its appearance is a predictable feature of many full-textured works of the nineteenth century. Most such notes create harmonic interval patterns similar to those of suspensions: 4–3, 7–6, 6–5, 9–8, and 7–8. When the pattern creates augmented or diminished intervals, it usually resolves in a way consistent with the resolutions of those intervals noted earlier.

Ex. 11-31. Appoggiaturas.

(Two - voice reduction)

Like most other decorative patterns, appoggiaturas may be accented or unaccented. Unaccented appoggiaturas occur in Ex. 11-32.

Ex. 11-32. Bach: Prelude in D Major (*Well-tempered Clavier*, Book I).

Escape Tones

Escape tones, approached by step and left by leap, are usually unaccented and occur most often within the phrase, rather than cadentially. Like appoggiaturas, escape tones are generally found in the upper of two voices, as seen here.

Ex. 11-33. Barret: Keyboard Sonata.

Escape Tones

Ex. 11-34. Bach: Two-voice Invention in E Minor.

Pedal Points

We have seen in this and earlier chapters how decorative pitches connect and embellish basic pitches of a melodic line. Pitches that form unstable intervals with a second part may be a part of the basic melody, thereby assuming a more structural role. One of the main considerations is metric placement and duration. In Ex. 11-35a dissonance is formed by pitches which are related to a recurrent basic pitch that is established by its repetition and metric placement.

Ex. 11-35a. Haydn: Sonata in E-flat, Minuet.

The note e^1-*flat* occurs throughout the passage, except in measure 7, as the lower member of an accompanimental pattern in the lower part. In the second measure it creates a persistent dissonance with d^2 in the upper line. This conflict continues through measure 3, and is finally resolved in measure 4. There is nothing *decorative* about the continued presence of the *e-flat* throughout the example, for it is a pitch of considerable structural importance. Its role is that of a *pedal* (or ground), which produces a strong tonal reference for the melodic activity above.[1] Two voices are implicit in the accompanimental pattern, as the harmonic basis reveals.

A b^1-*natural* occurs three times in the upper voice in measure 5 of Ex. 11-35a. Again, although we anticipate a resolution of this pitch to c^2, it is heard as a basic pitch.

---

[1] Whether they are sustained or articulated, pitches which create similar effects are called *pedal points*. Although more common to homophonic music, pedal points may be found in two-voice compositions as well. By definition, a pedal is a sustained or articulated note against which other melodic-harmonic activity takes place.

Ex. 11-35b. Harmonic basis of Ex. 11-35a.

Exercises

For more detailed assignments see *Materials and Structure of Music I, Workbook*, Chapter 11.

1. Continue Ex. 11-3, by Frescobaldi, for eight or so more measures in such a manner that several suspensions are introduced.
2. Analyze all decorative pitches in Ex. 11-5.
3. Invent an elaborate version of Ex. 11-17, using passing and neighboring tones as a basis for doing so.
4. Locate by ear any suspensions or retardations in Ex. 11-22.
5. Make a two-voice harmonic reduction of Ex. 11-24, showing the basic pitches of both voices (the two-voice frame) as well as the main harmonic functions of the example.
6. Use the harmonic basis of Ex. 11-35a, shown in Ex. 11-35b, as the basis for a two-part composition utilizing a pedal point similar to that of the original. Transpose the harmonic sketch to E major before proceeding. Introduce all forms of decorative activity dealt with in this chapter as a basis for creating an elaborate upper part.
7. Listen to one of Bach's Two-voice Inventions and write a short essay in which you discuss the types of decorative activity heard in the piece. Be as specific as possible.

12

CONTINUITY AND RECURRENCE IN TWO-VOICE MUSIC

In earlier study of melody (Chapters 1-8) several repetitive processes such as rhythmic repetition, motive repetition, and sequence were discussed. These same processes and others are equally fundamental to phrase and sectional organization in two-voice textures.

Both voices in Ex. 12-1 make acceptable melodies if performed separately. Both use repetitions of a short motive.

Ex. 12-1. Haydn: Op. 76. No. 6, I.

The activity fluctuates between the two parts, creating continuous eighth-note activity to the cadence. Both voices are punctuated by rests, and the different rhythms used make it easy for the listener to shift attention from voice to voice. This kind of patterning is fundamental to two-part music.

A similar motivic treatment occurs in Ex. 12-2, which involves a staggered distribution of activity between two voices, each of which is fashioned out of motive recurrence. The excerpt is also a canon.

Ex. 12-2. J.S. Bach: Canon, *Aria With 30 Variations* (Goldberg Variations), Variation 27.

In many two-voice textures rhythmic continuity derives from an accompanying voice, upper or lower, that provides a steady, recurring background for a more rhythmically varied main voice; such is the case in Ex. 12-3.

Ex. 12-3. Handel: Sonata No. 6 for Flute and Continuo.

An alternative to the preceding can be seen in the next illustration in which rhythmic recurrence (in the guise of sequential eighth-note motion) occurs in the main voice and the accompanying lower line supplies harmonic-rhythmic support.

Ex. 12-4. J.S. Bach: French Suite No. 2, Menuet.

A different kind of repetition organizes Ex. 12-5. The upper line unfolds entirely through successive patterns of three eighths. The less active lower part, which is essentially accompanimental, is differentiated from the upper line by accented longer notes. Contrary motion further contrasts the two voices.

Ex. 12-5. J. S. Bach: Two-voice Invention in G Major.

An example of motive organization is shown in Ex. 12-6, which contains two rhythmically repetitive but independent voices, each unfolding through sequential repetition of a motive. It is possible to perceive the beginning of each repetition at several points. This is true because the successive melodic units are alike, seem to overlap, and are not separated by rests or contrasting durations.

Ex. 12-6. Beethoven: Fugue, Sonata, Op. 110.

A subtler form of repetition occurs in the next passage in which Mozart has systematically modified either the rhythmic or pitch organization of the motive that recurs in the upper voice. Such procedures heighten interest considerably.

Ex. 12-7. Mozart: Piano Sonata in B-flat, K. 333, Finale.

Sequential activity in Ex. 12-8 in one voice is usually matched by a corresponding sequence in the other. Ex. 12-8 shows three statements of a one-measure pattern in the upper part, accompanied by a sequential lower part. The lower voice accompanies with a twice-stated pattern which also is repeated a second lower.

Ex. 12-8. J.S. Bach: Two-voice Invention in D Major.

A similar sequential organization occurs in exact form three times and then modified a fourth time in Ex. 12-9. As one might expect, the step relations of the voice movement create a step succession of harmonic roots.

Ex. 12-9. Hindemith: *Ludus Tonalis,* Fugue in E. (C) 1943 by Schott & Co. Ltd., London. Reprinted by permission.

Successive phrases are frequently built out of a pattern that is treated in the first phrase as an exact sequence and then "borrowed," so to speak, as a point of departure for a contrasting or "answering" phrase. The listener is led into the second phrase with material which is derivative from the first but not maintained to its termination. Such a technique of smooth phrase delineation is seen in Ex. 12-10.

Ex. 12-10. Corelli: Sonata da camera for Violin, Sarabanda.

The second phrase, which begins at measure 5, is *not* actually part of the sequence. Both the sequential root pattern (up a fourth—down a fifth) and the step progression formed by basic pitches in both voices is broken. However, the second phrase clearly begins with a restatement of the first half of the two-measure motive that has occurred sequentially in the upper part.

Imitation

Imitation results from the statement of a melodic pattern by one voice, and the restatement or answer of the same pattern (exact or modified) by another voice. The pattern imitated (usually a motive) is often heard first as a solo statement, thus underlining its role as an imitated subject. Compositions of two or more voices which systematically employ strict imitation are called *canons*.[1] Other types of compositions which employ imitative sections interspersed with non-imitative (free) sections include fugues, inventions, chorale preludes, ricercares, motets, canzonas, and others. We are concerned here with the principle of imitation rather than with the study of large musical forms in which imitation is found.

Shostakovitch has employed imitation at the octave in Ex. 12-12. The time lapse between statements is quite close—one beat.

Ex. 12-11. Shostakovitch: Symphony No. 5, Op. 47, I. (C) Copyright MCMXLV by Leeds Music Corporation, New York, N.Y. Used by permission. All rights reserved.

Although the imitating voice may enter at any pitch-interval above or below the initial statement of a pattern, imitation at the unison (beginning the imitative answer on the same pitch as the first statement), octave, fifth, or fourth, represents the norm. Furthermore, the imitation of a melodic unit may be strict, the answer duplicating the first statement in rhythm and interval, or it may be modified rhythmically or intervallicly. Three kinds of imitation are shown in Ex. 12-12, Ex. 12-13, and Ex. 12-14.

Ex. 12-12. Frescobaldi: Organ Ricercare.

---

[1] The term *canon* refers to "law," in this case denoting the "laws" of one voice dictating activity in the other.

Ex. 12-13. C.P.E. Bach: Keyboard Sonata.

Ex. 12-14. Shostakovitch: Symphony No. 1, Op. 10, II. (C) Copyright MCMXLVI by Leeds Music Corporation, New York, N.Y. Used by permission. All rights reserved.

Four measures of imitative dialogue precede three measures of homophony in this transitional passage by Beethoven in which a change of key from *E* Major to *B* Major is accomplished. Such passages typify those in which imitative and non-imitative composition occur side by side.

Ex. 12-15. Beethoven: Sonata for Piano, Op. 14, No. 1, III.

Points of imitation, that is, imitative phrase beginnings or sectional beginnings, often occur to bring about an interdependency of voices that is signalled by their mutual sharing of similar thematic material. Recurrence in such situations is a product of polyphonic restatement, in contrast to such repetitive devices as sequence, motivic repetition, or simple rhythmic repetition, any of which may be produced by a single voice.

Imitation at the fifth above signals the relation between voices established for the opening measures of the passage in Ex. 12-16a. The imitation of the lower voice is sustained in the top part for only three measures. In b, imitation at the octave is based on the opening six measures of the bass.

Ex. 12-16a. Josquin des Près: *Homo quidan fecit coenam magnam,* Motet.

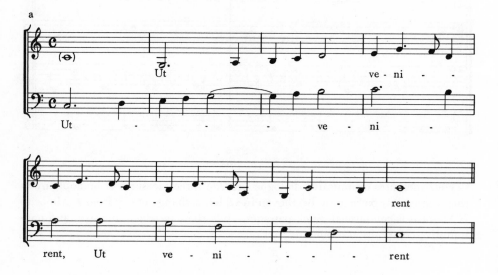

Ex. 12-16b. Josquin des Près: *Homo quidan fecit coenam magnam,* Motet.

As mentioned earlier, the systematic employment of imitation for an entire composition or section is called *canon*. In the movement that follows, a two-voice canonic relationship is maintained throughout; note that the composer consistently employs a reinforcement of the two-voice texture by coupling the violins and viola and cello in octaves. In such a passage the upper parts form a composite voice, as do the two lower strings, and the effect is of two, not four, parts.

Ex. 12-17. Haydn: String Quartet in D Minor, Op. 76, No. 2, III.

The excerpt from a two-voice composition by Lassus, Ex. 12-18, presents a good opportunity to see how motivic and rhythmic recurrence, sequence, and imitative processes can be integrated into a larger segment of a piece for two voices. Sing the piece, paying particular attention to the processes just cited. Then study the compositional detail of the piece, considering such factors as melodic motion and directional patterns, treatment of consonance and dissonance, and root relations.

Ex. 12-18. Lassus: *Sequentur Cantiones* (First Part).

The texture of this passage, written in the key of *G* Dorian, is contrapuntal, and imitation is maintained throughout. The music of both voices is developed, with rhythmic variations, out of the two motives heard first in the lower voice:

Ex. 12-19.

   the second motive is a

modified repetition of the first, transposed a perfect fifth above.

These motives are transformed rhythmically, through syncopation, augmentation, and diminution, to produce continuous motion distributed between two equal parts. Despite the similar melodic content of both parts, contrapuntal independence is maintained by staggering the entrances and avoiding the simultaneous use of identical durations. Not until the final cadence of the excerpt do the two voices converge rhythmically.

Even though no strong cadence occurs until measure 14, the music "breathes," because the voices rest at staggered locations. Thus the piece takes on shape, and the parts are more independent than they would be if they moved continuously from opening to close.

In many respects the techniques used to effect recurrence and unity in the composition by Webern that follows are analogous to those discovered in the Ex. 12-18, although they are far more subtly introduced. Listen to a recording of the Webern movement and study it carefully in an effort to learn how the composer has unified its linear detail. Such a study should remind one of the timelessness of composers' continuing search for unity.

Ex. 12-20. Webern: Five Pieces for String Quartet, Op. 5, II. Copyright by Universal Edition, Vienna.

Exercises

For more detailed assignments see *Materials and Structure of Music I, Workbook*, Chapter 12.

1. Use the opening motive of Ex. 12-1, by Haydn, as the basis of a section of two-voice imitative counterpoint for violin and viola. Write in a different key from the example.
2. Write a short canon, sixteen measures or more, based on the upper voice in Ex. 12-6.
3. Locate five variants of the main motive in Ex. 12-19 that occur in the continuation of the piece; write them on a separate sheet of manuscript and give a brief description of the relation of each to the original in measures 1 and 2.
4. Listen to a recording of Ex. 12-20 and study the piece carefully. Jot down for discussion as many factors as you can find that contribute to the melodic (linear) unity of the piece. Consider details of horizontal pitch organization as well as rhythmic figures.

13

THREE-VOICE COMBINATIONS

Our study of two-voice textures dealt with principles of organization that can be applied to any number of parts, thereby revealing the importance of a two-voice framework for any multi-part texture. Adding more voices creates new problems of spacing, part-clarity, and harmonic logic, but the basis for effective three-part combinations—coherent melodic structure—is not different from that of two parts. Except for the introduction of the chord as a unit of harmonic reference, the vertical alignment of three voices likewise poses no drastically new problems.

Rhythmic Association

The degree of individuality displayed by the separate parts of a three-voice texture can vary from total dependence to total independence. The term *homophony* is usually reserved for combinations in which a single part can be regarded as a principal melody, the remaining parts accompanimental. Whereas the slow-moving lines in Ex. 13-1 represent the most unobtrusive kind of homophonic association, the active parts of Ex. 13-2 are so thoroughly enmeshed with the motion of the top line that they, too, represent a form of homophonic texture.

Ex. 13-1. Schubert: Morgengrüss (*Die schöne Müllerin*).

Ex. 13-2. Mendelssohn: Song Without Words, Op. 19.

The Mendelssohn excerpt of Ex. 13-2 contains brief suggestions of part individuality, the rhythmic separation of the middle voice in measures 2 and 3, and the independent contour of the bass at several points. But on the whole, all three voices are relatively unified in pitch contour and rhythmic play: a *minimum* kind of counterpoint is present.

To justify the description "contrapuntal," a three-voice combination must contain parts that have some degree of individuality; and yet, all three must combine into a unified association. In fulfilling these basic requirements the parts can be combined into one of the three following dispositions:

Type 1: One voice dominating; remaining voices aligned as accompanying parts, varying one from the other only to an extent that preserves their separate identities.

Ex. 13-3. J.S. Bach: Three-voice Invention in E Major.

* dominating voice

Ex. 13-4. Hindemith: *Ludus Tonalis,* Fugue in E. (C) 1943 by Schott & Co., Ltd., London. Reprinted by permission.

* dominating voice (fugue subject)

Even in these two examples of the one basic type, some linear interest is displayed by the separate "subordinate" parts. The upper parts of the Bach excerpt form a simple foil for the greater melodic interest of the bass through the first three measures (the roles of the middle and bottom voices are switched in measure 4). The upper parts of the Hindemith excerpt are less subordinate in character, for they move in faster relative note values and cut more interesting lines in contrary motion to the bass.

Type 2: Two voices of about equal interest; a third voice decidedly subordinate.

Ex. 13-5. Franck: Symphony in D Minor, I.

Ex. 13-6. William Schuman: Symphony No. 3, Fugue. Reprinted by permission of Copyright owner, G. Schirmer, Inc.

In the Franck excerpt of Ex. 13-5, the two outer parts dominate because of greater rhythmic interest and imitation of patterns (the bass of measures 2 and 3 imitates the soprano of measures 1 and 2). The Schuman example is similar, for the disposition of melodic interest again is in the outer voices. But here the lower part does not contain imitative statements, nor is it quite as active as the top part.

Type 3: Three voices of approximately equal interest, each sharing the listener's attention in a "give-and-take" succession; frequently an imitative relationship.

Ex. 13-7. Handel: Suite in D Minor, Fugue.

Ex. 13-8. Lassus: Penitential Psalm No. 3.

Both the Handel and the Lassus textures contain imitation. In Ex. 13-7 the bass line imitates the top (beginning in the last half of measure 2), and the top imitates the bass (beginning in measure 3). During this exchange the middle voice winds through its own separate and quite individual motion. Ex. 13-8 contains imitative statements among all three voices at various points.

Almost any contrapuntal texture of three parts can be fitted into one of these three categories, but music does not normally remain set in a single disposition for long. The composer is free to shift or vary textural relationships. Consequently, it is often futile to describe an entire composition or large section by any one of these types.

Within a three-voice combination one line can dominate the other two by virtue of its more interesting rhythmic pattern. But faster motion alone does not ensure melodic domination over slower moving lines, unless this faster motion is couched in rhythmic patterns that are diversified enough to be interesting. The comparatively rapid motion of the "continuous basses" in many compositions of the Baroque era recedes into a subordinate "background" role because it also happens to move in rigidly uniform patterns.

Ex. 13-9. Handel: Trio Sonata, Op. 5. No. 4, Passacaille.

Both of the upper voices in Ex. 13-9 are marked by rhythmic diversity. This sets them off as conspicuous in comparison with the continuous eighths of the bass line. When rhythmic diversity is present in all three parts, the pattern of faster articulation usually dominates the texture.[1]

An exception to these rhythmic "rules of thumb" can occur when a melody that is well known to the listener is heard in slower motion than its accompanying parts. For instance, a familiar tune that serves as the melodic basis for forms in which variations occur simultaneously with the melody may draw more attention than voices of greater rhythmic interest.

The *chorale prelude* uses a pre-existent melody which, in many settings by composers, employs this contrasting relationship of slow voice accompanied by busy rhythms in remaining voices. In spite of its less interesting motion, its familiarity, coupled with emphasis of registration or instrumentation in performance, may still focus our attention on it as the dominating voice.[2]

Ex. 13-10. Scheidt: *Gelobet seist du, Jesu Christ.*

Chorale melody

Rhythmic Unity

The rhythms of the three separate voices normally are related; the voices share the same rhythmic divisions, although these divisions usually are not articulated simultaneously. In many three-voice textures (particularly in music of the Baroque period) the separate patterns, though different, produce periodic divisions of the meter's basic duration when added together. Note that the combined rhythms of Ex. 13-11 divide the basic duration ($\bullet$) into a continuous stream of quarters, while Ex. 13-2 contains divisions into sixteenths. The result of these combinations is a continuity of flow for the whole texture.

---

[1] All other factors being equal, we are prone to regard the highest voice of a combination as the most important—as the "melody."

[2] In organ chorale preludes the "melody" frequently is reinforced by octave couplings to strengthen it.

Ex. 13-11. Beethoven: Quartet in C-sharp Minor, Op. 131, I.

Ex. 13-12. J.S. Bach: Prelude in E Major (*Well-tempered Clavier,* Book II).

Although all part combinations do not consistently divide the metric basis into a set division, the separate voices often use the same (or closely related) patterns. Ex. 13-13 shows a less constant division of the basic duration. The result is a somewhat less-driving rhythmic propulsion than the passages of Ex. 13-11 and Ex. 13-12.

Ex. 13-13. Handel: Clavier Suite in E Minor, Sarabande.

Infrequently, the several parts move in identical rhythms, and separation of lines is achieved solely by individual pitch contours. This unusual way of maintaining line identity does not occur often in contrapuntal music. It will be discussed later as a possible means of pitch organization.

Voice individuality is most commonly achieved by contrasted note durations. Three parts composed of mixed long and short values offer the simplest and surest way of creating part separation. Combinations of three equally active voices usually incorporate a broad diversity of motion, in this way accentuating further the individuality of each part. The section shown in Ex. 13-14 contains parts whose rhythms typify this kind of individuality.

Ex. 13-14. Frescobaldi: Canzona for Organ.

Here each voice moves in its own individual rhythm, the occasional sixteenths acting as a minimum rhythmic bond between the two upper parts, but with no closer hint of kinship in evidence. Passages of this kind are infrequent in music of three parts, for most textures rely on a closer rhythmic union between at least two of the lines.

Stretches of a three-voice combination often are comprised of parts which move at different divisions of the basic duration. The Bach excerpt of Ex. 13-15 divides the quarter-note into eighths (bass voice) and sixteenths (middle voice) in a continuous relationship, while the top voice provides articulations of the basic duration itself.

Ex. 13-15. J.S. Bach: Fugue in E Major (*Well-tempered Clavier*, Book I).

The uniformity of each pattern adds up to a rhythmic thrust that is absent in music whose lines are formed by a greater variety of note durations (but each line is also less interesting *rhythmically* as a result). It is this simple 1 to 2 to 4 ratio of articulations (♩ : ♫ : ♬) that blends the three different parts together into such tightly unified association. (This kind of part-identity is most typical of music written during the late Baroque period.)

Aside from diversity of patterns created by fluctuating note-values, individuality of parts also can be obtained by contradictory divisions of the basic duration. Duplet patterns in one voice combined with triplet patterns in another creates a more severe separation of parts than two versions of a single metric division.

When the contrast is prolonged it is difficult for the listener to determine the fundamental metric division unless a third part reinforces one of the patterns.

In addition to contrasting or contradictory beat divisions, the displacement of accents in one part, by syncopation, forcibly differentiates that line from its associates. The ties across bars in Ex. 13-16 contribute to the clear rhythmic definition of each of the parts, as well as to the harmonic interest.

Ex. 13-16. J.S. Bach: *Art of the Fugue,* Contrapunctus IX.

The degree of unity of voices in a three-voice texture is also determined by the coincidence or non-coincidence of cadences in the separate lines. In general, a predominating voice establishes the pattern of cadence for all associated voices. Thus a chordal texture in which one voice dominates will display a uniformity of phrase length among the constituent parts, these lengths governed by the "melody's" cadences, as in the next example.

Ex. 13-17. J.S. Bach: *Vater unser in Himmelreich* (chorale harmonization).

On the other hand, textures of greater contrapuntal interest do not always display this singularity of cadential form; individual parts sometimes create their own phrase lengths and cadences separately. This condition avoids rhythmic stagnation by allowing continued motion in at least one voice while another pauses at its own formal junction. Ex. 13-18 is bracketed to show the phrase structure of each part, thereby revealing the variety of cadence locations that create a constantly mobile texture. Only in the sixth measure do all of the voices combine in a halt that creates a strong cadential effect. The imitation between the three voices further enhances this high degree of motion.

Ex. 13-18. Lassus: Penitential Psalm No.3.

In less imitative combinations, momentum is sustained at some phrase endings by continued motion in only one part. This singular movement reduces the conspicuous pause of the cadence, and it throws the active voice into stark relief against the inactive.

Ex. 13-19. Mozart: Sonata for Violin and Piano, K. 376, II.

Pitch Association of Three Parts

The introduction of a third voice to the musical fabric creates the possibility of a new reference unit of harmonic structure, the *chord*. Up until this time we have measured pitch associations by their intervallic content without relating them to chord structure.

We shall defer discussion of the chord until Chapter 14, for the present dealing only with the melodic principles that are pertinent to combinations of three relatively independent parts.

It is helpful to view a three-voice texture as a two-voice basis to which a third complementary part has been added. This added part forms a two-voice counterpoint with *each* of the original voices, and these two new associations follow closely the principles discussed for two-voice textures in Chapters 9, 10, 11, and 12. These contrapuntal relations of three voices are represented in Ex. 13-2 by brackets; where in a two-voice combination there is only one set of vertical relations, there are three sets in a three-voice texture.

Ex. 13-20. Three contrapuntal relations.

Top voice ————————————————————————————— ⎤⎤

Middle voice ———————————————————————— ⎦

Bottom voice ——————————————————————— ⎦⎥

Since the two outer voices of a three-part texture form the structural pitch limits—the "top" and the "bottom"—they constitute the vertical framework for the combination. For this reason, the success of a three-part union depends strongly upon the compatability of the outer voices, the two-voice framework.

The middle part in some combinations serves as a rhythmic and harmonic "cushion," filling in where outer parts take momentary pause or where they, alone, do not complete the desired sonority.

Ex. 13-21. Handel: Clavier Suite in E Minor, Courante.

In addition to rhythmic diversity (discussed on page 200), pitch contour is another melodic factor capable of seizing the attention of the listener. A contour of greater breadth will dominate another line that moves within a limited pitch range, unless the narrower voice has a more engaging rhythm.

A voice of limited contour, however, usually moves in slower, less diversified patterns, thus ensuring its more accompanimental role. Ex. 13-22 and Ex. 13-23 show two passages, each having one subordinate voice. It is true that the less obtrusive line in Ex. 13-22 is articulated in relatively brief values, but its *durational patterns* are the sums of the time between articulations, as well as the actual note values alone, thereby producing a slower motion in relation to the other voices.

Ex. 13-22. J.S. Bach: Fugue in C Minor (*Well-tempered Clavier,* Book I).

Ex. 13-23. Shostakovitch: Quartet, Op. 49, I. Used by permission of MCA Music, a division of MCA Inc., New York, N.Y. All rights reserved.

The Shostakovitch passage in Ex. 13-23 is noteworthy because it represents a kind of "bare minimum" counterpoint; its two lower lines lack interesting melodic contour and rhythmic diversity. The middle voice is, of course, a *pedal figure,* and thus represents the ultimate in *static* pitch contour. The bass is itself relatively static, for it consists of an *ostinato* pattern of the most rudimentary shape.

Individuality of pitch contour determines to a certain extent, then, the equality or inequality of linear interest discussed earlier. Three voices that form quite different pitch outlines, their rises and falls occurring at separate locations, create the greatest degree of contour separation.

Ex. 13-24 shows a three-part texture in which each line is rhythmically unique, separated from its associates by virtue of individual contour.

Ex. 13-24. J.S. Bach: Fugue in G Major (*Well-tempered Clavier,* Book I).

The two outer parts of a three-voice texture can be regarded as a framework that follows the same organizing principles developed in earlier sections devoted to two-voice textures. The potential cadence formulae remain identical, and the intervallic relations between the two lines retain cadential consonances except when decorative patterns form dissonances.

The middle voice forms a two-part union with each of the outer voices, as we illustrated with Ex. 13-20. Its relations with each of these parts is also that of a two-part texture, but a few extenuating circumstances create some notable differences when the three parts sound together.

For instance, the perfect fourth, which does not appear frequently as a basic interval in two-voice textures, appears commonly between the upper voices of three-voice combinations. The tonal instability of this interval precludes its occurrence between the lower two parts as a cadential consonance; when it is formed between the two upper parts it is normally accompanied by a major or minor third or a perfect fifth between the lower two parts.

Ex. 13-25.

A style of writing that makes extensive successive use of the interval combination shown in Ex. 13-25 can be found in the works of composers from many different periods of music history. Its effect is so striking when it occurs within a generally contrapuntal texture that it has been assigned the special name *fauxbourdon* ("false bass"). As we shall see in the following chapter, a more apt name might be *sixth-chord style*, because of the sixth formed between the outer parts.

Ex. 13-26. Anonymous: *Angelus ad Virginem.*

The octave, fifth, thirds, and sixths are the most frequent intervals on strong beats, with the fourth as a possibility between the two upper parts. Ex. 13-27 and Ex. 13-28 show two three-part combinations which, when reduced to their basic outlines, reveal this use of basic intervals and decorative patterns.

Ex. 13-27. Handel: Suite in E Minor, Gigue.

Reduction

Intervals	1.	8 — 6	3 — 5	3 — 5	3 — 3	3	6	8	3	3	3	3	8
	2.	6	— — 6		— —	6	4	6	5	3	6	6	6
	3.	3	— — 5		— —	5	3	3	6	8	5	5	3

Ex. 13-28. Landini: Ballata.

1	8	6	6	8	—	5	5 — 5	3	6	8
2	4	6	4	4	—	1	— 5	1	— 3	4
3	5	1	3	5	1	5	— 3	3	3	5

The interval combinations in Ex. 13-29 are most common as the pitch ingredients around which a three-voice union might be formed. The intervals are all reduced to a single octave compass for ease of reference; compound versions of each relation are just as possible.

Ex. 13-29. Consonances.

Ex. 13-29 continued.

Decorative Consonances

All other interval combinations which include seconds or sevenths, or which have fourths or tritones between the lowest and either of the other parts, usually arise from a decorative pattern of some kind. We shall deal with some of these matters in greater detail in Chapter 14, where we will discuss chord structure for the first time.

Spatial Distribution of Parts

The distances maintained by the voice pairs of a three-voice texture, and the overall pitch range enclosed by these combinations, are both determined by the particular sound desired by the composer and the relative contours of the individual lines. Two outer parts that move in predominantly contrary motion inevitably will lead to fluctuating texture that varies from "narrower" to "wider." Similarly, lines of highly individual melodic contours render uniformity of spacing impossible. The very nature of counterpoint dictates that any three-voice texture will normally encompass *at least* a full octave range, thus making individual part motion possible without constant impingement on the pitch territory of another voice. Three-voice combinations with very active lines usually cover more than this bare minimum.

In general, a particular section will maintain a relatively uniform spacing that further unifies texture. As basic types, two distributions of pitch levels to the various parts are common:

Type 1: Generally equidistant parts, no consistent couplings of any two of the three in evidence. Such a disposition will usually reveal considerable individuality of pitch contour and rhythm.

Ex. 13-30. J.S. Bach: Three-voice Invention in A Major.

In Ex. 13-30, each of the three parts remains within a clearly delineated range of activity, maintaining its unique patterns within its assigned region. An abstraction of the spacing characteristics in this passage shows more clearly the distribution of pitch activity within the three lines, all of which cover a total span of two octaves and a fifth.

Ex. 13-31. Spacing of parts in Ex. 13-30.

Textures of this type cannot remain for long in a single relationship of parts unless similar motion prevails.

Type 2: Two parts coupled in close range, the third part separated by approximately an octave (or more). (The coupling can obtain between the two upper or the two lower voices.)

Ex. 13-32. Schumann: Fugue on B.A.C.H.

Ex. 13-33. J. S. Bach: Fugue in D Minor (*Well-tempered Clavier,* Book I).

These two excerpts show the coupling possibilities in three parts, in terms of register. In the Schumann sample the upper parts are combined within close proximity, while the bottom part winds through a range approximately two octaves below the middle voice. The Bach excerpt is a reversal of the Schumann, for here the upper part is separated from the coupled pair of lower parts. In both instances, the separate part is more conspicuous by virtue of its highly contrasted octave position in the combination.

Features other than spacing can serve to emphasize a particular voice. Although the two upper parts in Ex. 13-34 are coupled in *range* as distinct from the bottom part, the longer durations of the upper line make it a distinct pattern from the other two. Here rhythm, not spatial coupling, is the distinguishing factor.

Ex. 13-34. Telemann: *Christus, der uns selig macht.*

In addition to the specific musical effect by the composer, voice distribution in a texture depends upon the instrument or instruments that play them. A distribution such as that in Ex. 13-35 is impractical for a piano because some of the spacings would be clumsy for the right hand. Ex 13-36 would be ineffectual for the piano, but for different reasons; here the problem would be clear articulation and separation of individual melodic strands. The constant voice crossings can be clear when played by flute and two violins (or by any combination of single-line instruments), but the articulation difficulties for the pianist would be ticklish. Added to this purely physical problem would be the lack of tonal contrast between the three separate voices, and the combination of objections make such a spacing most improbable for piano.

Ex. 13-35. Copland: *Appalachian Spring,* Bride's Dance. Copyright 1945 by Aaron Copland. Reprinted by permission of Aaron Copland, copyright owner, and Boosey & Hawkes, Inc., Sole Licensees.

Ex. 13-36. J.S. Bach: Suite No. 2 in B Minor, Rondeau.

In general, *heterogeneous*, or gapped spacings that contain no couplings of any kind are associated with highly contrapuntal textures in which individuality of parts is paramount. In more homophonic (*homogeneous*) combinations a closer spatial alliance of parts becomes essential. The effect of harmony is most readily achieved when parts are close enough to make them fuse into a block of sound.

A simple experiment will demonstrate the differences of spacings. If the combinations of Ex. 13-37 are played by separate instruments, the more unified, compact effect of (a) contrasts discernibly with the more disparate sound of combination (b).

Ex. 13-37.

Aside from the differences of tone quality produced by the register changes for the top and bottom parts in (b), the wider separation alone reduces the effect of tonal fusion that is more apparent in the closer-knit alliance of (a).

Exercises

For more detailed assignments see *Materials and Structure of Music I, Workbook,* Chapter 13.

1. Plan a three-part rhythmic texture for percussion (clapped hands will suffice for performance if necessary) that consists of three complementary patterns.

Model:

2. Look through piano, choral, orchestral, and chamber music to find passages of rhythmic association which correspond to one of the types discussed early in this chapter.
3. Find two parts (or extract them from a composition) which will serve as an outer framework for a three-part texture. Add a third part in complementary pitch and rhythm patterns.
4. Write an eight- to ten-measure passage in which the top voice dominates, the two lower voices are relatively subordinate and are coupled together in register. Write another passage in which the bass dominates and the two upper voices are coupled.
5. Analyze a number of contrapuntal textures (Bach, Handel, Mozart) for basic pitches in three separate voices. Construct a three-voice basic framework as an abstraction of the texture. Then decorate the resultant framework to create a different composition.

14

CHORD STRUCTURE

With the addition of another part to a two-voice texture we can recognize a new unit, the chord, as a basis of pitch organization. This will not represent a major change in method, for chords are collections of intervals, and they are classified by the kinds of intervals they contain, by *sonority* types. The relative stability of a chord is determined by the intervals which comprise it and by the relation it bears to other chords surrounding it.

In Chapter 2 we discussed the relative *stability* and *instability*, the relative *consonance* and *dissonance* of intervals. As a general rule, a consonant, *stable* chord is one that contains only consonant intervals, while a dissonant chord contains one or more dissonant intervals.

Ex. 14-1 shows four different chords, the last three of which are considerably more dissonant than the first. Note that each of these last three contains at least one unstable interval.

Ex. 14-1. Chords.

The more complicated the interval structure within a chord, the greater the chord's dissonance. Thus we could make a scaling of harmonic sonority that would extend from the most consonant sound combination, the octave, to the most dissonant, in which all twelve pitches of the chromatic scale might sound together in a biting combination.

Ex. 14-2. Chords.

215

Not only is chord (b) more dissonant than chord (a), its many different pitches (and thus many different intervals) also impart to it a high degree of *density* (in this particular spacing) that a few-toned chord would not have.

Between these two sonorities of Ex. 14-2 lies the gamut of chord types that are found in most music. The bulk of our musical heritage has used a restricted harmonic palette that lies closer to the ⅝ sonority of Ex. 14-2a than to Ex. 14-2b, but composers since the beginning of our century have considerably broadened the possibilities toward the dissonant side of the scale. One of the recognizable trademarks for any composer is the chord combinations to be found in his music and the way these sonorities are linked together into harmonic successions. Many of our subsequent discussions in this book will be concerned with the recognition and classification of chord types.

Any chord that can be reduced to no more nor less than three different notes is called a *triad*. That is, even a chord made up of five different *tones* might still be reducible to a triadic basis if two of the five pitches are octave replicas of two others.

Ex. 14-3. Triads.

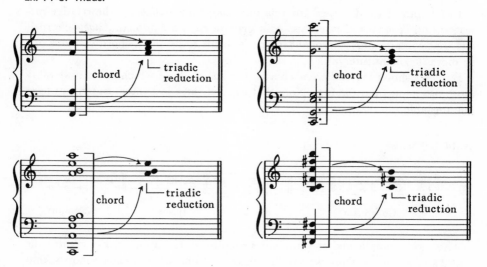

Western music is unique in its development of a concept of chords—the "vertical" plane of sound in music—in addition to the purely melodic or "horizontal" plane. In non-Western cultures the simultaneous soundings of different tones are regarded (if at all) only as the result of coincidences between the several strands of melody. Some of the "chords" of the Siamese music shown in Ex. 14-4 "just happen," for they are not derived from any manner of predetermined chord progression, and the musicians who perform such music make no effort to plan their improvisations so that particular tones coincide at all vertical combinations. A similar result sometimes can be heard in the improvised web of lines created by jazz musicians as each instrumentalist contributes his own melodic strand to the total result.

Ex. 14-4. Siamese Orchestral Piece: *Kham Hom* (Sweet Words), *Historical Anthology of Music*, Volume 1; Copyright by Harvard University Press. Reprinted by permission.

But in our composed music, harmonic motion pervades musical structure, adding another dimension to tonal organization. The simplest units of harmonic structure are triads of relatively consonant quality. They are the only chords which consist of intervals no less stable than major and minor thirds, so they are among the most stable chords. These are the *major* and *minor triads*, each of which consists of a perfect fifth divided by a third.

Ex. 14-5. Triads.

It is the location of the constituent thirds that determines major or minor quality in triads: when the first third above the root is major, a *major triad* results; when the first third above the root is minor, a *minor triad* results.

Two others of the simpler triad types are known as *diminished* and *augmented*. These designations are derived from the interval that encompasses their outer tones, the diminished and the augmented fifths respectively.

Ex. 14-6. Triads.

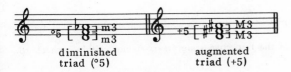

Both of these triads are relatively unstable, for they lack the intervallic simplicity that creates a clear root effect. Neither contains a perfect fifth or fourth, and the diminished triad contains the relatively unstable tritone. Since both the augmented and diminished triads involve equal-sized intervals (minor thirds in the diminished triad, major thirds in the augmented), they are ambiguous and lack the clarity of tonal focus that creates a root effect.[1]

Major and minor triads are stable, and so they are more important to our present study. Furthermore, they will form the basis of many other chords that will be discussed later. Note that major and minor scales yield more major and minor triads than diminished and augmented.

Ex. 14-7.

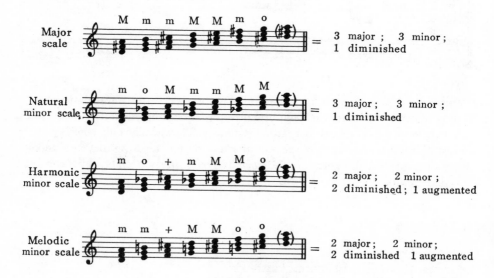

Each of the chords of Ex. 14-7 is a *diatonic* chord for the particular scale it is built within.[2] Thus the triad *g-b-d* is diatonic to *D* major, but it is non-diatonic (or *chromatic*) for *d* natural minor; and the triad *B-flat-D-F* is a diatonic chord of *F* major, nondiatonic for *C* major.

Although the major, minor (and less so the diminished and augmented) triads are the harmonic staples of music of the past eleven hundred years, any three different pitches must be regarded as potential triad material. The chord succession in Ex. 14-8 shows six three-note chords, or *triads*, only the last of which is similar to one of the four types we have been discussing. The remaining five triads are relatively dissonant combinations which are essentially products of the linear motion of the three lines.

---

[1] We shall use the term *prime* for the fundamental pitch of chords which do not possess roots.
[2] Since only pitches of the respective scale are contained within each chord.

Ex. 14-8. Hindemith: *Ludus Tonalis,* Fugue No. 4 in E. (C) 1943 by Schott & Co., Ltd., London. Reprinted by permission.

In addition to sonority type—major, minor, diminished, or augmented—of the classified forms, another vital bit of information about a chord concerns its relation to other chords. That is, chords are like people in that they "behave" or reflect their own identities only in relation to other chords, and these familial relationships are a necessary aspect of chordal description.

In tonal music the individual chord's relation to the tonic pitch is denoted by the roman numeral that represents the scale position of the chord's root. If we build a triad on each degree of the major or minor scale, we can identify the resultant chords according to their relationships to tonic *within that scale*.

Ex. 14-9. Chord nomenclature in relation to tonic.

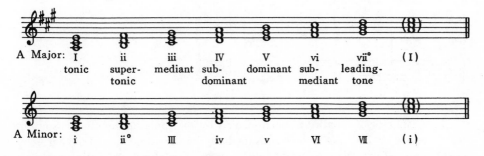

The two essential facts to be known about a particular triad within a tonality are its *sonority* and its *tonal function*. Therefore, it is important that a distinction be made here between capital and lowercase roman numerals, for these, in conjunction with the ° sign for diminished and the + sign for augmented, are concise ways to indicate the two basic facts about any diatonic triad:

Numeral Type (capital or lowercase, plus ° or + when applicable) shows basic sonority.
Thus V or IV denotes major triad
vi or ii denotes minor triad
ii° or iv° denotes diminished triad
III + or II + denotes augmented triad

Numeral Value shows scalar degree relationship to tonic pitch.
Thus V (or v) denotes a root tone that is a perfect fifth above (or perfect fourth below) tonic.
I (or i) indicates the triad built on the tonic pitch.

Chord Succession

Within a tonality, the most important chord is the tonic (I or i, depending upon major or minor sonority), for it is the only chord that can render total stability within a progression. Just as almost all tonal melodies end with their *tonic pitch*, so almost all multi-part music ends with a *tonic chord*; it is the sonority that can best produce the relaxation of tension normally associated with musical termination.

Aside from the tonic, any other *stable* triad (of major or minor sonority) is a potential tonic, for if emphasized enough, another chord can replace a former tonic as the center of pitch focus: modulation takes place.[3]

The next most important chord within a tonality is the *dominant* (*V*), because in the traditional key schemes of major and minor (and in some modes) this triad coembodies the important *dominant* and *leading tone* melodic relationships. The combination of these two pitches in the same sonority creates the simplest chord relationship in a key scheme; it is this chord in conjunction with a tonic chord that most clearly delineates an intended tonality. When the two are combined in a weak-strong metric relation there can be little doubt about intended tonal focus.

Ex. 14-10. V to I chord progressions.

This simplicity of tonality pattern formed by the tonic-dominant relationship (or its reverse, V-I) causes it to serve as the basis for a great portion of the harmony in the music of our Western tradition. This basic two-chord association has been used to accompany every conceivable kind of melody, from the modest child's song to art works of considerable complexity.

Ex. 14-11a. Folksong: *Have You Ever Seen a Lassie?*

---

[3] Review at this time the discussion of pitch significance in Chapter 2, pp. 20–25.

Ex. 14-11b. Beethoven: *Dance.*

Any digression from the *tonic* chord is, in a restricted sense, a weakening of tonality. However, the root of the dominant chord does not contradict the role of the tonic pitch *as tonic,* for the root of their melodic relationship lends emphasis to the tonic pitch. This can be illustrated if we note in Ex. 14-12 that the interval formed between the two roots is a fifth or fourth, and the root of both of these intervals is the same pitch, the root of the tonic chord.

Ex. 14-12. V to I chord progressions.

The change that occurs when one chord gives way to another is called *harmonic succession* or *harmonic progression.* The motion of chordal change imparts another element of psychological movement to musical tones; the change away from the tonic chord establishes a certain degree of expectation and tension; the eventual return to tonic provides fulfillment and relaxation of movement.

If the harmonic structure of a composition remained solidly imbedded in only the tonic chord, no effect of harmonic tension could result, and the important feeling of completion that results from departure and eventual return to a tonic would be missing. The total effect would be dull and static if significant rhythmic or melodic or textural contrasts did not compensate for this harmonic sameness.[4] Viewed as melodies, bugle calls suffer from this severe harmonic limitation, for they are the mere spinning-out of a single chord pattern that is based on the instrument's harmonic series.

---

[4] See Richard Wagner's Prelude to the Opera *Das Rheingold* for an example of a complete musical section that operates within a single chord, in this case the E♭ major triad.

Ex. 14-13. Bugle Call: *Reveille.*

A major: I - ⌐

A similar negation of harmonic motion might be desired for particular kinds of music that serve distinctive functions within a musical or social setting. One way of emphasizing the implied motion of one musical section is to precede it by a section that lacks harmonic changes. The excerpt of Ex. 14-14, from a toccata by Monteverdi, illustrates the avoidance of forward propulsion that can result.

Ex. 14-14. Monteverdi: Toccata, from *L'Orfeo.*

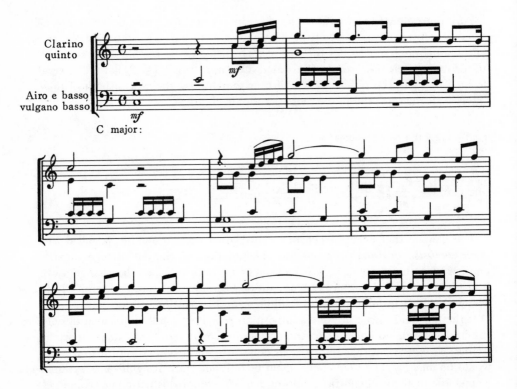

Most music incorporates harmonic successions of one kind or another. In some textures the chord structure is organized in vertical blocks, each of which moves to another, thereby achieving direct harmonic change, as in Ex. 14-15a.

Ex. 14-15a. J.S. Bach: *Alle Menschen müssen sterben.*

D: I   vi   I   IV   V   I - - - - - - ii   I   ii   V   I

But in other textures the chords might appear in melodic outlines, these arpeggiated patterns adding up to particular chords (as in Ex. 14-15b).

Ex. 14-15b. Schubert: *Der Müller und der Bach.*

In order to understand better the harmonic content of a piece of music, it is customary to analyze the various chords that constitute the harmonic successions and to plot this data in graphic form. The roman numerals mentioned earlier are indispensable for denoting sonority types and root relations within a tonality. Ex. 14-16 shows a simple analysis of a musical phrase.

Ex. 14-16. Haydn: Sonata No. 18, I.

Ex. 14-16 continued.

ii   i   ii   V   VI   (iv)   vii°   i

In some patterns of music, as in Ex. 14-16, it is impossible to assign a chord name with absolute assurance, either because the constituent pitches are so brief, or because there is more than one possibility of analysis. Measure 5 is subject to interpretation because the highly mobile top line of the first two beats might imply a iv or a i chord. If we return to our guide of basic melody analysis, *e* is revealed as the most important pitch, so the iv chord is a most likely interpretation of *implied harmony*. In ways such as this, basic melody analysis and harmonic analysis are mutually complementary techniques for gaining musical insight.

Chord Position

The structural names for the various parts of triadic chords are derived from the intervals they contain. Thus the three parts are called *root*,[5] *third,* and *fifth.* These terms are meaningful as designations when derived from the *simple* or *fundamental* position of the triad, all notes in their closest relations, as illustrated in Ex. 14-17.

Ex. 14-17. Structural chord names.

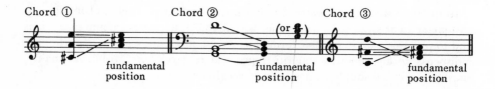

Chord ①   Chord ②   (or ♯)   Chord ③

fundamental   fundamental   fundamental
position   position   position

Even when the position of a chord changes, the individual parts are still named according to their unexpanded relations in the fundamental triadic representation. Each of the chords in Ex. 14-18 consists of the same root (*E-flat*), the same third (*G*), and the same fifth (*B-flat*), even though vastly different chordal textures are present.

---

[5] With the exception of diminished and augmented triads and other rootless chords which will be discussed further on page 227.

Ex. 14-18.

Even when more than three pitches make up the chord, if some are duplications of triad notes, then the basic structure is still the *fundamental triad*. Thus the chord type remains the same although voicing and texture change.

Ex. 14-19.

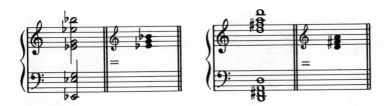

Chord Inversion

The simpler chord types (such as major and minor triads) can be turned upside down and internally reordered without appreciably changing their basic sonority. This is corroborated by the fact that these topsy-turvy arrangements do not alter root effects in any appreciable way. We can see that the same harmonic root is retained in any distribution of the notes of a major triad.

Ex. 14-20. Chord inversion.

For the reasons illustrated above, any distribution of tones is known by the name of its fundamental (simplest) reduced form. Thus both chords in Ex. 14-21 are *F major triads*, even though *f* is not at the bass position in either arrangement.

Ex. 14-21. Inverted chords.

Chord (a) is in *first inversion,* while chord (b) is in *second inversion.* These denotations refer to the number of note shufflings away from the fundamental *root position* that are required to achieve the particular chord form. That is, beginning with the simple *root position,* the first inversion requires one redistribution of notes, the second inversion requires two.

Ex. 14-22. Inverted chords.

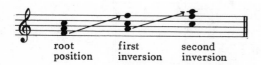

root   first   second
position   inversion   inversion

Another explanation for the three possible triad positions would recognize the *root,* or *prime,* as lowest member in a root position chord; the *third* as lowest member in a first inversion; and the *fifth* as lowest member in second inversion.

The representation of chords usually indicates the internal distribution of chord members. This is done by appending arabic numerals to the roman designation of root tone; these numerals denote interval distances above the bass note. A complete representation would be as follows:

It is important to note that these numerical designations are derived from the intervals above the bass *as if the chord were all contained within a single octave.*

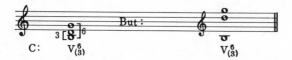

This system of chord symbolization is usually abbreviated. When no arabic numerals accompany a chord designation, it is assumed that the sonority is in *root position*, or $\frac{5}{3}$ in structure. And the designation $\frac{6}{3}$ is normally simplified into just "6", which, in most cases,[6] can also be taken to mean "first inversion triad." The full designation $\frac{6}{4}$ is necessary, of course, for the second inversion triad, in order to distinguish it from the first inversion.

As mentioned earlier, diminished and augmented triads lack the perfect fifth (or fourth) and the unequal thirds that create the root effect of major and minor triads, but the theory of inversion is normally extended to these sonorities also. The principle that governs chord invertibility is derived from the notation of tones in stacked thirds. In other words, a chord is in *root* (or *prime*) position when all of its members can be stacked one above the other in successive relations of thirds. Therefore, chords 1a, 2a, and 3a in Ex. 14-23 are not in fundamental position, but their rearrangements in 1b, 2b, and 3b reveal their "non-inverted" forms.

Ex. 14-23. Inverted chords.

We shall study other principles of chord structure later when our harmonic material includes more than the simple triad. But for the present, the principle of inversion is helpful in that it simplifies the problem of chord classification according to structure.

To determine the structural type of any chord, one must first locate the root or prime of the combined intervals. With major and minor chords this process can be simplified by a search for perfect fifths or fourths or, when these intervals are missing, thirds or sixths; the root pitch of either of these combinations will be the root for the whole chord. Lacking any of the above evidence (as in diminished and augmented triads), the principle of superposed thirds produces a workable answer. The process is illustrated below.

Ex. 14-24. Locating roots of chords.

---

[6] This method of symbolization breaks down with some more complex chords which are not discussed until Volume II.

When a three-pitch chord does not contain a *fifth* or *fourth*, the next simplest interval, the major or minor third (or sixth) determines the root. Many three-voice textures contain these non-triadic structures because individual voice motion rules out the simultaneous occurrence of three different chord members. Notice that Ex. 14-25 ends with a two-note sonority (or *diad*) because the composer demanded certain resolutions of the melodic tendencies already established.

Ex. 14-25. Chorale: *Wer weiss, wie nahe mir.*

Tonality: g i   i   V   i   V   VI ii° V   (V)   v   III iv   i VI i   V   i

Melodic-Harmonic Synthesis

Few compositions of any scope reveal the simplicity of chord structure and voice movement found in Ex. 14-25. In much music our awareness of chords is so affected by melodic elements that melody and chords form an inseparable synthesis, each reflecting the other, each delineating and clarifying the other. In other words, chords and melodies do not operate in music as mutually exclusive properties. Because of this, examples such as the following cannot be explained satisfactorily in exclusively harmonic or melodic terms.

Ex. 14-26. Beethoven: Quartet in F Major, Op. 18, No. 1, I.

If we attempt to isolate chords from this passage merely by noting the sonorities heard as vertical coincidences *on each beat*, we shall have to acknowledge that some chords (such as those on the first beats of measures 2, 3, and 4) do not represent the harmonic structure of the passage. Secondly, by trying to reconcile both the *b-naturals* and the *b-flats* that sound together in measures 1, 3, and 4 within a single chord, we would produce an implausible representation of the harmonic organization.

Actually this passage is best understood harmonically as the melodic animation of a single chord:

The top voice unfolds the upper three notes of the chord (*e, g,* and *b-flat*) within a range of two octaves. Rhythmic interest is provided by the syncopated entrances of these same three notes in the first three articulations. The viola part is rhythmically coupled with the top voice and melodically reiterates the three lower notes of the chord in pairs (*c, e,* and *g*). The technique used in these two voices is, of course, arpeggiation of basic associates—the melodic spinning out of a simple chord.

The second violin and cello parts are organized in a different way; they are more explicitly *melodic*. Both voices establish an imitative association and both span an octave that is filled in by pitches which pass within this boundary. The *b-naturals* are simply part of the *passing groups* that embellish *C*'s, and they can be regarded as brief leading tones which, in view of their brief duration, do not conflict with the more basic (the more *harmonic*) *b-flats* sounding above. It is not difficult to see here that it is partly due to the continued reemphasis on *c* in these two parts that the harmonic function of V_7 in the key of *F* and the structural weight of *C* is made clear.

We might conclude, then, that *chord* in this example can be described best as the vertical frame that channels the passage; it is through essentially melodic means, however, that this frame is established.

The next excerpt appears to involve a change of harmony on each successive eighth note.

Ex. 14-27. Beethoven: *Missa Solemnis.*

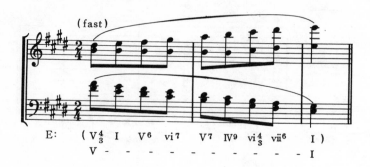

But again, harmonic explanation can be made with accuracy only by acknowledging melodic elements which project and prolong a single harmonic meaning, in this case the progression of V–I in *E* major.

Note that the upper voice spans a ninth from leading tone to tonic, while the alto reiterates b^1 before passing by step up to the tonic, melodically expressing a 5–1 relation. The two lower parts are coupled and move by step in parallel thirds. Each voice forms a melodically satisfying approach to the closing tonic chord, and each voice (or coupling) displays a fundamentally melodic character: step movement prevails.

The listener is swept along by the movement of parts in this short passage; the sonorities created by the moving voices, grouped around the repeated b^1 in the alto, contribute to the momentum and sense of expectancy of the dominant effect without replacing it. The passage is a contrapuntal elaboration of dominant—tonic movement, prolonged by stepwise (passing) movement and a repeated pedal tone on the dominant. The "chords" which occur as each voice carries out its stepwise elaboration of the dominant pattern must be viewed as *passing chords*; they are not a basic part of the harmonic structure. The inaccuracy of a detailed description of each of the vertical alignments as chords in such a passage can best be understood by listening to the passage.

Melodic elements are not always as significant as in the two examples cited here. Any chordal analysis of music must, nonetheless, acknowledge the coordinate relationship between melody and harmony in creating musical structure.

Exercises

See Chapter 14 of *Materials and Structure of Music I, Workbook,* for more detailed exercises.

1. Practice spelling major, minor, diminished, and augmented triads from a given note as root or prime. Think through the component intervals of each chord before spelling with note names. For example:

    B-flat augmented triad:
        Augmented triad = augmented fifth

                                            major third
                                            major third

$$\begin{cases} \textit{B-flat—F-sharp} \text{ augmented fifth} \\ \textit{B-flat—D} \text{ major third} \\ \textit{D—F-sharp} \text{ major third} \end{cases}$$

Spelling: *B-flat—D—F-sharp*

2. Analyze a passage chosen by the instructor, denoting each chord by its proper symbol. Sample:

Schumann:

G major: V   vi   V   I   IV₆   I⁶₄   V   I

3. In class or informally with a friend, listen to major, minor, diminished, and augmented triads played on the piano or organ and identify as to sonority.

   a. Identify which member of the major or minor triad is in the top of the chord.

   b. Identify which member of the major or minor triad is in the bass of the chord.

4. Using a three-voice texture, write a passage that is based on the following chord progression. Write the outer basic framework first, add the middle voice, then elaborate each basic melody to create an effective but simple contrapuntal texture.

   G major: I/I₆/V/vi/V₆/I/V/I//

5. Plot a simple chord progression of about four measures in length, one chord per measure. Using an instrument (or voice), improvise a simple melody that corresponds to the selected chords. Use a simple repeated rhythm for all pitch patterns.

   Example:

Progression :   I | vi | V | I   ‖

Rhythm :   ♩. ♪♩

I   vi   V   I

i   VI   V   i

15

CONTINUATION OF THREE-VOICE COMBINATIONS

Spacing

In Chapter 13 we dealt with some aspects of spacing in three parts. Let us now turn our attention to more specific guides to the distribution of three voices.

The overtone series is a useful point of reference for the spacing of three voices:

The similarity between the natural intervallic arrangement of the series (widest intervals at the bottom) and the most common arrangement of vocal parts (greater distances between lower voices) is evidence of still another relationship between musical practice and the inherent properties of musical sound.

Ex. 15-1. Marenzio: Madrigal.

In the madrigal shown in Ex. 15-1 we find a typical distribution of parts. The upper voices lie generally within an octave of each other, while the two lower parts are occasionally as far apart as two octaves. While subject to individual vocal ranges and melodic contour, the outer voices seldom are farther apart than two octaves and a fifth, as mentioned earlier in Chapter 13. Two octaves is a much more common limit. An interesting exception to this rule of thumb can be seen in measure 2. Here the soprano and alto move in contrary motion to the interval of a minor tenth. This exception to the rule is the logical result of a primarily contrapuntal association involving contrary motion.

Most three-voice works reveal considerable variety of spacing procedures. This can be seen by comparing the first and second phrases (measures 1–2 and 5–7) of the Marenzio example. Throughout the first phrase the voices are deployed so that different intervals occur between voices on nearly every beat. The second phrase begins with parallel movement in all voices, thus establishing a contrasting textural relationship between two successive phrases. Parallel motion in triads, as in measure 5, is seldom found in three-voice writing. The effect is of melodic duplication of one voice in two accompanying voices, rather than independent contrapuntal movement. The example illustrates a texture in which one voice predominates, with the other voices serving as accompanying parts.

In Ex. 15-2, a *C* major triad has been spaced for several different three-voice combinations. As can be seen, some of the spacings are performable by *only one* or *two* combinations of three-voice groups, because of vocal range limits.

Ex. 15-2. Three-voice distribution of a C major triad (root position and first inversion).

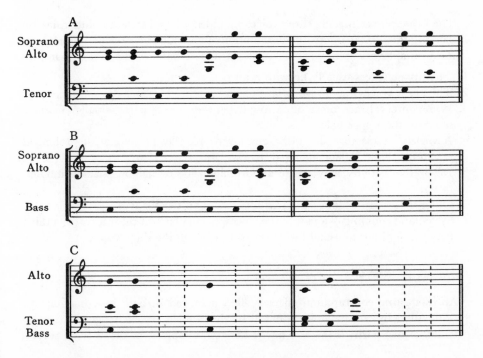

Ex. 15-2 continued.

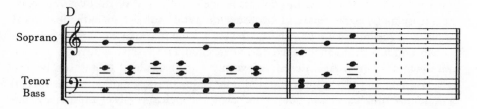

Exceptional spacings sometimes occur as the result of decorative pitches. These unusual separations occur most often in weak metric positions, and they do not attract the same attention or create the sense of imbalance that would result from their use in accented positions or longer durations. Several examples of more exceptional spacings which result from melodic decorative activity are in Ex. 15-3.

Ex. 15-3. Exceptional three-voice distribution.

The principles of spacing three voices should not be taken as absolute rules, but rather as guides to the intervallic distribution of melodic movement between parts. These principles are useful in achieving a clarity and balance of pitch relationships.

1. The upper voices usually lie within an octave or less.
2. The lower voices may move as far apart as required by melodic considerations.
3. Wider intervals are more often found between lower parts; smaller intervals separate the upper voices.
4. A variety of spacings should be employed; parallel movement, if prolonged, negates melodic independence of parts.
5. Decorative activity may create abnormally wide or narrow spacing momentarily.
6. Outer voices are seldom separated by more than two octaves.
7. Systematic coupling of a pair of the voices, particularly at the interval of a third, may bring about unusually wide separations from the third voice.

Crossing Voices

An interesting contrapuntal effect is often achieved in both instrumental and vocal textures by crossing voices, that is, by the momentary exchange of the range positions of two parts. If the alto moves above the soprano or below the tenor, for example, the voices involved in the high-low exchange are said to have *crossed*. Crossing most often occurs between adjacent parts, and it is usually the result of the fulfillment of a particular melodic pattern.

Voice crossing most often occurs *within* a phrase, although cadences involving crossed parts, or phrase beginnings using this procedure can be found. A typical example of crossing is seen in Ex. 15-4.

Ex. 15-4. Byrd: Madrigal.

Contrapuntal and Homophonic Textures

The possibilities for organizing three voices are, as we have seen, almost unlimited. No two works are identical, nor do any two derive their musical interest from identically developed compositional techniques, no matter how similar their outer surfaces may appear. Nonetheless, just as the most complex contrapuntal activity will adhere to certain harmonic formations, so even the most simply developed homophony will rely on rudimentary principles of counterpoint, if only because they are implicit in the most basic aspects of musical organization.

Ex. 15-5a illustrates an unadorned homophonic texture.

Ex. 15-5a. D. Scarlatti: Sonata in C major.

A predominant upper part is accompanied by repeated pedal c's in the left hand and a middle voice is developed entirely out of motion from e^1 to its upper neighbor f' and back to e'. The harmonic activity, featuring a harmonic rhythm of one chord per measure, consists of three chords: tonic, subdominant, and a tritone, all organized above a tonic pedal. The contrapuntal resolution of the tritone occurs in measures 5 and 8, while each voice maintains at least some degree of rhythmic independence. It is, in fact, through the incorporation of decorative activity that the work derives its minimum contrapuntal motion. Stripped of these decorative elements, the piece would appear as in Ex. 15-5b.

Ex. 15-5b. Reduction of Ex. 15-5a.

The point is that even the simplest homophonic texture may reveal elements of organization that reflect contrapuntal relationships, however mild and unprepossessing.

Contrapuntal writing dominates the texture of Ex. 15-6a.

Ex. 15-6a. J.G. Walther: *Herzlich thut mich verlangen.*

Each voice maintains rhythmic independence, and each successive entry is imitative. All three parts are unified by conjunct motion. Cadences, occurring at bars 4, 8, and 12, are weakened by continuous motion in one or more voices, so that the effect of the example is of one broad, continuously unfolding contrapuntal section, that reaches a terminal cadence in measure 12.

Harmonic relationships are much in evidence in this music. Harmonic rhythm, too, contributes to the forward motion of the counterpoint. It is, as a matter of fact, primarily through *deceleration of harmonic rhythm (from two chords per measure to one chord per measure)* that the cadences and phrase endings are distinguished in measures 4, 8–9, and 12.

Ex. 15-6b shows a simple reduction of the Walther excerpt. It becomes clear through a study of the reduction how harmonic relationships, here in the form of triads and diads (two-note combinations), form a framework for melodic activity. Note also that the principles of three-voice spacing discussed earlier are evident in this keyboard composition.

Ex. 15-6b. Harmonic reduction of Ex. 15-6a.

Doubling in Three Voices

The harmonic result of the vertical alignment of three contrapuntal voices at any one instant is not always a complete triad, even though triads represent the core unit of harmonic organization. In many instances melodic movement demands the doubling of one note in another voice, often an octave or two removed in register. Such doublings are seen in the Frescobaldi toccata (Ex. 15-7).

Ex. 15-7. Frescobaldi: Toccata.

Where doubling occurs in a three-voice chord, the resulting sonority is usually a consonance. Several such combinations are shown in Ex. 15-8.

Ex. 15-8. Doubling in three-voice chords.

Although either note of a consonant interval may be doubled, it is most frequently the *root*. Doubling of the interval root usually occurs in consonances whose roots are strong members of the tonality such as tonic and dominant. By doubling these pitches the composer emphasizes and helps to clarify the prevailing tonality.

More freedom has been exercised in doubling members of decorative consonances, whose roots, as we have described, are less evident. Either member of a decorative consonance may be doubled; the choice is usually determined by melodic considerations.

Common doubling procedures are illustrated in Ex. 15-9. The piece is in *d* minor, and both of the endings for the opening section of the sonata (which is repeated) are achieved through transient-terminal cadences to the dominant. In both instances the cadential pitch *a*, the dominant, has been doubled.

Ex. 15-9. Corelli: Sonata in D Minor, Giga.

It is important to point out that in tonal music leading tones, pitches that form tritones, decorative pitches, and altered tones generally are not doubled in three-voice textures. In other words, pitches which suggest continued movement and create instability are not reinforced. When exceptions to this basic consideration occur, they are usually located in weak metric positions, thus attracting less attention. Two exceptional doublings, involving the interval of the fourth above the bass, are seen in Ex. 15-10. Here the doubling of a fourth results from simultaneous use of decorative tones which coincide on weak portions of the beat.

Ex. 15-10. Doubling.

Decorative Patterns

Decorative activity in three voices is consistent with and in proportion to the rhythmic activity of parts. It may be located primarily in one prevailing part, as in Ex. 15-11, distributed between two coupled voices, as in Ex. 15-12, or it may be couched in voices of equal activity, as seen in Ex. 15-13 by Hindemith.

Ex. 15-11. Beethoven: Quartet in F Major, Op. 59, No. 1, I.

Ex. 15-12. Buxtehude: Prelude in E Minor.

Ex. 15-13. Hindemith: *Ludus Tonalis,* Fugue No. 8. (C) 1943 by Schott & Co., Ltd., London. Reprinted by permission.

In some instances, such as Ex. 15-14, decorative patterns may represent a colorful aspect of the organization of voices whose function is mainly accompanimental.

Ex. 15-14. Mozart: Piano Concerto in C Minor, K. 491, I.

A study of the preceding illustrations by Beethoven (Ex. 15-11) and Buxtehude (Ex. 15-12) will reveal that, as in two-voice textures, passing and neighbor tones comprise the most common forms of melodic embellishment. Such a statement applies to a vast amount of music as is illustrated by the excerpt by Hindemith (Ex. 15-13). Here, despite a more complex rhythmic and harmonic fabric, decorative pitches are approached or resolved by step. Each independent voice forms a cohesive and meaningful musical line, and the three parts fit harmonically into an intelligible tonal whole. The importance of the tonality frame, *d—f-sharp—a,* as the primary points of pitch focus, can be heard clearly.

The importance of passing and neighbor tones in melodic patterns such as the sequence and imitation cannot be overstressed. An interesting sequential use of passing tones is found in Ex. 15-15 from a motet by Ockeghem.

Ex. 15-15. Ockeghem: *Ut hermita solus.*

Double passing tones in thirds occur on the second half of beat three in measure 1. At the same point, the bass, moving in contrary motion, ascends through a passing figure to *a*. Consecutive dissonances are heard on both parts of the beat, but each dissonance is resolved by step to a member of the prevailing harmony, a *d* minor triad. A similar treatment of passing tones is heard in measure 2, organized around an *a* minor triad.

Syncopated upper neighbors, moving in parallel tenths, form an entirely consonant embellishment of the prevailing *d* minor sonority in Ex. 15-16. The importance of members of the tonality frame, here d^1 and *a*, as doubled tones in three-voice writing, is significant.

Ex. 15-16. Ockeghem: Motet.

Note that g^1 and *b-flat*^{1} are upper neighbors to the basic pitches f^1 and a^1, despite their triadic agreement with d^1, because of their short duration. The root progression of the entire example could be expressed as ![music notation] . This is a good example of how a composer may organize an extended contrapuntal passage around a simple harmonic framework.

A logical outgrowth of decorative activity is the "decorative sonority." Such sonorities are those whose harmonic significance is essentially to embellish structural chords, the most common of which are passing and neighboring decorative chords.

Example 15–17(a) illustrates considerable use of decorative chords in a contrapuntal texture for three voices. The reduction, Ex. 15-17(b), provides a basis for assessing the significance of the various sonorities that are either structural or decorative. Chords arising from the incorporation of suspensions have been included in this reduction, although it should be clear that such sonorities are themselves the result of the elaboration of simpler chords (triads) by means of rhythmic displacement.

Ex. 15-17. Haydn: Sonata in E-flat Major, II.

Textures involving the deployment of three voices in the manner of Ex. 15-17 are frequently regarded as distillations of four parts. Such interpretations are open to question, but there seems little doubt that the style of keyboard composition of the preceding example might easily be viewed as a condensation of four-voice progressions. We shall deal with this question in later chapters.

Suspensions in Three-voice Textures

Suspension figures account for a great variety of on-the-beat dissonance in three-voice writing. All of the types of suspensions found in two parts occur in three-voice music, but some, such as the 9–8, are more common in three voices than in two. Ex. 15-17 affords an excellent study of suspension patterns in a three-voice texture.

The excerpt in Ex. 15-18 contains several suspensions. Perform the example, paying particular attention to the way the music is impelled forward by the suspensions, whose resolutions coincide with the introduction of a new voice.

Ex. 15-18. J.C. Fischer: Fugue in E Major.

At measure 11 a 4–3 suspension occurs in the middle part. The top voice is consonant with the bass. However, the instability created at this point (in measure 11) is not solely a product of the perfect fourth between the bass and middle voice. On the contrary, it results from the 2–3 suspension created between the middle and upper voices. Although it is common to identify this typical configuration of three parts as a 4–3 suspension, it is equally important to be aware of the double nature, so to speak, of this and other suspension figures. The voice above the bass that is not participating in the suspension figure usually forms a consonance with the bass (or lowest sounding part). This aspect of the suspension in three voices is clearly illustrated in measures 9, 11, 12, 15, 19, 20, and 21 of Ex. 15-18.

We noted in our study of two-voice combinations that the lower voice sometimes changes pitch while an upper voice suspension resolves. The "change of bass" is a common feature of suspensions in three-voice textures, too, as a glance at Ex. 15-17 reveals.

Ornamental Resolutions of Suspensions

Resolutions of suspensions are frequently elaborated through the interpolation of pitches which prolong or embellish the dissonance. In bar one of Ex. 15-19, the resolution of the suspended e^2 has been decorated by motion to two interpolated pitches, a^2 and f^2-sharp. D^2 is the note of resolution of the dissonance, but its arrival has been delayed by the intervening activity. Decorative pitches, consonant or dissonant, which enhance the resolution of a suspension are frequently called *changing tones*. Ornamental activity, such as the type seen in Ex. 15-19, is not basic to the suspension pattern and need not be included in an intervallic analysis.

Ex. 15-19. Mozart: Piano Concerto in A Major, K. 488, I.

A variety of suspension patterns enhance the illustration by Walther shown as Ex. 15-20.

Ex. 15-20. J.G. Walther: *Herzlich thut mich verlangen.*

The following summary of principles which characterize the use of suspensions should be noted:

1. 4–3, 7–6, 6–5, 9–8 and 2–3 figures occur in three-voice compositions.
2. Secondary suspensions often occur between the two upper voices in conjunction with suspensions above the bass.
3. The note of resolution is not generally sounded against the dissonance on the same level as the dissonance. It frequently occurs in a different octave. This is always true with 9–8 suspensions, sometimes in 7–6 patterns.
4. Suspended tones are not doubled.
5. Change of bass may occur with the suspension.
6. Suspensions are frequently ornamented by the interpolation of changing tones, which constitute elaborations of the suspension figure.
7. Suspensions may occur as diatonic or as altered pitches.

In the hands of some composers (such as Beethoven, for example) the suspension has been more freely treated. Ex. 15-21 incorporates several unusual suspensions in an interesting three-voice texture.

Ex. 15-21. Beethoven: Sonata in A-flat Major, Op. 110, Fugue.

Other Forms of Pitch Decoration

The escape tone, the appoggiatura, and the anticipation are less frequent forms of melodic embellishment in three-voice compositions. The techniques associated with their use do not differ significantly in three-voice writing from their treatment in two voices. The same dissonant-to-consonant intervallic movement formed by the suspension, i.e., 9–8, 7–6, 6–5, 4–3, is created by appoggiaturas, although they occur more rarely than suspensions. Accented unprepared dissonances are uncommon until the nineteenth and twentieth centuries, although they can be located in scattered instances before the nineteenth century. Escape tones, anticipations, and appoggiaturas are illustrated in a variety of musical styles in Ex. 15-22. A further similarity between two- and three-voice procedures lies in the fact that examples of these forms of decoration occur most often in the top voice.

Ex. 15-22a. Binchois: *De plus en plus.*

Ex. 15-22b. J.S. Bach: Sinfonia in E-flat.

Ex. 15-22c. J.S. Bach: Fugue in G Minor (*Well-tempered Clavier,* Book 1).

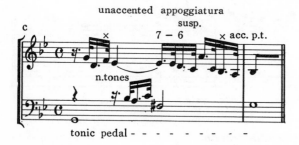

Ex. 15-22d. Beethoven: Opus 18, No.2.

The tone of resolution is usually not sounded along with the appoggiatura, therefore, the sequence in Ex. 15-23 will almost never be found.

Ex. 15-23.

Exercises

See Chapter 15 of *Materials and Structure of Music I, Workbook,* for more detailed exercises.

1. Write ten different spacings of the *D* major triad for each of three different combinations of three voices, such as soprano, alto, and tenor.
2. Use examples in this chapter for sight-reading vocally and at the piano.
3. Analyze all decorative patterns in Ex. 15-6a.
4. Transpose the tenor (middle) part of Ex. 15-6a up a whole-step; then add an upper and lower part in the style of Ex. 15-6, using appropriate decorative patterns. Analyze your work, accounting for chord roots and decorative pitches.
5. Use Ex. 15-21 for aural recognition of decorative pitches.
6. Add two voices above the bass line in Ex. 15-1. Include examples of every type of suspension in the setting. Transpose the bass down a major second before beginning the setting.
7. Write a contrapuntal setting (in three equal voices) based on the harmonic reduction in Ex. 15-5b. Use imitative entries in each part.

16

HOMOPHONIC TEXTURES:
NON-CHORD TONES

In our consideration of musical organization to this point our emphasis has been on combinations of individual voices. We have seen how linear patterns may be combined and how, in three-voice writing, these combinations produce chords.

All music is not conceived as combinations of independent melodic lines; in much music one line is prominent, while subordinate lines (often in corresponding rhythms) produce an accompanying harmony. Such textures are called *homophonic*. We shall consider this term as the opposite of *contrapuntal*, since the latter describes music in which the separate parts are of relatively equal melodic interest.

The following example is homophonic; there is one dominating melody and the remaining texture forms a chordal background that complements the important top voice. Notice that the two-voice framework is still a significant structural feature of the total texture.

Ex. 16-1. Schubert: "Ständchen" (*Schwanengesang*)

Even when one voice is of decided prominence, the other lines certainly may be "melodic," in the sense that they contain some elements of rhythmic or contoural independence. In textures such as the following the overall effect is not exclusively that of counterpoint or of pure homophony; the result is rather that of a succession of block harmonies interwoven with some isolated rhythmic activity and lines of simple melodic distinctiveness.

Ex. 16-2. Palestrina: *Adoramus te Christe.*

Two - voice framework

Example 16-3 shows still another kind of homophonic texture, this one achieved through only two lines which are rhythmically differentiated. The lower part outlines simple chords, while the melody unfolds with simple decorative patterns (upper neighbors) around a basic pitch line that belongs to the chords of the lower part.[1]

Ex. 16-3. Beethoven: Sonata in G Major, Op. 79, III.

Two-voice framework

---

[1] The accompanimental figuration of this passage is typical of classic-period works, both as piano and string patterns. It is called an *Alberti bass,* after the composer Domenico Alberti, who apparently pioneered its use.

It is clear, then, that homophonic textures vary from clear-cut combinations of a melody with block-chord accompaniment to less obvious examples in which contrapuntal elements are present, mainly as isolated spurts of rhythmic independence in one or more of the subordinate voices. The common element of all is a singularity of melodic interest and, frequently, a common bond of rhythmic motion.

Textural Considerations

In earlier chapters we discussed fundamental principles that govern contrapuntal associations. For the present we shall be concerned with tones related as blocks of harmony rather than as combined horizontal lines which, as may happen, produce discernible chords. It will be apparent that many of the principles related to the connection of chords have their basis in principles discussed earlier in terms of voice motion. It would be fallacious to regard the ground rules of harmony as unrelated to principles of counterpoint. We shall begin with principles of a generalized nature and proceed to more specific matters that are determined by particular circumstances.

Voice Ranges

It is customary to designate the four parts of a texture according to the voice names of choral music, even when human voices are not involved. Thus four parts are named, from top to bottom, *Soprano, Alto, Tenor,* and *Bass.* (See page 121 of Chapter 9 for the usual ranges of these voice parts in the chorus.)

Notation

In notating parts for any combination of four voices, choral or instrumental, the score can be "closed," in that it consists of all parts written together on two staves, soprano and alto combined in the treble clef, tenor and bass combined in the bass clef, as shown in Ex. 16-4.

Ex. 16-4. Closed scoring.

Observe that the stems of individual parts indicate which voice the particular note belongs to. Even when parts cross, this expedient shows the proper orientation of the lines.

Doubling of Pitches

If we limit our harmonic resources to triads for the present, a four-voice texture necessitates the duplication of one member of each triad, and in some instances (because of linear factors or the desire for a particular sonority) one member might even be tripled or quadrupled. This doubling can be accomplished at the octave, double octave, etc., as well as at the unison.

Ex. 16-5. Doubling in triads.

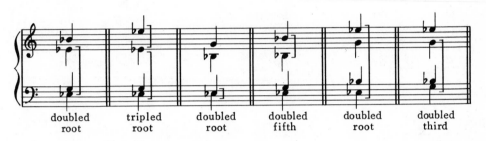

| doubled root | tripled root | doubled root | doubled fifth | doubled root | doubled third |

At best, rules of doubling represent the practice of a particular composer, the "norm" of an era of composition, or merely the unique sonority desired by the composer at a particular moment. Furthermore, individual voice motion frequently determines the constituent members of any particular sonority. However, when sonority alone is the determining factor, the following can be regarded as general guides:

Triads in Root Position
    (a) Major   root doubled
    (b) Minor   root doubled (or third)
    (c) Diminished   third doubled ($^{\circ}\!\frac{5}{3}$ seldom occurs)
    (d) Augmented   third doubled (seldom occurs in any form)
Triads in First Inversion
    (a) Major   root doubled
    (b) Minor   third doubled (or root)
    (c) Diminished   third doubled (or fifth)
    (d) Augmented   third doubled (seldom occurs)
Triads in Second Inversion
    (a) Major   fifth doubled (bass pitch)
    (b) Minor   fifth doubled
    (c) Diminished   third doubled (or fifth)
    (d) Augmented   fifth doubled (or third)

Doubling the root of a major or minor triad emphasizes that chord's stability. In the case of tonic, subdominant, and dominant triads, this doubling procedure also reinforces an important scale degree, 1, 4, or 5. Since these tones remain constant (do not vary with change of mode), they act as the fixed tonal elements of any key. As a consequence, they are often doubled within a four-pitch chord rather than some other tone.

As can be deduced from the chart above, certain duplications are generally avoided. For example, we expect the leading tone of a key (when that key has been established) to resolve by step upward. To double this tone in a chord would exaggerate this expectation. And in chords containing a tritone (the diatonic chords ii° in minor, vii° in major and in melodic and harmonic minor) the member that is *not* a part of the tritone, the third, is usually doubled.

Ex. 16-6. Doubling in tritone chords.

In homophonic textures the principles of doubling just cited can be overruled if the linear progression of a particular voice would be hampered. In Ex. 16-7 the sixth chord (*E* major triad) contains a doubled third, even though this third also is the leading tone of the key. The extenuating factors are the melody's dip to *e* in the subsequent chord (thus not resolving its *g-sharp* leading tone) and the more graceful line created in the tenor voice by the step ascension of *f-sharp—g-sharp—a*. Note that the cadential tonic chord in measure 2 contains the doubling of its root, *a*, but notice further that the third measure contains the V chord again with the doubled third. Once more the circumstances are evident, for both of the *g-sharps* are a result of step motion in the soprano and tenor lines.

Ex. 16-7. Praetorius: *Ich dank dir, lieber Herre.*

Spacing of Four-voice Textures

The same voice distributions apply to four-voice combinations that were discussed in relation to three voices in Chapters 13 and 15. However, the addition of another part makes possible a greater variety of voices, as well as a fuller texture.

As we noted earlier, wider intervals appear more frequently at the bottom of a texture than between the upper voices. Intervals greater than an octave are found often between the bass and tenor; they do not appear as frequently between adjacent upper voices, alto—soprano, tenor—alto.

Two basic types of spacing traditionally have been applied to the dispositions of four voices: the term "close" applies to any arrangement in which the three upper members of a chord are in their closest possible positions. In such arrangements the soprano and tenor voices normally lie no more than an octave apart.

Ex. 16-8. Close spacing.

The term *open* is used to denote distributions in which the three upper parts are not arranged in their closest possible relations. In such arrangements the soprano and tenor notes will usually (though not always) lie more than an octave apart.

Ex. 16-9. Open spacing.

The designations of *close* and *open* are helpful, but they are such general descriptions that many kinds of spacing are not adequately identifiable by them. We can apply the term *homogeneous* to any distribution, close or open, that makes use of approximately equal intervals between the adjacent voices.

Ex. 16-10. Homogeneous spacing.

The opposite of homogeneous, *heterogeneous,* refers to any chord in which the members are spaced with unequal gaps between them. Notice that most heterogeneous spacings are automatically also *open.*

Ex. 16-11. Heterogeneous spacing.

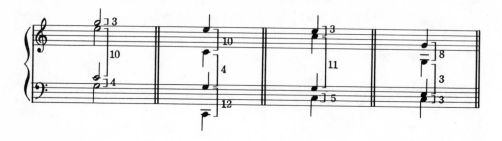

A four-voice texture in which separate pairs of adjacent voices are coupled together (as described in the discussion of spacing in Chapter 13) would be a *heterogeneous spacing.* These kinds of arrangements are more typical of instrumental textures than of vocal. The use of certain heterogeneous distributions depends upon the available pitch range covered by participating instruments; obviously a combination of piccolo, clarinet, trumpet, and tuba possesses greater potentiality for heterogeneous spacings than do the soprano, alto, tenor, and bass vocal choir.

Ex. 16-12 contains five different settings of the first phrase of "America." Each passage has been written to illustrate a particular distribution of voices. Adoption of some of the spacing principles for this particular passage imposes occasional crudities of texture and voice movement one might wish to avoid. It would be inappropriate, however, to judge the relative merits of the five settings, for the success of any one could be decided only in terms of its fulfillment of a particular musical need.

Examples (a) and (b) are similar to choral textures used frequently for this kind of communal song; but the remaining settings might be more appropriate for other uses. Each version should be played or sung several times (avoid using the piano if possible) followed by a discussion of the various factors that contribute to its musical effect.

Ex. 16-12a. Open homogeneous; chordal distribution.

Ex. 16-12b. Close homogeneous; emphasis on brilliance of sonority.

Ex. 16-12c. Heterogeneous coupling; Soprano—Alto; Tenor—Bass.

Ex. 16-12d. Homogeneous; emphasis on low register (somber timbre).

Ex. 16-12e. Open homogeneous; emphasis on linear harmony.

Composers control the spacing properties of their music with the same care lavished on chord structure, melodic pattern, and rhythmic motion; the appropriate chord could be inappropriate if its spacing were not matched with the desired effect. In this respect, spacing, individual voice range, and dynamics are inseparable factors. Example 16-13 shows a passage in which all three of these factors are combined in a complementary union that creates a sense of placid solemnity. Note that all four voices lie within the lower reaches of their respective ranges, that the spacing is generally homogeneous, and that the dynamic level is *piano*.

Ex. 16-13. Beethoven: *Missa Solemnis,* Gloria.

The excerpt in Ex. 16-14 illustrates the way a single musical phrase might shift quickly from one kind of distribution to another. Here the upper and the lower pairs of voices are coupled; after a beginning that is open, the couplings move together into a tight formation.

Ex. 16-14. Dello Joio: *Song of Affirmation,* Part 1. Copyright 1953 by Carl Fischer, Inc. Reprinted by permission.

The opposite condition, a close spacing moving progressively to an open, could be equally appropriate in another musical situation. Furthermore, abrupt shifts from one spacing to another are most appropriate when the nature of a passage demands variety rather than unity for its intended effect. In general, however, a single kind of vertical distribution prevails within any musical phrase or passage.

Harmonic Succession

In homophonic textures chord structure is the main organizational determinant, while in contrapuntal combinations the melodic logic of individual lines emerges as most significant. Because of this added emphasis on the vertical harmonic unit, the way in which chords are juxtaposed becomes an important issue. In some passages the rate of chord change is conspicuously periodic, thereby lending an effect of simplicity to the whole texture.

Ex. 16-15. Schubert: Impromptu in A-flat Major, Op. 90.

In some works this consistency of harmonic change joins with other elements to create a tightly-knit structure. The compositions from which the passages in Ex. 16-16 are extracted are almost totally organized upon the rate of harmonic change established in their initial measures.

Ex. 16-16a. J.S. Bach: Prelude in C Major (*Well-tempered Clavier,* Book I).

Ex. 16-16a continued.

Ex. 16-16b. Mendelssohn: Song Without Words, Op. 102, No. 3.

Nonetheless, strict uniformity is not always the case. In most works (or at least sections) a generally uniform pattern of chord change is retained, but deviations from this norm occur, in some cases to fit particular melodic patterns, in other cases to intensify climactic sections through an acceleration of harmonic rhythm.

The passage in Ex. 16-17 is typical of many phrases of the Classical period. It displays a deviation from an established rate of chord change, but this deviation itself becomes a new "norm." Observe that the rate of change beginning at *d* is approximately three times faster than in the preceding phrases, thus producing a kind of "harmonic accelerando."

Ex. 16-17. Mozart: Symphony in G Minor, K. 550, III.

When the rate of harmonic change is rapid (relative to the rhythms of participating voices), a feeling of greater momentum is imparted to the whole texture. On the other hand, a relatively plodding rate of change effects relaxation.

Contrapuntal Considerations (Voice Leading)

Although linear matters are not paramount in homophonic textures, the joining of one chord with another is normally achieved by means of predictable motion from one chord tone to the next. The individual chord members are links in separate unfolding chains of lines, even if those lines are sometimes of negligible melodic interest. In this sense, linear considerations are pertinent.

Except for unique instances, all lines of a four-voice texture do not move in parallel motion, and it is obviously impossible for *all* voices in such a texture to move in contrary or oblique motion in relation to one another. In the usual four-voice homophonic texture a general balance of all of these possible relationships is maintained.

In achieving this balance the following principles hold true:

1. Consecutive (parallel) fifths and octaves usually do not occur between any two voices, particularly between the outer voices.

Ex. 16-18. Parallel motion.

Parallel octaves   Parallel fifths   Contrary octaves

2. Fifths and octaves usually are not approached by similar motion in the same voices, particularly in the outer voices. This occurs occasionally at cadences, but even here one voice almost always moves by step to the cadential sonority.

Ex. 16-19. Similar octaves and fifths.

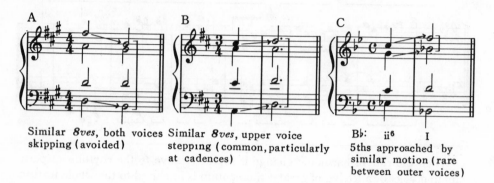

Similar *8ves*, both voices   Similar *8ves*, upper voice   B♭:   ii⁶   I
skipping (avoided)   stepping (common, particularly   5ths approached by
                               at cadences)   similar motion (rare
                                                                   between outer voices)

3. A tritone created by two voices normally resolves in the manner established earlier, i.e., the °5 contracts, the +4 expands.

Ex. 16-20. Resolution of tritones.

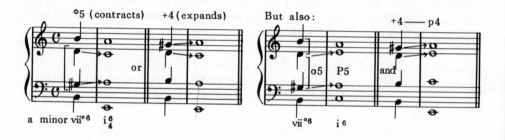

4. Voices usually maintain their range identities by not overlapping immediately into the range of adjacent voices.

Ex. 16-21. Overlapping voices.

5. The outer voices of a texture create an effective two-voice counterpoint; the inner voices are in many instances reduced to subsidiary lines.

Ex. 16-22. Schumann: *Freue dich, O meine Seele.*

6. When linear considerations do not preclude it, every vertical point contains a full complement of chord tones, root (or prime), third, and fifth. When this possibility is overruled, a simpler sonority might well result: diad, unison, or octave doubling, etc. (The composer's desire for a particular sonority also can overrule this norm of the complete chord.)

7. When two successive chords contain one note that is common to both (or in some instance more than one), this note is retained in the same voice part unless melodic considerations demand another mode of linkage.

Ex. 16-23. Common tones between chords.

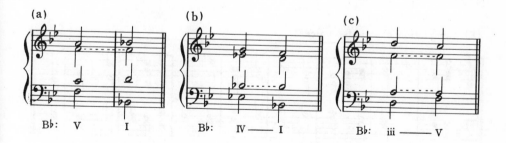

A step-by-step working procedure for the homophonic setting of a given melody is shown in Ex. 16-24. The result is only one of many possible solutions to the given problem. These settings are planned as simple choral arrangements without recourse to any procedures which would create more forceful musical statements. The chordal resources deliberately have been limited to diatonic triads.

Ex. 16-24. Working procedure for setting of melody.

(A) Melody

(B) Added basic pitches for bass voice creating a two-voice framework

(C) Bass voice completed

Implied I   V   vii°   I   (I⁶)   ii⁶ (ii)   iii   vi⁶   iii   IV⁶V⁶ I   ii   V   I
chords:

(D) Sketch of pitches for middle voices

(E) Completion of middle voices

(F) Decorative patterns added for more contrapuntal texture

Non-chord Tones

In harmonic textures, decorative patterns are better described as *non-chord tones:* melodic tones that do not belong to the underlying chord. It will be apparent that their primary purpose is increased melodic activity and that their melodic characteristics are similar in all types of textures; the passing tone and the suspension retain their unique properties whether in contrapuntal or chordal textures. But we can now consider decorative patterns from two standpoints: their melodic (horizontal) structure and their relationship to the accompanying chord (vertical).

The following chart is a slightly expanded and redefined version of the earlier outline given on page 115. The characteristics of the various non-chord tones are stated here in terms of their harmonic context.

Outline of Non-chord Tones

Type	Approached by	Left by	Direction and other characteristics	Rhythmic placement
Passing tone	step	step	Same direction; connects two chord tones. Multiple passing tones fill in wider spaces between chord tones.	Unacc. or acc.
Neighbor tone	step	step	Direction changes; returns to same chord tone.	Unacc. or acc.
Appoggiatura	skip	step	Direction may or may not change.	Acc. is more frequent
Escape tone	step	skip	Direction may or may not change.	Usually unacc.
Neighbor group	———	———	Pattern is step-skip-step; a figure formed with both upper and lower neighbors of a chord tone.	Unacc. or acc.
Anticipation	step or skip	rearticulation	Approached from either direction.	Unacc.
Suspension	rearticulation or tie	step	Preparation on weak metric location, suspension on strong, and downward resolution on weak.	—
Retardation	rearticulation or tie	step	Same as suspension but with upward resolution.	—
Pedal point	—	—	May be sustained or rearticulated in any voice. Commonly upon tonic or dominant.	—

We can now view the passing tone as a *non-chord* tone that is approached by step from a chord member and resolves to another chord member by step in the same direction. The intervallic progression still suggests the *stable–unstable–stable* pattern. The only aspect of the analytic process that is in any way different is that concerned with the vertical relationship: the members of each successive chord must be identified so that we can distinguish the non-chordal material.

Ex. 16-25. Passing tones.

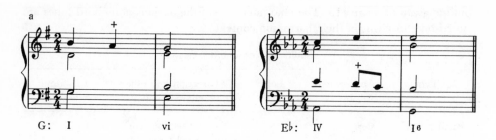

Neighbor tones fulfill a similar role in relation to a chord: they are *non-chord tones* (approached by step from a chord member) which return to the same chord member.

Ex. 16-26. Neighbor tones.

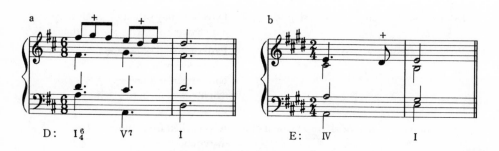

The escape tone is a *non-chord tone* (usually unaccented) that is approached by step from a chord member and left by leap. As first described in Chapter 8, it may be left by leap in either direction, but a change of direction occurs most frequently. The appoggiatura, on the other hand, is a *non-chord tone* approached by leap from a chord tone, but left by step. Again the direction of resolution is variable, but a change from the approach is most frequent.

Ex. 16-27. Escape tones and appoggiaturas.

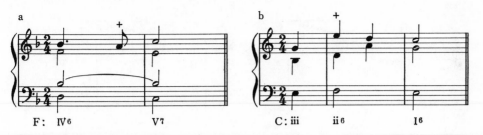

The anticipation, as its name implies, acts as a preview of the subsequent chord tone. Metrically the progression is from weak to strong.

Ex. 16-28. Anticipation.

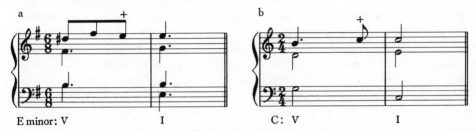

The following excerpts should be studied in terms of their use of the non-chord tones discussed thus far.

Ex. 16-29. Mozart: *Le Nozze di Figaro,* "Deh vieni, non tardar."

Ex. 16-30. Mozart: Variations on a Menuet by Duport, Var. I.

Ex. 16-31. Weber: Overture to *Euryanthe.*

The suspension presents a slightly different set of considerations in the light of our review of decorative patterns in homophonic contexts. In two- and three-voice textures we described suspensions by noting the intervals formed between the suspended tone and the other voices. With more complex textures, however, it is no longer necessary to determine all of the intervallic relationships. Instead, we shall refer to most types of suspensions only by measuring the *suspended tone* and *its resolution* from what appears to be the characteristic dissonance-consonance pattern formed. The following types, two of which are illustrated in Ex. 16-32, are among the most common: 4—3, 9—8; 7—6, and 2—3. In many instances this characteristic pattern will be formed between the suspension voice and the lowest part of the texture.

Ex. 16-32. Brahms: Violin Sonata in G major, I.

Dissonances often are formed between the suspended note and members of the chord other than the bass. In measure 3 of the above example a 7–6 suspension occurs between the highest note in the piano part and a lower voice, in addition to the 9–8 suspension formed with the bass.

Suspensions formed by the lowest voice are measured as before: from the suspended note and its resolution to the upper member of the chord that forms the characteristic dissonance. This type of suspension, illustrated in Ex. 16-33, is one of the most frequent. A complete description of the intervals present within this suspension would be $\frac{5-6}{2-3}$. For simplicity we can reduce this figuration to 2–3 alone.

Ex. 16-33. Pachelbel: *Nun lasst uns Gott, dem Herren.*

In the suspension pattern composers have often avoided doubling the resolution tone, particularly when it is a leading tone or other chromatic tone (as in many 4–3, 7–6, and 2–3 suspensions). In other harmonic contexts, as the preceding examples demonstrate, this caution is unnecessary.

Pedal Point

Pedal point—sometimes just "pedal" or "organ point"—is an excellent example of a technique that composers have used extensively, a technique that is not peculiar to any single musical style. In its simplest form a pedal figure consists of a tone that is sustained through a succession of chords. It usually occurs in the lowest voice but it is found occasionally in the highest or an inner part. The term itself implies, however, that its most frequent use is in the bass.

An early example of this technique is the Perotin excerpt shown below. The lowest voice merely sustains a single pitch, above which the other two voices move in a strictly measured rhythm.

Ex. 16-34. Perotin: Three-voice Organum, *Alleluia.*

The tone that forms the pedal may or may not be a member of the successive chords that occur above it. In the following it is the tonic; as such it is a member of both the tonic and subdominant triads, but it is foreign to the dominant (as in measure 4).

Ex. 16-35. Haydn: Quartet in B Minor, Op. 64, No. 2, IV.

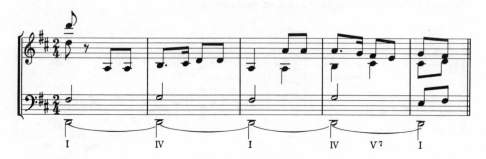

Pedal tones are not always sustained. Rearticulated pitches produce the same harmonic effect in a slightly "busier" way, as in Ex. 16-36.

Ex. 16-36. Haydn: Quartet in D Major, Op. 50, No. 6, I.

The tonic and dominant pitches serve the pedal function most frequently, particularly in music of the eighteenth and nineteenth centuries. Whatever pitch is used, the pedal tone becomes a kind of static pillar of reference, the associated chordal weavings acting as decorative patterns which prolong motion but do not effect real changes in the harmonic structure of the passage.

The tonic pedal often appears near the beginning of a movement (as in the previous example by Haydn) or near the end. Both are locations in which the composer usually wishes to solidly establish the tonic. An examination of the Preludes and Fugues of Bach's *Well-tempered Clavier* will disclose his fondness for the closing tonic pedal. Used in this manner the pedal gives the impression that the harmonic progress of the composition is closing, the moving voices are merely elaborating previous material in a prolongation of the cadential pattern.

Ex. 16-37. J.S. Bach: Fugue in C Minor (*Well-tempered Clavier,* Book I).

On the other hand, the dominant pedal is used with telling effect as a signal of the return of the tonic key. For obvious reasons, this is often found just prior to a closing section. The following passage contains a pedal on the dominant.

Ex. 16-38. Reger: Toccata in D Minor.

More than one pitch may act as a pedal. Sometimes the tonic and dominant are combined, as in the following example.

Ex. 16-39. Schubert: *Die Winterreise,* "Der Leiermann."

Pedal point is a uniquely effective way of maintaining tonal stability. In passages employing pedal, tonal orientation remains unswerving despite the presence of chords quite foreign to the pedal pitch. In this sense chords which move over (or under) a pedal are *decorative chords* (passing chords, neighbor chords, etc.), and as such they prolong the harmonic meaning of the pedal tone and the key it represents.

Even more complicated uses of the same basic technique occur. Ex. 16-40 contains a passage in which two violins arpeggiate a *C* major triad through three measures, under which viola and cello move in parallel minor sevenths. Note again that it is the unchanging triad arpeggiation, the pedal, that provides the stable element; the moving sevenths form a decorative motion.

Ex. 16-40. Shostakovitch: Quartet, Op. 49, III. By permission of the International Music Company, New York.

Accented Non-chord Tones

To this point we have generally limited our discussion of non-chord tones to such aspects as approach, resolution, direction, etc. And yet an equally significant feature of their effect lies in their placement in "accented" or in "unaccented" locations. *Strong* metric locations always serve to intensify a dissonant tone. Hence, accented non-chord tones appear to possess more melodic "thrust" than unaccented ones.

Nineteenth-century harmonic practice featured the use of accented non-chord tones—appoggiaturas, accented passing and neighbor tones, rearticulated suspensions—often combined with one another. The following chorale prelude on a familiar German Christmas chorale exemplifies this highly expressive and intense melodic/harmonic style.

Ex. 16-41. Brahms: *Es ist ein Ros' entsprungen.*

In choosing between various styles of non-chordal material, a composer can select from two distinctive principles of melodic writing: accented non-chord tones highlight the dissonant properties of the music and focus attention upon the melodic tensions. Unaccented non-chordal usage, on the other hand, makes smooth the harmonic connections and results in a less obtrusive use of melody.

Simultaneous Non-chord Tones

Non-chord tones do not always occur singularly. A great degree of harmonic mobility can be created when two decorative patterns occur together, particularly when they are articulated simultaneously. The simple combination of an anticipation along with the resolution of a suspension, for example, produces a sharp dissonance colorfully known as the "Corelli clash." (In spite of the name, it was used by other Baroque composers as well!)

Ex. 16-42. Corelli: Sonata, Op. 2, No. 4.

Other non-chord tones are frequently combined, particularly when they are of the same type—double passing tones, double neighboring tones, etc. Example 16-43 contains a double suspension. This type of pattern is particularly common when two lines are moving in parallel thirds or sixths.

Ex. 16-43. Mozart: Motet, *Ave verum corpus.*

A more complex combination occurs when an entire chord is suspended above a foreign bass note. In Ex. 16-44 the first beat of the final measure contains a diminished triad suspended over an arpeggiated tonic chord. The third tone(the *g'*), unprepared in the previous chord, is added to the upper parts to form a more complete sonority.

Ex. 16-44. Mozart: Sonata in D major, K. 311, I.

A non-chord figure containing a so-called *free tone* (which in terms of melodic analysis would be merely a secondary pitch) occurs when a pitch that is clearly foreign to the prevailing chord is approached and left by skip. The cadence shown in the following example actually is similar to the bi-chordal effect illustrated in Ex. 16-45; the lower line is merely an arpeggiated tonic triad, part of which forms dissonant relations with the chord in the upper voices.

Ex. 16-45. Free tone.

In some musical passages it is not easy to make an absolute judgment about what is "chordal" and what is "non-chordal." We can note such a passage from an earlier example, shown again below for our present purposes.

Ex. 16-46. Schumann: *Einsame Blumen* (Waldszenen).

We might ask what is the chordal basis (or bases) for measure 3. Is the progression here VI—iv, with the *c″* of the top voice an appoggiatura? Or is the whole measure best described as founded in IV, the *b′-flat* and *a′* functioning as successive passing tones between *c″* and *g′*? The answer to this problem is best sought through a basic-melody analysis, as well as attention to the total set of melodic/harmonic patterns. The two lower parts, through skips, outline the IV chord (*C—e-flat—g*). The boundary tones of the melody are easily accommodated into this chordal unit, for they are the root and fifth (*C—G*). As a consequence, the entire measure can be described most accurately as a IV chord over which two consecutive passing tones add melodic interest.

In some instances the total set of voices will not favor one interpretation of harmonic structure over another. When this occurs, the simplest explanation should be chosen *if a choice must be made*. The potentiality of a dual (or even triple) analysis indicates the probability of an ambiguous passage, in terms of harmonic structure, thus making a precise analytical distinction irrelevant anyway. The essential purpose of analysis, after all, is to support and to intensify our understanding of musical organization *as an aural experience*.

Non-chord Tones in Twentieth-century Harmonic Contexts

Obviously the identification of non-chordal material becomes more difficult as harmonic language becomes more complicated. Nevertheless these principles of melodic activity are of value in analyzing the music of our century. As the following example demonstrates, clear passing and neighbor patterns can be discerned despite a more complex chordal structure than in the previous examples. Used judiciously this analytic approach is still relevant for a great deal of the music of the twentieth century.

Ex. 16-47. Bartók: Improvisations, Op. 20, I. Copyright 1922 by Universal Edition; Renewed 1949. Copyright and Renewal assigned to Boosey and Hawkes, Inc. Reprinted by permission.

Exercises

For more detailed assignments see *Materials and Structure of Music I, Workbook,* Chapter 16.

1. Find several examples to illustrate each of the following homophonic textures:
    a) a dominating melody with a chordal accompaniment;
    b) block harmonies with isolated rhythm activity;
    c) two-line texture, the lower outlining chords (similar to Ex. 16-3);
    d) a texture in which contrapuntal and homophonic elements are blended.
2. Using the harmonic progression of Ex. 16-22 as a harmonic basis, create piano settings illustrating homophonic textures (a), (c), and (d) of Ex. 1 above.
3. Taking an *F* major triad as a harmonic unit, see how many different four-part arrangements you can devise using customary vocal ranges, doublings, and spacings; do the same with a *d* minor triad in first inversion.
4. Using the chord progression of Ex. 16-2 as a harmonic basis, write two different four-part vocal phrases (SATB) according to the guides given for spacing, doubling, and voice leading.
5. Choose passages from music you know from which to describe the patterns of harmonic rhythm.
6. Perform each of the versions of "America" appearing in Ex. 16-12 by singing the on-the-beat chords in arpeggiated form (bass up) making suitable octave transpositions in order to fit your own vocal range.

17

TONIC, DOMINANT, AND SUBDOMINANT CHORDS; HARMONIC PROLONGATION

With this chapter we begin the study of the relationships formed by the various chords with respect both to each other and to the tonal center. The possibilities for chord progression are manifold; the *probabilities* (as we can observe from the musical repertoire) are fewer. We will note typical uses of chords and some important exceptions.

We saw in Chapter 14 that each scale degree may function as the root of a chord and that the number of this scale degree may be used to identify the chord. Descriptive labels, such as *tonic, subdominant,* and *dominant,* are also convenient means of designating chords without naming specific pitches. Thus we can see identical harmonic relationships even when the actual pitches are different.

Ex. 17-1.

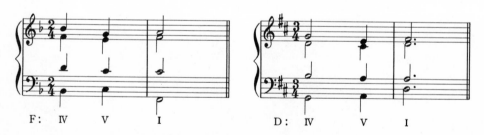

Tonic and Dominant Triads

The harmonic relationship exemplified by the progression dominant to tonic (V—I) is perhaps the single most meaningful relationship in traditional harmonic music. It has been said that this progression is not only the basis for understanding most triadic relationships but also (by extension over long time spans) the basis for most musical forms in the era dominated by tertian harmony.

Before examining individual examples, let us consider the significant properties of these chords and the overall effect of the progression:

Characteristics of I: a chord embodying the tonal center and representing stability, the starting point and the goal of most harmonic progressions.

Characteristics of V: a chord located a fifth above the tonal center and representing instability; although the dominant sometimes serves as a temporary goal for harmonic progression (in interior sections of some compositions), its typical role is to progress to the tonic. In this sense it represents the "activist" element in music.

Characteristics of the progression V—I: instability moving towards stability, root motion by a descending perfect fifth (or ascending perfect fourth), forcefully defining the key and emphasizing the finality of the tonic chord. Melodically, the progression of leading tone to tonic (scale degrees 7–8) complements this harmonic activity. In differing textures, the above features can be seen in Ex. 17-2 and Ex. 17-3.

Ex. 17-2. Schubert: Impromptu, Op. 90.

Ex. 17-3. J.S. Bach: French Suite No. 3, Menuet.

The harmonic action evident in these examples is one of the important *propulsive* elements in music (along with rhythmic activity, melodic motion, etc.) and helps to produce the sense of dynamic growth and momentum that is so effective in music. Action implies *direction* as well as motion. In this sense there are but a limited number of tonal directions:

1. *towards* tonic—a "homing" effect produced by the approach to and arrival at the tonal center, a drive towards stability and finality.
2. *away from* tonic—a "departing" effect aimed at exploring the resources of the key; variety and instability are its characteristics.

3. *interim* progressions—successions of chords that either vacillate around a particular scale step or move in a sequence that does not emphasize any particular stopping point. Their effect can be either nondirectional or multidirectional; in either case the progression is not as firmly rooted in the tonic key as in the preceding. One finds this type of harmonic activity in developmental passages where conclusive harmonic action is often avoided.

Illustrations of the above:

Ex. 17-4. Haydn: Symphony No. 95, Menuetto (towards tonic).

Ex. 17-5. Haydn: Symphony No. 86, I (away from tonic).

Interim progressions, since they generally involve more complicated harmonic language, are beyond the scope of our present discussion. We can, however, make the following generalizations and observe a typical example in Ex. 17-6:

1. They are often sequentially organized.
2. Clarification of the tonic is avoided.
3. They are often accompanied by tonal change and chromaticism.

Ex. 17-6. Haydn: Capriccio in G Major.

Inverted Tonic and Dominant Triads

Although the general harmonic meaning of a chord remains unchanged when its root is not in the bass, its effect and melodic characteristics are somewhat different. The specific effects of second-inversion triads will be explored in a later chapter, and we will confine our present inquiry to the properties of I and V in first inversion.

Typically the voicing of a chord with its third in the bass has two general results: the harmonic effect is slightly weakened, and the melodic aspects of the bass line are emphasized. First-inversion chords seem more supple and often follow the root-position form. The melodic force of the bass line is seen most clearly in V_6: the leading tone in the bass points strongly to the tonic pitch.

Ex. 17-7. Purcell: *Dido and Aeneas,* "Shake the Cloud."

Ex. 17-8. Rameau: Rigaudon.

Ex. 17-9. Handel: *Judas Maccabaeus*, "Rejoice, O Judah."

Ex. 17-10. Beethoven: Quartet in E Minor, Op. 59, No. 2, I.

Other Forms of Tonic and Dominant

The preceding examples have shown that (a) the tonic triad embodies the major or minor quality of the key and (b) the dominant triad is generally major, containing the raised seventh scale degree—the leading tone—in minor keys.

Until the close of the Baroque era (roughly 1750) composers customarily closed minor compositions with a major triad, a cliché named the *Tièrce de Picardie* (the "Picardy" Third) for reasons that remain obscure. This practice emphasized the conclusiveness and consonant qualities of the major tonic triad.

Ex. 17-11. J.S. Bach: *Orgelbüchlein,* "Puer natus in Bethlehem."

Occasionally the minor dominant chord (v) will be used, as in Ex. 17-12; the subtonic is employed instead of the raised leading tone, so the chord remains in its diatonic form. This practice imparts a modal flavor to the harmony and is far less common than progressions involving the major dominant triad.

Ex. 17-12. Vaughan Williams: *Mass in G Minor,* Kyrie. Reprinted by permission of the copyright owner, G. Schirmer, Inc.

The Subdominant Triad

It has become traditional to explain the triad on the fourth scale degree as a so-called "under-dominant"—the literal meaning of the term *subdominant.* This conjures up a neat picture of the tonic at the center of all harmonic progression with dominants both above and below:

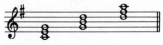

G Major:

This explanation, unfortunately, is not supported by the musical facts as we shall soon see. We shall discard this archaic explanation in favor of some observations that can be substantiated through our study of the usage of the subdominant triad in music.

Characteristics of IV: a chord that has two important roles, (a) as an "approach" chord to V and (b) as a means of prolonging or ornamenting another chord. IV often tends to lead away from the tonic rather than towards it (compare the progressions V—I and I—IV). Thus it too may serve as a temporary tonal goal, often near the end of a composition. Furthermore the chord is highly variable in quality, especially in nineteenth-century music (see Ex. 17-14 and Ex. 17-15); this interchange of mode is often heard in Romantic music.

Examples of the Subdominant in Root Position and First Inversion

Ex. 17-13. Haydn: Quartet in E Major, Op. 20, No. 6, I.

Ex. 17-14. Brahms: *Sehnsucht.*

Ex. 17-15. Schumann: Symphony No. 2, Finale.

Ex. 17-16. Handel: Concerto Grosso, Op. 6, No. 1, I.

Ex. 17-17. Schumann: Quintet in E-flat Major, Op. 44, II.

Ex. 17-18. Schubert: Sonata in A Major, Rondo.

The following extended example reveals that it is possible to create a substantial composition using *only* I, V, and IV. Through the use of decorating and prolonging techniques, a limited chord vocabulary can form the basis for extended passages of music.

Ex. 17-19. Schubert: Sonata in G Major, IV.

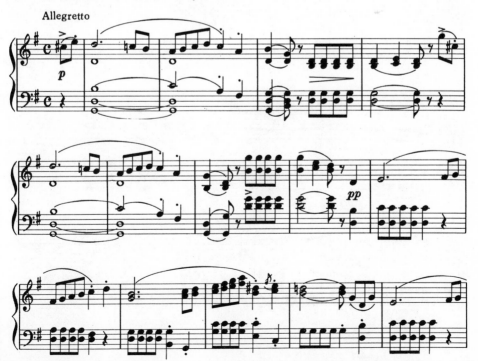

Ex. 17-19 continued.

Harmonic Prolongation

We have generally considered a "chord" to be a *simultaneous* combination of pitches—a vertical event. In analysis, however, it is also helpful to view a chord as a set of pitches that can appear successively; in this sense a chord may also be a horizontal event. As long as the pattern of sounds conforms to the chordal framework, we recognize them as belonging to a single chord.

Composers have developed many devices for spinning out the effect of a single chord over a long time span. Ex. 17-20 contains such a passage. Despite all the rhythmic activity, the harmonic motion is quite slow.

Ex. 17-20. J.S. Bach: Prelude in G Major (*Well-tempered Clavier,* Book I).

Ex. 17-21. Analysis of Ex. 17-20.

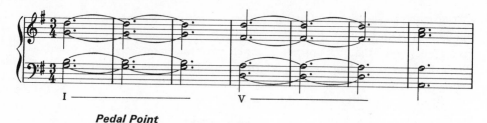

Pedal Point

Pedal point is a highly effective way to prolong the influence of a pitch. With this technique a composer can use the tonic and dominant chords as organizing points in large musical forms. The three examples that follow illustrate characteristic uses of pedal as a prolonging technique.

Ex. 17-22. Buxtehude: Prelude in E Minor (tonic pedal used at the opening of a composition to establish the tonic key and support the gradual "unfolding" of the tonic triad).

Ex. 17-23. Franck: Pastorale in E Major (tonic pedal used at the end of a composition to spin out the final tonic chord and emphasize its finality).

Ex. 17-24. Mozart: Sonata in B-flat Major, K. 333, III (dominant pedal, rearticulated, used to build up suspense and prepare the return to the tonic).

Passages of prolongation (especially of V) abound at the ends of transition and development sections. The effect of resolution is intensified through its long delay. Ex. 17-25 employs a variety of prolonging techniques—repeated note patterns, arpeggiation, sustained chords, scale lines, pedal, neighbor tones—and builds up excitement and intensity before resolving. By these means the dominant triad is projected over a span of fourteen measures and stands as a significant structural point in the unfolding of the composition.

Ex. 17-25. Beethoven: Sonata in C Major, Op. 53, I.

The passage quoted in Ex. 17-26 has a similar purpose—to prolong the dominant and delay the ultimate resolution to *E* major. Techniques here include arpeggiation, alternating V and i chords, and scale passages.

Ex. 17-26. Beethoven: Sonata in C Major, Op. 53, I.

Through these examples we can see that a chord has musical meaning on several levels of musical architecture. Not only are tonic, dominant, and subdominant triads important as chord-by-chord details but also in their larger role in musical form. The harmonic action that occurs on this highest level of musical structure is the propulsive force that gives shape to the entire composition.

Exercises

For more detailed assignments see *Materials and Structure of Music I, Workbook,* Chapter 17.

1. Practice spelling I, IV, and V chords in a variety of major and minor keys.
2. Find examples of harmonic prolongation in the repertoire for your instrument.
3. Write an 8-bar melody outlining tonic, dominant, and subdominant triads.
4. Listen to a recording of *Frühlingstraum,* by Schubert, and identify the I, IV, and V chords used in the opening section of the song.

18

FURTHER STUDY OF HARMONIC RELATIONS; HARMONIC RHYTHM; SECOND-INVERSION CHORDS; THE SUPERTONIC

Most of the musical examples in the preceding chapter were drawn from the years 1650–1900, a period in which chord relationships were constructed within the framework of the major/minor key system. We should not infer, however, that these harmonic relations are an exclusive property of this period. Some contemporary music, as the following example demonstrates, reveals a similar type of harmonic organization.

Ex. 18-1. Copland: Sonata for Violin and Piano. Copyright 1944 by Aaron Copland. Reprinted by permission of Aaron Copland, Copyright Owner, and Boosey & Hawkes, Inc., Sole Licensees.

The following phrase, dating from the middle of the sixteenth century, is clearly in *d* minor. The final cadence emphasizes *D* as the tonic, and the other chords— all root position triads—belong to the diatonic materials of this key and, in their total effect, affirm the tonality.

Ex. 18-2. Palestrina: *Veni, Sancte Spiritus.*

Example 18-3 presents a picture more typical of sixteenth-century compositions in a chordal style. Here the choice of *one* key is difficult, although *e* minor is the most likely. Complicating factors appear, however, in the second and third measures; the use of the minor dominant and the emphasis upon *G* and *C* suggest other alternatives. It seems clear, though, that the cadence, viewed against all that precedes it, is i-V rather than iv-I.

Ex. 18-3. Ingegneri: *Ecce quomodo.*

Harmonic Rhythm

The temporal aspect of harmonic progression is an essential part of the analytic process. We have seen in earlier chapters that *duration* is an effective means of producing emphasis in music; thus the duration of a chord is an important part of its effect. The term "harmonic rhythm," therefore, is best defined as the *rate of harmonic change.*

The following examples illustrate an uncomplicated passage and an analysis in terms of harmonic rhythm.

Ex. 18-4. Viotti: Violin Concerto in A Minor, I.

Ex. 18-5. Harmonic rhythm analysis of Ex. 18-4.

Harmonic rhythm generally fluctuates considerably in the course of a composition. The next two examples, taken from the same movement, differ greatly in their rate of chord change. In Ex. 18-6 the harmonic rhythm is extremely slow, since the same basic chord (the tonic triad) is prolonged for four and a half measures in a very slow tempo. The changes in Ex. 18-7 occur more rapidly.

Ex. 18-6. Brahms: Violin Concerto, II.

Ex. 18-7. Brahms: Violin Concerto, II

Ex. 18-8. Harmonic reduction of Ex. 18-7 (solo line omitted).

In this latter passage Brahms has used an accelerated harmonic rhythm to heighten the intensity and excitement, along with increased rhythmic activity in the various parts and a dynamic *crescendo*. All of these elements combine to propel the music towards the climax. Reductions similar to Ex. 18-8 can be helpful in plotting the harmonic rhythm of complex passages.

Harmonic rhythm is, at times, even more variable than the preceding examples suggest. When a single chord is prolonged for an extended period of time (cf. Wagner's orchestral prelude to *Das Rheingold*—136 measures of a prolonged E-flat major triad in a moderately slow tempo), harmonic rhythm as such ceases to exist. The harmonic flow is static. On the other hand, when the harmonic rhythm becomes as rapid as in Ex. 18-9, the harmonic changes may cease to be separately audible. This can produce the effect of a harmonic "blur" in which the separate chords are used not as functional progressions but as passing chords.

Ex. 18-9. Reger: *Kyrie eleison.*

The use of pedal point is a further consideration when studying harmonic rhythm. Not only does its use make the concept of chord inversion meaningless, but it can also "camouflage" the harmonic rhythm. Our ears depend upon the bass so much in identifying a harmonic progression that the basic harmonic framework is obscured when a pedal is present. The "pedal fugue" of Brahms' *A German Requiem* is a prime example. This composition employs a rich and varied harmonic vocabulary—all, however, over a tonic pedal sustained throughout the movement by the bass instruments. The beginning of this movement is quoted in Ex. 18-10.

Ex. 18-10. Brahms: *Ein deutsches Requiem,* "Der gerechten Seelen."

Tempo is an important factor in determining the harmonic rhythm. Harmonic structures that would be dismissed as "passing chords" at a rapid tempo must be considered as basic units in the harmonic scheme at a slower tempo. If, for example, the tempo of Ex. 18-9 were significantly slower, the effect of the succession of chords would be considerably different: their harmonic separation as individual chords would be more apparent to the listener.

Tempo also poses a practical problem for the composer: to sustain the motion of the music, most composers choose a faster harmonic rhythm in very slow tempi. Conversely, fast tempi often necessitate a slower harmonic rhythm. Psychologists tell us that as listeners we possess both a maximum and a minimum threshold of perception—if chords are too widely separated (as by rests), we will have difficulty in relating them; if they occur at too rapid a speed, we cannot perceive them as separate events. The consideration of tempo, then, is crucial to both the compositional and analytical process.

Once the predominant harmonic rhythm of a composition has been established, one may draw some conclusions regarding its use as a creative technique. An increase in the rate of harmonic change can be used to produce a crescendo of harmonic activity as effective as a dynamic or textural crescendo. It is not surprising to note that the speed of harmonic rhythm in most compositions increases when approaching a cadence (cf. the next four examples). These excerpts, from different eras of music history, demonstrate this practice.

Ex. 18-11. J.G. Walther: Concerto in B Minor (interior).

Ex. 18-12. J.G. Walther: Concerto in B Minor (cadence).

Ex. 18-13. Franck: Symphony in D Minor, I (interior).

Ex. 18-14. Franck: Symphony in D Minor, I (cadence).

We can make other observations about the use of harmonic rhythm as a determinant of musical form. Its rate is noticeably faster in formal sections that are developmental rather than expository. Likewise, sections that display an uncertain or unstable tonality often make use of a relatively rapid harmonic rhythm. A composer frequently differentiates between his thematic materials in a composition by setting them in differing rates of harmonic motion.

In contrast to these procedures, a composer often chooses a slow harmonic rhythm for sections in which a theme is stated as a whole or in which a single key is emphasized. Obviously it is easier to reinforce a tonality if the harmonic changes are relatively slow. Thus harmonic rhythm can be an agent of form in music and can influence both thematic and tonal aspects.

Melodic motion is another element that can influence or be influenced by harmonic rhythm. When the melodic element is prominent or very active in a composition, a slower harmonic rhythm is often present. The reasons for this are clear: a too rapid harmonic change would obscure the melodic patterns and might inhibit the choice of melodic tones. Conversely, sections in a fast harmonic rhythm rarely display a strong melodic element. These problems emphasize the fact that melodic and harmonic interest within a single section are rarely of equal significance; one or the other usually predominates.

Second-inversion Triads

The student of music literature will notice that triads appear less often in second inversion than in either root position or first inversion. A probable reason for this exists in the intervallic structure of the chord: major and minor triads in root position and first inversion contain at least *one* cadential consonance between the bass and upper parts (specifically, root position contains both a perfect fifth and a third; first-inversion triads contain a third and one decorative consonance—a sixth). Only the second inversion contains *no* cadential consonances above the bass; it is constructed entirely of decorative consonances (the sixth and the perfect fourth). Hence it is a less stable sonority.

The perfect fourth, in particular, sets this inversion apart. The fourth has been treated as an unstable interval throughout much of music history and normally has not been used above the bass without some special treatment to cushion its effect (introduction by step motion, resolution as a suspension, etc.).

Whatever the reasons behind this practice, we find relatively few second-inversion triads in contrast to a profusion of root position and first-inversion sonorities. When second inversions are used, they are generally the product of non-chord tones. The three uses of six-four chords we will examine are the "cadential" six-four (I_4^6), the "passing" six-fours (V_4^6 and I_4^6), and the "embellishing" six-four (IV_4^6).

The Cadential I_4^6

By far the most frequent use of any second-inversion triad is as a preparation for an authentic cadence; hence the label "cadential." In this context the tonic is the only chord found in the $\frac{6}{4}$ position. Its approach and resolution demonstrate the restrictions composers have placed upon its use. This harmonic cliché is illustrated in Ex. 18-15.

Ex. 18-15. Mozart: Violin Sonata in E Minor, K. 304, I.

This example of i_4^6 can easily be interpreted as a combination of non-chord tones: the E suspended from the previous chord and the G an accented passing tone. To continue this line of reasoning we could logically conclude that this is merely an embellished V, that the "real" harmonic progression is from iv_6—V—i. Examples such as this have led some musicians to deny that this usage of the six-four chord produces a tonic function at all.

However, not all examples of the cadential I_4^6 are as easily explained. Ex. 18-15 illustrates, though, the salient features found in virtually every occurrence of the cadential I_4^6. One of the most significant of these is the metrical placement of the six-four—usually on a strong beat, resolving immediately to V on the next beat. The notes that form the intervals of the sixth and fourth generally resolve, as they do here, down by step to the nearest tones of V. Another characteristic is the doubling of the bass note (the dominant) in another part. These same features are present in Ex. 18-16.

Ex. 18-16. Haydn: Quartet, Op. 9, No. 2, Menuet.

Ex. 18-17 illustrates the cadential i_4^6 in a much thicker texture—six voices. The same principles of doubling and melodic motion can be seen even under conditions of greater textural density.

Ex. 18-17. Bach: Six-voice Ricercar, *The Musical Offering.*

The previous examples have illustrated the standard resolution from I_4^6 to V. Ex. 18-18 contains an unusual treatment of I_4^6 in which it occurs at the culmination of a prolonged pedal point on the dominant (during which there are several other examples of I_4^6), and resolves to I without first proceeding to V. The voicing of the parts is also interesting: the dominant pedal appears only in the orchestral parts. A further unusual feature is the complete absence of leading tones in both the choral and orchestral parts.

Ex. 18-18. Beethoven: *Missa Solemnis,* Kyrie.

The following summary of the characteristics of the cadential I_4^6 should be helpful:

1. It usually occurs in a strong metric location.
2. The dominant tone is in the bass.
3. It resolves to V or V_7.
4. The bass is doubled in an upper part (when there are more than three parts).
5. The upper voices, other than the doubled tone, usually resolve down by step.

Passing Six-four Chords

The second-inversion triad is sometimes used as a link between two more basic chords (basic because of their duration, metric location, or other factors) or in extended examples of similar motion. In cases such as this, as in Ex. 18-19, the entire sonority may be viewed as an aggregate of non-chord tones or as a decorative chord. It is frequently of very short duration. In plotting the harmonic rhythm, however, it is helpful to recognize that a separate harmonic unit has been formed. Passing six-four chords are found on the tonic and, less frequently, on the dominant.

Ex. 18-19. Stamitz: Sinfonia in E-flat Major.

Ex. 18-20 also illustrates a typical passing I_4^6. In contrast to cadential six-four chords, passing six-fours occur most frequently in "weak" (metrically unaccented) locations.

Ex. 18-20. Corelli: Concerto Grosso, Op. 6, No. 11, Sarabande.

Examples of V_4^6 used in passing are rare. The following, however, illustrate the usual procedure: V_4^6 appears between I_6 and I or vice versa. Examples from music literature are not numerous enough to justify detailed conclusions about their doubling and other characteristics, but the general melodic principles governing the use of six-four chords usually are relevant.

Ex. 18-21. Haydn: Quartet in G Minor, Op. 74, No. 3, III.

Ex. 18-22. Beethoven: Sonata in C Major, Op. 2, No. 3, III.

Embellishing Six-four Chords

A third frequent type of six-four treatment is as an "embellishing" chord, or, described from a melodic viewpoint, as a double neighboring tone grouped over a stationary bass tone. In this context IV_4^6 is the only chord that appears with any frequency. As in the final cadence of Ex. 18-23 it is used to prolong the final tonic chord.

Ex. 18-23. Embellishing six-four chord.

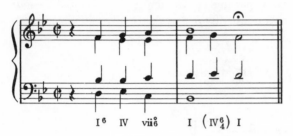

Numerous examples of IV_4^6 can be found in works from the Classical period. In many of these the chord occurs virtually at the beginning of the movement, as in Ex. 18-24. In this context it helps to focus attention on the tonic note and thus tends to establish solidly the key of the movement. In an obvious sense, it functions as a pedal figure on the tonic pitch.

Ex. 18-24. Haydn: Symphony No. 102, IV.

A similar, yet more elaborate, example appears in Ex. 18-25. The IV_4^6 occurs briefly in the first measure and again in a more prominent and extended role in measure 3.

Ex. 18-25. Cannabich: Sinfonia in B-flat Major, II.

Other Uses of Six-four Chords

Music thoroughly embedded in the major-minor tonal system has sometimes used the suspenseful effect of the I_4^6 as a preparation for the cadenza in instrumental concertos. The orchestral interlude that precedes the cadenza customarily ends with a I_4^6 sustained by a fermata, as in Ex. 18-26.

Ex. 18-26. Beethoven: Piano Concerto No. 4, I.

The harmonic progression interrupted by the cadenza is resumed at the end of the cadenza. The soloist usually ends with a trill or some other prolongation of V; this resolves with the entrance of the orchestra on the I chord. There are, of course, some striking exceptions to this procedure,[1] but they are in the minority.

The appearance of six-four chords can be a useful aid in harmonic analysis, especially in the sometimes difficult problem of determining the key. Since they are relatively infrequent, a six-four chord of even a beat's duration usually appears within a context of tonal stability and often points unmistakably to the dominant of the key. In the absence of other evidence, it seems most logical to interpret an isolated six-four chord as I_4^6, unless the context clearly contradicts this analysis. Cadences ending with a six-four chord are not common in music of any period. An unusual example of such a cadence occurs in Ex. 18-27 (the cadence is, of course, an interior one). The cadence appears to be the result of the extended dominant pedal point in measures 4–6.

Ex. 18-27. Verdi: *Aida,* "Ritorna Vincitor."

---

[1] See Beethoven's Piano Concerto No. 3, I, bar 481, for a brilliant and unusual exception.

In Ex. 18-28 a six-four chord appears as the structural climax of a section. Although the overall tonality of this excerpt is not as clear as eighteenth- and nineteenth-century standards would demand, the relationships between the individual chords are, for the most part, the most traditional of all root relationships—the perfect fifth, and the chords are mostly major and minor triads. The enharmonic spelling of the six-four chord (*g-sharp* = *a-flat*; *d-sharp* = *e-flat*) appears to be for the convenience of the eye in its organization of the melodic line.

Ex. 18-28. Bartók: Concerto for Orchestra. Copyright 1946 by Hawkes & Son (London) Ltd. Reprinted by permission of Boosey & Hawkes Inc.

The Supertonic Chord

In Chapter 14 we learned that triads can be built on any scale degree. We have also seen in previous chapters that the triads on the first, fourth, and fifth scale degrees delineate the mode, *e.g.*, in major keys, I, IV, and V are major triads. In this sense these three triads confirm the scale basis of a composition. The other triads of the harmonic spectrum can be identified initially by their quality (i.e., as major, minor, etc.). In this chapter we will discuss only one of these, the *supertonic*.[2] Our discussion will focus primarily on its appearance in major and minor, even though its use is not restricted to these two scales.

The supertonic triad is minor in a major key, setting it apart from the major triads I, IV, and V. In Ex. 18-29 the second scale degree appears as the bass note in measure 5; it is also the root of the chord. Since *G* is the tonic of this excerpt, the minor triad on *a* is supertonic. However, the relationship of the *a* minor triad to the tonal center is not strongly confirmed until the *G* major triad is heard in measure 8. Thus, in retrospect, it can be related to *G* and understood as *ii*. The ii chord also contains the fourth and sixth scale degrees, so it can be used to harmonize either the second, fourth, or sixth scale degree.

---

[2] *Supertonic* literally means "above the tonic."

Ex. 18-29. Beethoven: Piano Concerto No. 4, Op. 58, III.

In minor keys the supertonic triad is diminished. We have seen that the diminished triad is less stable than either the major or the minor triad, that its characteristic interval, the diminished fifth, is generally resolved to a smaller interval, and that the fundamental of this chord is a *root* in only a broad sense.

In Ex. 18-30, the lowest note, the *prime*, of the chord is doubled after the resolution of *g* in the soprano voice. The diminished fifth (*f-sharp—c*) moves to an octave (*B—b*) in similar motion, making clear that *f-sharp* is in fifth relation with the root *b*. The characteristic resolution pattern of this interval is not used. This is often true in minor when the ii° functions in the same way as the ii chord in major, in root relation of a fifth with the dominant chord.

Ex. 18-30. Carl Loewe: *Der Pilgrim vor St. Just,* Op. 99, No. 3.

The second scale degree is frequently the root of a major triad. Because a tritone is created between the third of this chord and tonic, a major triad on the super-tonic has a different function from that of its *unaltered* counterpart. It will be discussed in detail in Chapter 23.

Ex. 18-31. Bach: Chorale, *Ermuntre dich, mein schwacher Geist.*

The difference in quality distinguishes ii (or ii°) from I, IV, and V; however, this does not explain the tonal relationships that can exist between them. Because of the tones in common, ii (ii°) is *related* to both the subdominant and the dominant. It has two tones in common with IV, one tone in common with V.

Ex. 18-32. The supertonic triad.

Like the subdominant, the supertonic frequently functions as a "predominant" chord, i.e., a chord used to approach the dominant, both cadentially and within a phrase.

Another strong relationship can be established between ii and V, because their roots form a fifth relationship. This is the same root relation that exists between V and I. The roots of IV and ii are a third apart, a relationship that is not present between any paired arrangements of I, IV, and V.

One important structural role of the supertonic chord arises because it has a tone in common with V and because its root forms a fifth relation with V. Root relations by fifths tend to define harmonic activity, as in the V-I progression. This is also true when ii moves to V. If a half cadence is used to demarcate the end of a section, the use of ii before V emphasizes the harmonic caesura because of the root relationship.

The ii chord frequently appears in an unaccented metric position when it precedes V. Consequently, V is emphasized both by the root relationship and by the rhythmic placement. Both of these factors appear at the end of Ex. 18-33. Note also that ii has two notes in common with V_7.

Ex. 18-33. Mendelssohn: Song Without Words, Op. 85, No. 5.

In Ex. 18-33, ii is preceded by IV. Thus ii appears between two different chords, each of which has at least one tone in common with it. In this sense ii can link IV to V through these common elements.

As its root position form, the first inversion (ii₆) of the supertonic triad frequently precedes V. In the three-part illustration (Ex. 18-34), the two lower parts move in parallel thirds until the dominant is reached (measure 3) in the lowest part. However, instead of a subdominant root, the fourth scale degree (measure 2) forms the third of the supertonic chord.

Ex. 18-34. Mozart: Quartet in A Major, K. 464, II.

In Ex. 18-35 the upper three parts move in similar motion in measures 1 and 2. When the fourth scale degree appears as bass in measure 2 the upper three voices move in contrary motion, creating a ii₆ chord.

Ex. 18-35. Kuhnau: *The Battle Between David and Goliath.*

The succession ii$_6$—V represents a fusion of the patterns IV—V and ii—V because the bass motion up a second is characteristic of the root relation between IV and V, and because the fifth root relation is also present. In this sense, ii$_6$ and IV are used interchangeably to harmonize the fourth and sixth scale degrees, and to precede V. The bass motion up a second is an important melodic factor; the use of ii$_6$ instead of IV provides the harmonic element of the fifth relationship, while still retaining the melodic second of the bass line.

A simple experiment can be performed with Ex. 18-36 to bear out the preceding discussion. Here ii$_6^°$ is used in the realization of the keyboard part; consequently, *a* in the violin part (end of measure 4) is a passing tone.

Ex. 18-36. Corelli: Violin Sonata in C Major, III.

If we change ii$_6^°$ to iv, *b* would be a passing tone. Either chord could be used. However, ii$_6^°$ creates a change in harmonic rhythm that corresponds to measure 3 and supports the drive to the cadence on V.

Ex. 18-37. Corelli: Violin Sonata in C Major, III.

The occurrence of ii$_6$ (ii$_6^°$) is often characterized by the harmonic sixth between the two outer voices, placing both the root (or prime) of the chord and the fourth scale degree in prominent positions. Instead of the characteristic diminished fifth of ii°, an augmented fourth is created between the prime and some other part.

Ex. 18-38. Brahms: Symphony No. 4, IV.

In this excerpt ii°_6 moves to i, and the tritone resolves typically. The bass motion in measures 2 and 3 outlines 4—1, supporting an upper voice motion 2—3. The motion by step in the upper voice balances the motion by skip in the lower voice.

A ii°_6 chord in a major key is shown in Ex. 18-39. The middle part, because of its chromatic motion, has considerably more independence than if the minor supertonic had been used. Notice that the augmented fourths in the upper two parts (*) move by similar motion to other augmented fourths. Here it is the descending chromatic pattern of the middle voice which heightens the drive to the supertonic.

Ex. 18-39. Chopin: Mazurka, Op. 7, No. 2.

Oblique and contrary motion are the prime organizing forces in Ex. 18-40. Beginning in measure 5 the root movement ascends by seconds, leading to IV in measure 7.

Ex. 18-40. Brahms: Sonata in F Minor, Op. 5, V.

A similar root relation is illustrated in Ex. 18-41; each of the chords is in root position.

Ex. 18-41. Debussy: *Bruyères,* Permission for reprint granted by Durand et Cie., Paris, copyright owners, and Elkan-Vogel Co., Inc., Philadelphia, agents.

That composers of tonal music have commonly relied on fifth-related chords as the basis for key-defining progressions has been amply illustrated in this and other chapters. The harmonic succession ii—V—I is typical of such activity. Note the recurrence of the pattern in Ex. 18-42.

Ex. 18-42. Mozart: Sonata in B-flat Major, K. 333, III.

A final excerpt will afford the reader an opportunity to study the supertonic in various guises—diatonic and mutated, in juxtaposition with the dominant, the dominant seventh, the I_4^6, and other chords in both major (C major) and minor (A minor) keys. The importance of the supertonic as a "pre-dominant" chord in cadences is reflected in the harmonic progression that concludes the first phrase.

Ex. 18-43. Mozart: Rondo in A Minor, K. 511.

Exercises

For more detailed assignments see *Materials and Structure of Music I, Workbook*, Chapter 18.

1. Examine the harmonic rhythm of Beethoven's Piano Sonata, Op. 2, No. 2, Scherzo and Trio. What (if any) differences exist in the harmonic rhythm of the Scherzo and its Trio? Do the harmonic changes coincide with the metric accents throughout? Compare measures 1–4 and 17–20 of the Trio: does the harmonic rhythm differ?

2. In music of various composers, find several examples of the main kinds of second-inversion chords discussed in this chapter (*cadential, passing, embellishing*). Also find examples which do not fit the definition of these three types.

3. Write several textural versions based on the cadential pattern shown below. Do these in major and minor keys and in different meters. Write the two-voice outer framework first for three- and four-voice examples.

   Progression: IV–I$_4^6$–V–I ‖ *or* ii$_6$–I$_4^6$–V–I ‖

4. Write a four-voice homophonic setting for the following chord progression: G minor:

G minor:

i   iv$_4^6$ i   i^6 V   i iv i   iv V   i   i iv$_4^6$ i   i iv$_4^6$ i   ‖

5. Ear-training procedures: Continue the following drills from previous chapters.
   a. Recognition of intervals, melodically and harmonically
   b. Recognition of triad quality, soprano and bass factors
   c. Harmonic dictation for roman numeral designation and chord inversion
   d. Harmonic dictation for roman numeral designation and one or both of the outer voices
   e. Melodic and rhythmic dictation with continuation of syncopation and increasing complexity of rhythm
   f. Intensive drill in rhythmic reading and sight-singing

6. Make your own outline (from the discussions in this chapter) of the harmonic characteristics of the supertonic triad, paralleling the summaries of I, IV, and V in the previous chapter.

7. Spell, write, play, and sing the chords that could appear on the second scale degree of any diatonic scale.

8. Use the harmonic rhythm of Ex. 18-29 as the basis for a four-part vocal composition. Write in a contrapuntal texture with or without a text.

9. Reduce Ex. 18-37 to a two-voice framework. Then use this framework as the basis for a six-measure phrase for piano.

10. Write a new melody for all or part of Ex. 18-42. Then create a new accompaniment for the melody you have written.

19

THE DOMINANT SEVENTH;

DIMINISHED $^6_3$;

HARMONIC CADENCES

A significant feature of tertian harmony is the possibility of creating many different types of sonorities by combining various types of thirds. We have seen that four common varieties of triads (M, m, °, +) can be created using only major and minor thirds. Obviously, this process can be extended to include more complex sonorities. Generically, any four-tone sonority is a *tetrad*; when its components can be arranged to form a series of consecutive thirds, we refer to it as a *seventh chord*. Ex. 19-1 contains several possible combinations.

Ex. 19-1. Tetrads (x = a seventh chord).

Seventh chords, because of their potential for adding harmonic color and melodic tension, became an important part of the composer's vocabulary in the seventeenth, eighteenth, and nineteenth centuries, reaching peak usage between 1825 and 1900—an age characterized by harmonic color and variety. Throughout this historical evolution towards greater harmonic complexity, one type of seventh chord was used with greater frequency than all the rest: the major-minor or "dominant" seventh chord.

Ex. 19-2 illustrates the dominant seventh chord in its simplest arrangement. Its terminology derives from the intervals contained in the chord: a major triad and a minor seventh built on the same root pitch (*D*), hence the term "major-minor" (Mm) seventh. When this chord is built on the dominant, we shall refer to it as V₇.

Ex. 19-2. Mozart: Concerto in G Major, K. 453, I.

Melodic Tendencies in V₇

Unlike triads, the dominant seventh chord contains a strong set of melodic impulses or "tendencies." It is characterized both by mild dissonance (the interval of the seventh) and tonal instability (the tritone formed by third and seventh of the chord). Historically, we can see that composers have often cushioned the effect of dissonance through stepwise preparation and resolution. Early examples of V₇, as illustrated in Ex. 19-3 and Ex. 19-4, demonstrate this procedure: the dissonant seventh is approached by step or prepared in the same voice and resolved by descending step.

Ex. 19-3. Tye: *Come, Holy Ghost* (seventh approached by step).

Ex. 19-4. Scheidt: *Allein Gott in der Höh sei Ehr* (seventh prepared in the same voice, suggesting a suspension).

In Ex. 19-5 the dominant seventh is introduced in such a way that the chord's seventh must be regarded as a chord member rather than as a result of linear activity. Its metric location, duration, and approach (by leap) confirm the fact that the seventh is an integral member of the chord and not merely the result of linear impulse.

Ex. 19-5. Monteverdi: *Ohimè, se tanto amate.*

The tritone found in the major-minor seventh chord is an equally important factor in the chord's resolution. Traditionally the interval resolved in one of two ways:

When notated as an augmented fourth, it expands to a sixth.
When notated as a diminished fifth, it contracts to a third.

The usual result is that (1) the leading tone is resolved upwards by step and (2) the seventh is resolved downwards by step.

Ex. 19-6. Resolution of the V_7.

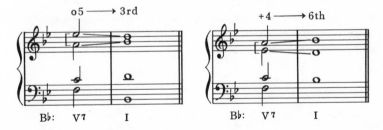

This resolution pattern is sometimes not adhered to. A composer may resolve the leading tone downward to the fifth of the tonic chord in order to obtain a complete triad on the resolution chord. This is seldom done, however, when the leading tone is in an exposed melodic position.

Ex. 19-7. Variant resolution of the diminished fifth in the V_7 chord.

Figuration of V₇ and its Inversions

As with triad inversions, we shall indicate seventh-chord inversions by figured bass symbols. Since we are dealing with a more complex sonority, however, the figurations must be more complete. For the four positions of the dominant seventh (and for all seventh chords in general), we will use the following figured bass symbols.

Ex. 19-8. Figuration of inversions of the V₇.

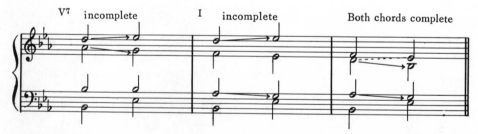

In Ex. 19-8 the figures in parentheses are unnecessary to the identification of the chord and, consequently, are generally omitted both from the figured bass and from the analytical symbols. Note that the numerical relation that represents the interval of the *seventh* (or its inversion, the *second*) is *always* included—$^7-^6_5-^4_3-^4_2$ respectively.

Inverted forms of V₇ are almost invariably complete. On occasion, though, V₇ appears with the fifth missing and root doubled. Similarly, when V₇ does appear in complete form, its chord of resolution is often incomplete. Ex. 19-9 contains three typical versions of this progression.

Ex. 19-9.

These progressions illustrate the conflict that often exists in music between *harmonic* and *melodic* goals. Completeness of sonority is a prime harmonic goal; likewise, smooth melodic motion and resolution of unstable intervals are important melodic goals. When it is not possible to achieve both of these objectives in a musical situation, the composer must decide in favor of one or the other. In the first two progressions of Ex. 19-9, harmonic values are subordinate to melodic purposes; in the third the tritone is not resolved.

Inversions of V$_7$

The following examples illustrate typical uses of V^6_5, V^4_3, and V^4_2. Each excerpt should be carefully examined for (1) preparation and resolution of the seventh and (2) treatment of the leading tone.

Ex. 19-10. Haydn: Quartet in D Major, Op. 50, No. 6, I.
          V^6_5–I with characteristic tritone resolution.

Ex. 19-11. R. Strauss: *Breit über mein Haupt.*
          V^6_5 to I with seventh prepared in the preceding chord.

Ex. 19-12. Tchaikovsky: Violin Concerto in D Major, I.
          V^6_5 as a neighbor chord to I (tritone approached and left by contrary motion).

Ex. 19-13. Haydn: Quartet in C Major, Op. 54, No. 2, II.
          V^6_5 with delayed resolution to i.

Ex. 19-14. Bruckner: Symphony No. 7, II.
     V^6_5 with bass note approached by skip.

Ex. 19-15. V_7 interpolated between V^6_5 and i.

Ex. 19-16. Mozart: Quintet, K. 516, III.
     V^4_3 (relatively infrequent) used as a passing chord between I and I_6.

Ex. 19-17. Schumann: Piano Concerto, Op. 54, II.
     V^4_3 to I_6 with seventh resolving upwards by step (a common feature in resolutions
     of V^4_3).

Ex. 19-18. Brahms: Symphony No. 3, I.

V^4_2 to I_6, the seventh approached and left in the manner of a *neighboring tone*.

Ex. 19-19. Beethoven: *Coriolan* Overture.

V^4_2 with seventh approached and left in the manner of a *leaning tone*.

Ex. 19-20. Pachelbel: *An Wasserflussen Babylon.*

V^4_2 with seventh prepared as a *suspension*.

Ex. 19-21. Wagner: *Lohengrin,* "Ha, dieser Stolz."

V^4_2 with seventh approached and left as a *passing tone*.

Ex. 19-22. Beethoven: Sonata in C Minor, Op. 13, III.

V_2^4 to I_6 with characteristic leap of a fourth in one upper voice.

Summary of Characteristics of V_7

1. It is built on the dominant, resolves generally to tonic, and is often preceded by ii, IV, V, or I.
2. In its resolution, V_7 is more intense and reveals stronger melodic tendencies than V.
3. It is complete when inverted. V_7 is incomplete at times for melodic reasons (fifth omitted, root doubled).
4. Resolution tendencies:
   a. The seventh resolves down by step.
   b. The leading tone resolves up by step.
   c. When spelled as augmented fourth, the tritone expands to a sixth.
   d. When spelled as a diminished fifth, the tritone contracts to a third.
5. The seventh is approached and left by a melodic pattern that suggests one of the following decorative-tone figures:
   a. the passing tone
   b. the suspension
   c. the neighbor tone
   d. the appoggiatura (infrequent)
6. Exceptions to the downward resolution of the seventh are made
   a. when the resolution occurs in another voice (Ex. 19-21).
   b. when the resolution is decorative.
   c. when the resolution is delayed (Ex. 19-13).
   d. when V_3^4 progresses to I_6 (Ex. 19-17).

The vii$_6^{\circ}$ Chord

The diminished triad on the leading tone bears a marked resemblance to the dominant seventh chord, since all of its members are also members of V_7. Walter Piston and others have argued that it is actually a *dominant* chord, and that its root is missing (this root would be the dominant). One cannot deny the similarities between vii° and V_7, but we must regard this triad as a separate chord in its own right. As discussed in Chapter 14, we shall regard the lowest member of this chord as its *prime*, for the sonority does not possess a root.

Like most diminished triads, vii° rarely appears in any inversion other than first. The bass thus is not a member of the prominent tritone that characterizes this chord. A typical progression involving vii$_6^{\circ}$ is shown in Ex. 19-23.

Ex. 19-23. Brahms: Violin Sonata in A Major, I.

The obvious similarities between vii$^\circ_6$ and V$^4_3$ account for their frequent inter-changeability. Their sound is virtually identical, creating an aural problem in distinguishing the one from the other. In most contexts vii$^\circ_6$ and V$^4_3$ are equally appropriate, for they create the same aural expectations.

Ex. 19-24 and Ex. 19-25 illustrate customary doubling practices in the vii$^\circ_6$. These procedures, however, apply equally to any diminished triads. When either root or third is in the soprano, composers have preferred to double the third (the one member that is not a part of the tritone). The fifth of the chord, however, is customarily doubled when it is in the soprano. Obviously, melodic considerations can preclude one or the other of these procedures.

Ex. 19-24. Pachelbel: *Aus tiefer Not.*

Ex. 19-25. Buxtehude: *Herzlich thut mich verlangen.*

In writing the vii$^{\circ}_{6}$, particular care should be taken *not* to double the chord's prime—the leading tone—for reasons mentioned many times in previous chapters.

Despite the similarities between the vii$^{\circ}$ triad and the various inversions of V$_7$, composers have preferred to use the dominant seventh in all but one inversion. Ex. 19-26 illustrates the various possibilities and the general preference. Surprisingly enough, there are very few exceptions to these conclusions. It seems likely that the exposed tritone in both vii$^{\circ}$ and vii$^{\circ}_{4}$ was a decisive factor, as well as the greater functional stability of the chord when the dominant tone is present.

Ex. 19-26. Comparison of dominant seventh and vii$^{\circ}$ inversions.

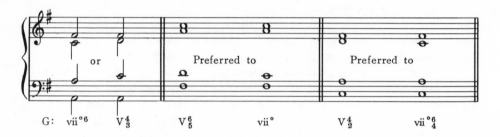

G: vii$^{\circ 6}$ V$^4_3$ V$^6_5$ vii$^{\circ}$ V$^4_2$ vii$^{\circ 6}_{4}$

Harmonic Cadences

Harmonic progression is but one of the means by which the composer can create the feeling of conclusiveness that he desires at the cadence. We observed earlier that a single melodic line can attain a convincing and satisfying cadence through certain manipulations of pitch and duration, and these same factors produce similar effects in two and three voices. We noted also that merely a cessation of motion can produce a cadential effect.

In recognizing cadences in harmonic texture it is important to remember that chordal succession *alone* cannot produce a cadence; it must be coupled with other factors—reduced motion, metric placement, etc.—to achieve this condition. We will attempt now, however, to identify various types of cadences with greater precision than before (as, for example, in melodic cadences), since we are now concerned with the entire harmonic content of the music.

Cadences that we designated as *terminal* abound in the music of the seventeenth, eighteenth, and nineteenth centuries but in several subvarieties. One of the most frequent of these is the *authentic* cadence, a cadence produced by movement from dominant to tonic. This rather general description leaves a great deal of variety in the exact procedure used by composers. Possible variants exist in the type of dominant sonority (V, V$_7$), the soprano line (including such cadence lines as 7–8, 2–1, 2–3, 5–8, etc.), and the bass line (including 7–8, 2–1, 5–8, etc.). The following examples illustrate various uses of the authentic cadence.

Ex. 19-27. Beethoven: Septet, Op. 20, Menuetto, I.

Ex. 19-28. Mendelssohn: Symphony in A Minor *(Scotch)*, I.

Ex. 19-29. Mozart: Symphony in A Major, K. 114, Menuetto.

Ex. 19-30. Mozart: Requiem, Offertory, *Domine Jesu Christe.*

Ex. 19-31. Buxtehude: Instrumental Sonata, *Jesu, Meine Freude.*

A second type of terminal cadence is known as *plagal*, which is produced by movement from subdominant to tonic. The downward root relation of a perfect fourth is characteristic of the plagal cadence and may clearly be recognized in the typical "Amen" following many hymns. In its effect the plagal cadence is fully as conclusive as the authentic cadence, often following an authentic cadence at the conclusion of a movement or composition. Ex. 19-32 clearly demonstrates a plagal cadence concluding a composition.

Ex. 19-32. Brahms: *Alto Rhapsody.*

Progressive cadences may also be classified more precisely into diffe;ent types, suggesting continued motion in a number of different ways. A frequent manifestation of this is the *half* cadence, in which the final chord is the dominant. Since composers have approached the dominant in any number of ways, there are countless varieties of half cadences. In Ex. 19-33 the cadence is little more than the reverse of the familiar authentic cadence V—i.

Ex. 19-33. Mozart: *Mass in C Minor,* K. 427, "Domine Deus."

Other diatonic (or even chromatic) chords may precede the final dominant chord, however.

The iv₆ commonly occurs in a particular species of half cadence[1] that is known as the "Phrygian cadence." Its name stems from the typical cadential descending semitone found in the Phrygian mode. The characteristic features of this cadence, illustrated in Ex. 19-34, are first the chordal progression iv₆ (or iv) to V, and second the contrary motion between the outer voices, expanding or contracting to the octave of the dominant. This cadence is common in minor keys, less frequent in major.

---

[1] Another kind of progressive cadence, the *deceptive,* is discussed in Chapter 21.

Ex. 19-34. Handel: Concerto Grosso, Op. 6, No. 2.

Phrygian cadences are often seen as interior cadences, less often as terminal cadences. Occasionally, however, Baroque composers used Phrygian cadences at the end of one of the inner movements of their sonatas, concertos, or suites, suggesting a close harmonic connection with the following movement.

Exercises

For more detailed assignments see *Materials and Structure of Music I, Workbook*, Chapter 19.

1. Practice spelling Mm seventh chords on various roots.
2. Write out V_7 chords in four voices, using at least five different spacings; resolve each chord to tonic.
3. Find examples of authentic, plagal, and half cadences in the repertoire for your instrument.
4. Find examples of V_7, V_5^6, V_3^4, and V_2^4 from the repertoire for your instrument. Examine these for (a) preparation of the seventh, (b) resolution of the tritone, and (c) completeness. Find examples of all four types of seventh preparation.
5. Continue the aural practice suggested in recent chapters, concentrating upon recognition of the dominant seventh in root and inverted positions. Learn to identify these chords both as isolated sonorities and in progression.

20

TERNARY FORM ;
THROUGH-COMPOSED FORM

In music, as in all of the arts, various fundamental formal designs are used, each having its own particular characteristics. The comprehension of musical design depends largely upon the way some patterns recur within a composition. In earlier chapters we saw that repetition is frequently used to unfold and unify the smaller sections of a melody; this is also true of the larger parts of most formal structures.

Formal plans can be understood by the ways in which they incorporate repetition and contrast. One common scheme involves a restatement of all or part of an opening section. Simply stated, such musical structures follow the plan of *statement-contrast-restatement*. The trademark of this particular symmetrical structure is "three parts," two of which are the same or similar. Depending on the length of the total composition, each part contains at least one or more phrases.

Ternary form is a formal plan that involves three distinct sections, each of which may be different (as *A B C*), involve repetition (*A A′ B*) or restatement (*A B A*). In this chapter we shall discuss those ternary designs characterized by restatement. When the third section is a restatement of the opening section, it may be a literal or varied restatement that is distinctly separated from a contrasting middle section. The middle section in ternary form frequently is a definite and separate musical unit. This is particularly true when we listen to compositions in which several phrases are combined to produce each section.

Ex. 20-1 displays clearly a division into three parts. The change of melodic rhythm at measure 5 provides a striking rhythmic contrast as does the elaborately "decorated" melody of the second section. Both factors counterbalance the emphasis given to the rhythmic motive of the first section.

Ex. 20-1. Schumann: *Album for the Young*, Folk Song.

Even though the increased activity in measure 5 is immediately apparent, other factors work hand in hand to produce contrast. The entire composition is in *D*, but the section beginning at measure 5 is in *D* major instead of *d* minor. This mutation produces a significant contrast with the opening section. Since *D* major is associated only with the second section, it is another factor that delineates the form when *d* minor returns in measure 13.

Another contrasting element is the larger range of measures 5–12 and the linear triadic outlining. In this instance the opening accompanimental figure is used in each section (with some modifications). The retention of the accompanimental figure, and the retention of the basic pitches of measures 1 and 2 in measures 5 and 6, unifies this passage. It is evident that the principal contrast of the *B* section is provided by the change in melodic rhythm, mode, and the scherzo-like character.

The restatement (measures 13-20) is varied by changing the register (measures 13-14) and by doubling the melody in octaves (measures 17-20). This heightens the effectiveness of the return by avoiding the monotony of a literal restatement.

Frequently, however, the third section of a ternary form is a literal repetition of the first. If this is the case, the restatement need not be written out and it is indicated by *da capo* (*D. C.*)[1] at the end of the second section. Sometimes the indication *Dal segno* (*D. S.*)[2] is found at the end of the second section, as in Ex. 20-4. This means that the repetition begins at some indicated point (where "the sign" appears) rather than at the beginning. The sign usually looks something like the following: 𝄋

Even though Ex. 20-2 is longer than Ex. 20-1, its formal design is the same basic *A B A*. Similar relationships delineate the larger sections, but there are notable differences. For example, two distinctive accompanimental patterns are used in the Chopin. The first, measures 1–16, is distinguished by a durational accent on the second beat in the inner parts. In the second section, measures 17–33, the rhythm is distinguished by a downbeat pattern, as well as a change in the rhythm of the melody. And as a final confirmation of sectioning, tonal contrast between the two sections is achieved by modulation to a new tonal center. In Ex. 20-1 tonal contrast was produced by mutation.

Ex. 20-2. Chopin: Mazurka in C Major, Op. 33, No. 2.

---

[1] Repeat from the beginning, or "from the head."
[2] Repeat "from the sign."

Fine

D.S. al Fine

Another factor is present in Ex. 20-2 that tends to overshadow the other formal elements as a determinant of form. This is the change of texture.

The overall texture of both the Schumann and the Chopin examples is homophonic. We noted in Ex. 20-1 that the pitch range increased in the second section. This increase alters the texture slightly by changing the space between the melody and its accompaniment. In Ex. 20-2 the textural change in measure 18 is more pronounced because the accompaniment changes character and is moved to a different register. The number of parts is essentially the same, but spacing starkly distinguishes the textural "top" from "bottom." The motion in parallel sixths and thirds (measure 24 and following) represents still another aspect of texture.

A cursory examination of Ex. 20-3 and Ex. 20-4 reveals in both cases a basic ternary plan, but a closer look at the structure of each section shows that the processes of unfolding are not the same in both pieces. Thematic material, tonality, rhythm, and total length are obvious differences.

Another difference is the way each section closes and connects with the restatement. The *B* section of Ex. 20-3 closes with a half cadence that is combined with a definite rhythmic halt. The listener's demand for a return to the beginning probably results from the instability of the half cadence and the extreme rhythmic contrast. In Ex. 20-4 the end of the contrasting section is not signaled as boldly because the rhythmic activity in the upper parts continues through to the beginning of the restatement. The two sections merge (elide), and it is not until the return is in progress that we become aware of it.

Literal restatement of all musical parameters does not need to occur to create a satisfactory return. For example, in some styles thematic restatement is associated with tonality restatement; in some styles this is not an essential ingredient. The second movement (*Grablegung*) from Hindemith's *Mathis der Maler* illustrates this well. The movement begins in *C* (shown in Ex. 20-3).

Ex. 20-3. Hindemith: *Mathis der Maler,* II. Copyright 1934 by B. Schott's Soehne-Mainz. Copyright © renewed 1962 by B. Schott's Soehne-Mainz.

The restatement, which overlaps with the close of the middle section, begins in *B* (Ex. 20-4) in a re-orchestrated version featuring brass. An interruption by *B*-section material after only two bars of restatement intensifies the musical drama. After the interpolation of the *B*-material the restatement takes up at the point where the interruption occurred.

Ex. 20-4 continued.

Contrary to the original statement of the *A* Section, which is in *C*, its restated version begins in *B* then moves to *B-flat* and ends in *F-sharp*. The movement closes with an extended coda in *C-sharp*. Even though the initial tonality does not recur, restatement is accomplished through thematic, textural, and dynamic means.

In many ternary movements sectional tonal unity is basic to the style; such may not be the case, as the Hindemith movement reveals. This departure from convention is not disturbing; on the contrary, tonality restatement is not required since the conditions for its presence are not established in any part of the movement. What is established is a pattern in which each section begins with a tonally simple context, which gradually becomes more complex and which returns to a simpler tonal context.

Each of the preceding musical examples illustrates ternary movements with restatements involving all or most of the musical parameters, and in which each of the sections of the tripartite design are of approximately the same length. Length in music, however, is as much a psychological response as it is a measurable fact, and sometimes a shorter section (in terms of measures or clock-time) may balance or perfectly complement a longer section. Similarly, the return effect so essential to *A B A* designs may be satisfactorily achieved by restating only a very small portion of the *A*-section.

Most of the essential melodic and accompanimental material is heard immediately in Schoenberg's Piano Piece, Op. 11, No. 1, the opening bars of which are shown in Ex. 20-5.

Ex. 20-5. Schoenberg: Piano Piece, Op. 11, No.1. Used by permission of Belmont Music Publishers, Los Angeles, California

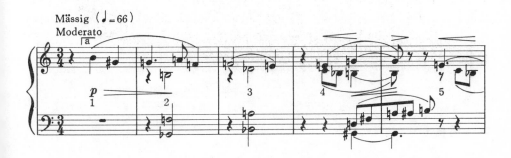

In the much shortened restatement (Ex. 20-6) the opening melodic material is presented at the original pitch level with octave coupling and in a new texture (the accompaniment is now in an arpeggiated form). Only the first two bars of the restatement are of this literal quality, which is sufficient for us to easily perceive the restatement.

Ex. 20-6. Schoenberg: Piano Piece, Op. 11, No. 1. Used by permission of Belmont Music Publishers, Los Angeles, California.

Once the return is accomplished the original three-measure phrase (Ex. 20-5) is extended to six. The apparent phrase lengthening is a telescoping of measures 1–8 and an organic extension of the basic melodic idea by the half-step step progression *e''*, *e''-flat*, *d''*. This step progression is accompanied by a fragmented version in the left hand (mm. 5–8, Ex. 20-6) derived from the three-note basic melodic shape, first by sequenced minor thirds, then a repeated major third.

Contrast in this movement is primarily the result of texture change, dynamic level change, and rhythm patterning. The melodic content of the middle (*B*) section is formed from the basic melodic material of the *A*-section; the accompanimental elements are octave displaced half-steps rhythmically grouped in such a manner that notes with longer duration form major thirds (as *B-flat* to *d* in measures 2–3, left hand part, Ex. 20-7) which is one of the interval components of the three-note pitch group, *b'*, *g'-sharp*, *g'* (mm. 1–2, Ex. 20-5).

Ex. 20-7. Schoenberg: Piano Piece, Op. 11, No. 1. Used by permission of Belmont Music Publishers, Los Angeles, California.

Each of the three-note groups in the right-hand part is a permutation of the basic three-note pitch group stated at the beginning of the movement; because of pitch level, the sixteenth notes form a counter-line to the parallel major thirds. In a similar fashion, the accompaniment operates at two different levels. The total textural effect is one of four intra-paired lines.

Both the *A* and *B* sections are made up of subsections that correspond to phrases and periods of tonal music. Tonality, however, is not an organizing factor in this movement. As has been indicated, texture, dynamics, and rhythm patterning are prime sectional delineators; unity results from recurrence of the basic melodic material in permuted versions in each of the three large sections that make up this piece.

Our discussion has emphasized the overall plan of ternary design, as well as some of the factors that demarcate or produce contrast between the sectional parts of the total form. As a matter of fact, it is very difficult to describe a piece of music without taking into consideration both the structural plan and the smaller factors that fill out this plan. Generally speaking, many compositions have a ternary structural design, just as many buildings are basically rectangles. However, we know that architects have adapted the rectangular structural principle to many different situations, and similarly, the ternary principle of statement, contrast, and return has been used in many quite different compositions.

Through-composed Form

Restatement is one principle of organization in most musical designs. However, there are compositions in which the return of larger formal units, such as a period or a section, does not occur. Broadly speaking, this means that no two parts of such a composition are identical in all respects. If this were adhered to consistently, the composition would be a series of contrasts without any sense of return or "rounding off" of the whole form.

The creation of a unified musical design depends upon many factors; large-scale repetition is only one of these. Compositions in which each section is essentially different are said to be *through-composed*,[3] to distinguish them from repetitive structural schemes. Through-composed compositions may contain several contrasting parts or sections; however, total length is ultimately limited by the listener's retention capacity.

Compositions based on the formal principle of non-repetition generally do not contain exact restatements. In Ex. 20-8 none of the five phrases is precisely like another; even so, it is a balanced structure. Each of the phrases is only externally different; within the separate phrases similarities exist that create unity.

Ex. 20-8. Gregorian Chant: *Sanctus.*

---

[3] The German form of this term, *durchkomponiert*, appears frequently in books that discuss musical form.

qui   ve - nit   in no - - mi - ne Do - - mi - ni.   Ho -

- - - - - - san - na in ex - cel - - - - sis.

Some of the phrases have similar contours, some pitch patterns recur (f'', e'', d'', e''). In addition, the tones focus decisively on F as tonic. Thus, even though this melody does not contain repeated or restated phrases, other factors make it a unified whole.

The through-composed formal procedure is used also for compositions that are longer than the melody of Ex. 20-8. Simply stated, the duration of a composition is determined by the length of each section. In a longer through-composed composition each section will comprise several phrases. Within each section repetition of phrases may occur, creating unifying elements within the section that differ from those found in all subsequent sections.

In Ex. 20-9 the four sections are clearly delineated by changes in meter, tonality, accompanimental patterns, texture, and rhythm. The key basis of this song, $e\ C\ g\ G$, is crucial for the delineation of the sectional design. The use of both g minor and G major also contributes to the tonal unity of the composition, through retention of the single tonic, counterbalancing the contrast of textural change. These major external differences make the form ($A\ B\ C\ D$) easy to comprehend as through-composed.

Internally, each of the sections is a highly unified structure. For example, A is subsectioned by phrases (*Intro.*, *a a' b*) with *a'* and *b* sharing melodic subphrases. There is also intersectional sharing of musical features, such as the long-short rhythmic figures, the exclusive use of four-measure phrases, and the use of repeated note figures both in the voice and accompaniment.

Ex. 20-9. Schubert: *Der Jüngling auf dem Hügel.*

Ex. 20-9 continued.

Ein Jüng ling auf dem Hü - gel mit seinem Kummer saß; wohl

ward der Augen Spiegel ihm trüb und tränen - naß, wohl ward der Augen

Spie - gel ihm trüb und tränen - naß

Mäßig

Sah fro - he Läm-mer spie - len am grü - nen Fel - sen-

Ex. 20-9 continued.

schwarzen Lei-chenzug, fing bit-ter an zu wei-nen, weil man, weil man sein

Rös-chen trug.   Jetzt ließ den Sarg man nieder, der

To-tengräber kam,   und gab der Er-de wie-der, was Gott aus sel-ber nahm, und

gab der Er-de wie-der, was Gott aus sel-ber nahm.

Ex. 20-9 continued.

Etwas geschwinder

Da schwieg des Jünglings Kla - ge, und be - tend ward sein

Blick, sah schon am schönern Ta - ge des Wie der sehens Glück. Und

wie die Sterne ka - men, der Mond her auf - ge- schifft, da las er in den

Ster - nen der Hoffnung ho - he Schrift, der Hoff - - nung

ho - he Schrift.

The potentials of this design principle are limited only by psychological practicality. It would be possible to create a form in which there is no repetition at any level, motivic, phrase, or sectional. However, that would be the exception rather than the rule. The distinguishing feature of through-composed design is large sectional contrasts. These gross contrasts often are softened by transferring characteristic patterns from one section to another.

Exercises

For more detailed assignments see *Materials and Structure of Music I, Workbook*, Chapter 20.

1. Listen to and study through compositions such as the following. Isolate those musical elements that play a prominent role in creating the ternary design of each work.
   a. Schumann: *Traumerei*
   b. Rachmaninoff, *Prelude*, Op. 3, No. 2
   c. Debussy, *La fille aux cheveux de lin*
   d. Mozart, "E amor un ladroncello" (*Così fan tutte*)
2. Write a short three-part (*A B A*) composition for a combination of four different instruments. Create a middle section that does not rely upon tonality change to provide contrast.
3. Make a detailed analysis of Ex. 20-8. What other patterns than those mentioned in the chapter are used to unify the composition?
4. Write a sixteen-measure through-composed composition for piano that uses a key scheme such as the following: G-flat major, parallel minor, G-flat major.
5. Locate, sing through, and analyze several through-composed compositions.

21

SUBMEDIANT AND
MEDIANT CHORDS;
HARMONIC SEQUENCE;
CHORD RELATIONS;
MUTATED CHORDS

Musical examples in the preceding chapter have often included chords not directly related to our discussion. The roots of these chords were either the third or sixth scale degrees. They represent the only two diatonic triads, iii and vi, that we have not yet discussed.

The quality of both the mediant and submediant triads differs, like that of ii and ii°, from I, IV, and V, making possible an immediate qualitative distinction. Other distinctions will become apparent as we examine the appearances of iii and vi in various contexts.

The Submediant and Mediant Chords

In major the submediant and mediant are minor triads. The submediant chord contains the sixth, first, and third notes of a scale, and is used to harmonize any of the three, whereas the mediant contains the third, fifth, and seventh scale degrees. In Ex. 21-1 the repeated *g* (the third scale degree) in the upper part is harmonized by both I and vi. The association of the two roots with *g* results in a change of harmonic rhythm that would not be present if only the tonic chord had been used for the first two beats.

Ex. 21-1. Beethoven: Piano Concerto No. 2, Op. 19, II.

In Ex. 21-2 the overall harmonic motion of the phrase is I → IV. The mediant connects I to IV at the submetric level in measures 1 and 3, and at the metric level it connects V with IV in measure 4. In both instances the half-step root relation gives added weight to the subdominant chord.

Ex. 21-2. Brahms: Symphony No. 4, III.

The primary organizing principle of Ex. 21-2 is contrary motion. The lower part in measures 1 and 2 is a mirror of the upper; it has the same intervallic structure. Fewer chords could have been used to support the melodic line; however, the contrapuntal (submetric) chords are a basic characteristic of the rhythmic-tonal drive of this phrase. Even though we can isolate a mediant chord in measures 1, 3, and 4, its role is as much melodic as it is harmonic.

In Ex. 21-3 the iii chord is in a prominent metric location; however, it is part of an upbeat pattern that deemphasizes its location in the measure. Since iii is used to harmonize the seventh degree, and since the V chord contains the lowered seventh degree, an alternating major-minor triad pattern is created.

Ex. 21-3. Ravel: Trio, IV. Permission for reprint granted by Durand et Cie., Paris, copyright owners, and Elkan-Vogel Co., Inc. Philadelphia, agents.

F#:   I   iii IV³ V

In a minor key the submediant and mediant triads are major in quality. Like its counterpart in major, VI is frequently associated with melodies that contain successive repetitions of the tonic note. As a consequence, VI is used frequently to create an active harmonic rhythm. This is seen in Ex. 21-4, where VI alternates with i in measure 2, harmonically interconnecting the two phrases by maintaining the harmonic rhythm of the preceding measures. The harmonic succession I–vi–iv is a typical phrase progression involving the submediant chord.

Ex. 21-4. Schumann: *Dichterliebe,* "Die alten, bösen Lieder."

c#:   V   i   V   i   VI   iv

The appearance of both VI and III in the second phrase of Ex. 21-5 produces a brief skirting of the relative major tonality creating a distinctive contrast with the first. The root movement of VI—III is similar to iv—i. Since this similarity exists, we can say that the iv—i of measure 3 is a sequential continuation of vi—iii; that is, a systematic harmonic pattern is immediately repeated at a different pitch level.

Ex. 21-5. Mozart: Requiem, K. 626, *Domine Jesu Christe.*

g: i   V⁶   i   VI   III   vi   i

In major or minor the submediant and mediant chords are frequently a part of a chord succession moving to the dominant. The half cadence that ends the first phrase in Ex. 21-6 gains harmonic prominence by the preceding root motion. The ii chord is structurally important because it relates directly to the dominant; and in this excerpt vi plays an important structural role because of its root affiliation with ii. Here vi is preceded by I; thus, each of the chords in measures 1–4 is related to the next with at least one common tone. Furthermore, root relationships by fifth occupy most of the phrase.

Ex. 21-6. Haydn: *The Creation,* "Now Vanish Before the Holy Beams."

The III chord appears between i and V in Ex. 21-7. The melody could have been harmonized with either i or V. Interpolating III enhances the harmonic structure, and maintains the harmonic rhythm established in the preceding two measures ($\frac{2}{4}$ ♩ ♩ | ♩ ♩ | ♩ ♩ | ♪). Notice that the resulting root movement outlines the tonic chord, thereby confirming the tonality; also note that each of the chords is related to its successor with at least one common tone.

Ex. 21-7. Brahms: Sonata in C Major, Op. 1, II.

Ex. 21-7 continued.

Roots:

Outline of tonic triad

In Ex. 21-8 IV appears between vi and ii, producing root movement in thirds. Consequently, each chord in measures 1 and 2 has two notes in common with its immediate predecessor. Notice also that the common tone relationship is not present in the supertonic plagal cadence, and that the phrase does not contain any fifth relationships.

Ex. 21-8. Wagner: *Parsifal,* Grail motive (Act I).

Sometimes the iii chord precedes tonic in a cadence. This places root movement by thirds in the important terminal position. The two tones of the iii chord which are shared with I (root and third of iii equal third and fifth of I) create a smooth relationship that borders on chord repetition. The presence of the leading tone in the iii chord provides the one factor that makes this relationship progressive.

Ex. 21-9 and Ex. 21-10 illustrate terminal cadences involving iii—I. Both examples are similar in cadential effect, but there is a notable distinction: in Ex. 21-9 the I chord is melodically outlined, whereas in Ex. 21-10 the iii chord is melodically outlined. Thus, even though the cadential harmonic pattern is the same in both excerpts, the terminal motion of each melody has a different character because of the chordal outlining.

Ex. 21-9. R. Strauss: *Ein Heldenleben,* Op. 40.

Ex. 21-10. Brahms: *Intermezzo,* Op. 10, No. 3.

B: iii   I

The submediant chord also appears in the role of a neighbor chord, and creates root movement by a second, thereby omitting the possibility of common tones. Ex. 21-11 shows vi as a neighbor to V, clearly indicated by its durational relation to V. Notice that the resultant motion by step in the bass adds variety to the phrase.

Ex. 21-11. J.S. Bach: *Ermuntre dich, mein schwacher Geist.*

G: I   IV   I   V   vi   V   I

In some contexts vi appears to "replace" I. The melody note marked (*) in measure 2 of Ex. 21-12 could be harmonized with the I chord. By using vi, however, the bass line in measure 2 conforms to measure 1, as well as adding a different harmonic color.

Ex. 21-12. J.S. Bach: *Aus meines Herzens Grunde.*

G: I   V   vi   IV

The appearance of vi as a cadential chord creates a particularly striking effect. It ends the second phrase (measures 5–8) in Ex. 21-13. The earlier harmonic and melodic activity of this phrase "predicts" that it will probably close on tonic, as does the first phrase. Furthermore, we have already heard the melodically outlined V_7 move to tonic in measure 4, so we expect the same resolution of the V_7 chord in measure 8. However, V_7 resolves deceptively to vi, rather than to the expected I chord. Since the expected harmonic pattern is evaded, harmonic deception results. The cadential succession V—vi is called a deceptive cadence, and is one other type of progressive cadence.

Ex. 21-13. Beethoven: Trio in B-flat Major, Op. 11, I.

More tonal activity leading to the expected tonic chord generally follows the deceptive cadence. In Ex. 21-14 a cadential vi appears in measure 8. Here the deception afforded by vi intensifies the eventual appearance of I, as well as enhancing the immediate repetition of previous material. Unlike the major-minor relation formed in major, the deceptive cadence in minor involves two successive major triads.

Ex. 21-14. Haydn: Quartet in D Minor, Op. 76, No. 2, IV.

V⁷   VI   i⁶

Since the root relationship between V and vi is a second, they have no tones in common. Therefore, V—vi, like the succession of all chords whose roots are a second apart, generally involves considerable contrary motion. The third of the vi chord (the tonic note) is generally doubled when it is preceded by V or V₇; the root obviously also can be doubled. In minor the root of VI is usually not doubled when it is preceded by the dominant, because the leading tone would then resolve to a tone an augmented second lower. Ex. 21-15 gives the usual doublings for both major and minor.

Ex. 21-15. Doubling in deceptive resolutions.

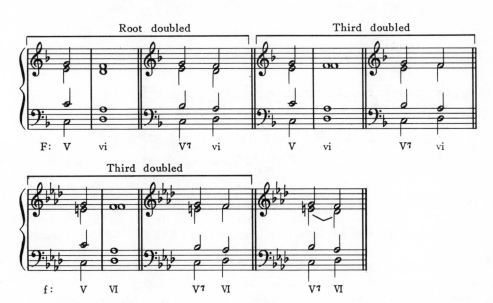

In Ex. 21-16 the vi chord ends the first phrase in harmony with the tonic note. Here vi is preceded by V₇, which harmonizes the second degree. Since the leading tone appears in the upper part, it is resolved to tonic. The fifth of the V₇ is part of a descending line and also moves to the tonic note. Consequently the third of vi is doubled.

Ex. 21-16. Schubert: Symphony No. 5, II.

Eb: I   V⁷ vi

When it occurs, the augmented mediant (III⁺) is generally found in positions similar to III. Any differences that result are produced by the augmented triad's distinctive quality and rootlessness. As we have observed in previous chapters, the inclusion of augmented or diminished intervals in diatonic tonal structures implies greater tension, because resolution to a point of stability seems desirable. Since the leading tone is a member of the triad, III⁺ generally resolves to chords that contain the tonic.

In Ex. 21-17 III⁺₆ is approached by contrary motion between the two outer parts. A logical chord at this point would have been III₆, but instead the tenor moves by step from *a* to *g-sharp* in the first measure. This forms the augmented sonority of the chord, at the same time directing attention to the *a* that follows on the second beat. This leading tone action of *G-sharp*—*A* propels the texture forward through iv to the dominant that eventually cadences on tonic.

Ex. 21-17. Bach: *Herr, ich habe missgehandelt.*

a: III⁺⁶ iv   V   ⁷   i

As in most unstable triads, the tones doubled are those that do not suggest resolution. Thus the third of an augmented triad (the note *E* in Ex. 21-17) is generally doubled.

The first inversions of both the vi and the iii chord appear in harmonic situations that are similar to their root position counterparts. Since the root of the chord does not appear in the lowest part, the resulting effect of harmonic change is considerably weakened in some contexts. For example, if vi₆ follows tonic, the root of I remains in the lowest part. Even though there is a *root change*, the tonic note, because of its tonal predominance, nullifies the effect of the harmonic motion. The result resembles a harmonic embellishment of the I chord rather than a change of harmonic function. Stated another way, the tonic note resembles a pedal, and any chordal change above it must be decisive to change the basic pattern of harmonic rhythm.

Ex. 21-18. I—vi$_6$.

The first inversions of both iii and vi are often used in passages that unfold the musical materials sequentially. In Ex. 21-19, iii$_6$ appears between vi and IV. Its use here coincides with the established pattern that alternates root position and first inversion chords. Therefore, even though the roots change in every measure, the harmonic rhythm, because of alternating inversions and root positions, is made up of greater and lesser accents.

Ex. 21-19. Mozart: Piano Concerto in F Major, K. 413, I.

Ex. 21-20 has two important features. First is the sequence formed over tonic and dominant pedals in measures 1 and 2. Superimposed on this strong root relation of I—V is a kind of "sub-progression" that accompanies *in harmonic sequence* the melodic sequence of the top voice.

Ex. 21-20. Massenet: *Manon* (Act III, Scene I).

Notice that the succession of I—vii°—vi in the first measure is followed by its sequence *at the dominant level* of V—IV—iii.

A second feature of Ex. 21-20 is its use of vi and iii as interior cadential chords which, though terminal in effect, relieve the passage of the monotony that would result if I had appeared more frequently in their stead.

Harmonic Parallelism

At times, extended passages of first inversion chords including iii$_6$ and vi$_6$ are found together with a scalar motion in the lowest part. When this occurs the melodic forces outweigh harmonic progression. This results partly from the root relations by seconds, the lack of common tone relationships, and the absence of strong bass progression. Passages such as that of Ex. 21-21 bear a direct relationship to the practice of *fauxbourdon* in the fourteenth and fifteenth centuries. In such passages harmonic relationships that are cadential in character are avoided; therefore, this kind of movement extends or lengthens a phrase by sequential patterns.

Ex. 21-21. Mozart: Sonata in C Major, K. 279, III.

C: IV⁶ iii⁶   ii⁶   I⁶ vii°⁶ vi⁶ V⁶   IV⁶ iii⁶ ii⁶ I⁶   (IV)   V   I

Harmonic parallelism places chords in a relationship more melodic than harmonic. As such, the individual root relationships are less significant than the total pattern as a sweep of motion. As in harmonic sequence, a systematic root pattern emerges. Sometimes an entire phrase is organized by parallel chords, as in Ex. 21-22.

Ex. 21-22. Puccini: *Il Tabarro,* Frugola's aria.

O e - ter - ni. in - na - mo - ra - ti, buo - na sera

In other contexts a series of parallel chords creates variety within the phrase, as in Ex. 21-23. In both Ex. 21-22 and Ex. 21-23 parallelism incorporates first inversion chords exclusively.

Ex. 21-23. Brahms: Variations and Fugue on a Theme by Handel, Op. 24, Variation I.

B♭: V   I   V   I⁶   ii⁶ iii⁶ IV⁶ V⁶ IV⁶——————V⁶   I

Parallelism is not restricted to inverted chords or root movement by seconds. In Ex. 21-24 root movement is by thirds, and each of the chords (except for the second) is major. In this excerpt it is difficult to distinguish between melody and harmony because the interval of the third characterizes both.

Ex. 21-24. Debussy: Preludes, Book I, "Les sons et les parfums tournent dans l'air du soir." Permission for reprint granted by Durand et Cie., Paris, copyright owners, and Elkan-Vogel Co., Inc., Philadelphia, agents.

Parallel fifths accompany a chordally outlined melody in Ex. 21-25. Because measures 3–5 constitute a harmonic sequence, some of the roots form an augmented second relationship. Notice that the effect of the parallel movement is partially counterbalanced by the contrary motion of the melodic pattern.

Ex. 21-25. Bartók: *Mikrokosmos,* Vol. V, No. 139. Copyright 1940 by Hawkes & Son (London) Ltd., Renewed 1967. Reprinted by permission of Boosey & Hawkes Inc.

More complex sonorities are involved in the parallel motion found in Ex. 21-26. In this passage the parallel chords move above an *ostinato*[1] figure. Both factors—parallelism and ostinato—create a static harmonic rhythm.

Ex 21-26. Stravinsky: *Le Sacre du printemps,* "Dance of the Adolescents."

Harmonic Sequence

The harmonic sequence is created by repeating a systematic root pattern at successively different pitch levels. Some skeletal versions of several patterns used in this procedure are given in Ex. 21-27.

Ex. 21-27. Harmonic sequence.

---

[1] A short, reiterated pattern.

In Ex. 21-27a the sequential pattern involves root movement up a perfect fourth, and its repetition a third lower. The pattern is broken here when root movement by a second appears between IV—V.

In Ex. 21-27b a pattern involving roots related by thirds is the basis for a harmonic sequence. Each unit of the sequence is connected by roots in a fourth relationship, and the interval of repetition is a third above.

First inversion and root position chords are alternated in Ex. 21-27c. The resulting root pattern is by fourths and fifths. Notice that in a harmonic sequence the leading tone "functions" like a root. Consequently, the vii$^\circ$ chord is assigned a status determined by its prime relation to the other diatonic triads.

Each of these illustrations involves a pattern of only two chords. The number of times a pattern is repeated is a matter determined by compositional necessity. One pattern might become dull if repeated too often, while another bears repetition because of its melodic and harmonic interest.

The phrase in Ex. 21-28 opens with a harmonic sequence. The pattern is based on the chord root relationship of a fourth and a bass pattern of root movement up a fifth. The melodic sequence is carried out between two different parts and is continued through measure 3, but the harmonic sequence ends in measure 2.

Ex. 21-28. Handel: Organ Concerto in F Major, II.

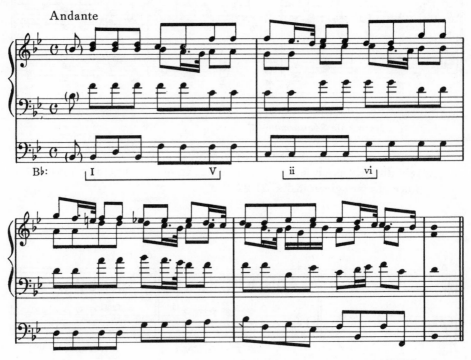

The harmonic pattern treated sequentially in Ex. 21-29 contains three chords. The root pattern is up a fifth, down a second; the interval of sequence is a minor third below. Since a minor dominant chord is used, the sequence contains only minor chords, whereas the initial statement contains only major chords.

Ex. 21-29. Brahms: Sonata in F Minor, Op. 5, I.

In Ex. 21-30 both root position and first inversion chords are used. The sequential pattern begins with vii°, indicating again that the leading tone functions as a root when it appears as part of a harmonic sequence.

Ex. 21-30. Schumann: *Album Leaf,* Op. 124, No. 4.

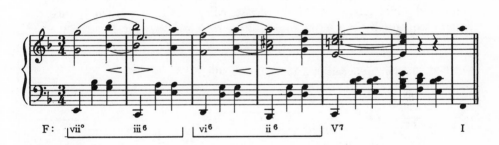

Harmonic sequences often involve non-diatonic chords. When this occurs the repetition can be the harmonic replica—equal sonorities as well as duplicated root relations—of the original statement. In Ex. 21-31 the basic harmonic pattern is I—V₇—I; the sequence has the same structure transferred up a second.

Ex. 21-31. Beethoven: Sonata in E-flat Major, Op. 81a, III.

Harmonic sequences play an important formal role in many compositions. Our discussion here is merely an introduction to this aspect of organization.

Tonal Relations in Major and Minor Keys

There are two significant aspects about the relation between any two chords: the pitches (if any) shared by both chords, and the kind of root relations formed between them. Each triad of a single scale has at least one tone in common with another triad from that scale.

The principal types of root relations that may exist between any two triads are:

1. down a fifth
2. down a fourth
3. down a third

4. up a second
5. down a second
6. up a third

The root movement up a fourth is an inversion of down a fifth, just as root relations of a sixth and a seventh are inversions of the third and second, respectively. Triads whose roots form a fifth relation have one tone in common, such as *V—I*. If the root relation is a third, as in *ii—IV* or *I—vi*, there are two tones in common. But if the root relation is a second, as in *V—vi*, there are no tones in common.

In tonal music, root movement[2] down a fifth is considered to be one of the strongest harmonic relations, and it is a fundamental relation used to establish major and minor tonalities. Within phrases composers have commonly used this pattern sequentially in a series known as the *circle of fifths*, as in Ex. 21-32.

Ex. 21-32. Beethoven: Sonata in C Minor, Op. 13, III.

---

[2] The root relations and movements described here are always in relation to the tonic of a key; thus *I—V* is root movement down a fourth (up a fifth) whereas *V—I* is down a fifth (up a fourth).

Root movement down a fourth is said to have lesser harmonic weight than down a fifth. This is amply demonstrated by any plagal cadence. Ex. 21-33 shows intra-phrase down-a-fourth root relations.

Ex. 21-33. Chopin: Nocturne, Op. 37, No. 1.

Root movement down a third is usually considered as having less progression strength than down a fifth or fourth. This is heard clearly in the progression of *I* to *vi* (mm. 2-3, Ex. 21-34) or in measures 3–5 of Ex. 21-37 in the progression I—ᵇVI—iv. Root movement up a third can be observed in Ex. 21-2.

Ex. 21-34. Beethoven: Sonata for Violin and Piano in F Major, Op. 24.

When root movement up a second occurs as in the deceptive cadence, it is a strong progression; when it occurs within the phrase it does not create as strong a rhythmic effect (see Ex. 21-25 and Ex. 21-26). Root movement down a second has more melodic than harmonic character (as in Ex. 21-28); thus it is useful where strong harmonic progression is not desired.

In summary, chord relations in major and minor keys can be described in terms of common tones and in terms of root relations. Root relations also can be described in a scale of qualitative weight from stronger to weaker:

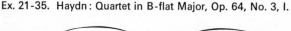

> *Stronger:*   down a fifth
> down a fourth
> down a third
> up a second (as in deceptive cadence)
> *Weaker:*   down a second

Mutated Chords: ♭III and ♭VI

Earlier in this chapter we saw that the mediant and submediant chords add new qualities to the harmonic palette. Harmonic color also is expanded by using chords that result from chromatic inflection, such as the minor tonic and the minor subdominant in a major key. Incorporating the chromatically inflected third and sixth scale degrees into the musical fabric gives the impression of "mixing" elements of both the major and minor modes. Initially, the resulting chordal and melodic digressions are regional, or "coloristic," in effect; structurally, these digressions prolong harmonic activity.

Frequently the progress of a composition is enhanced when repeated phrases are mutated by chromatic inflection. As in Ex. 21-35, the effect is that of juxtaposed modes, but the total impression is a blending that does not distort or change the structural tonal relationships. On the contrary, the mixture increases the available tonal possibilities.

Ex. 21-35. Haydn: Quartet in B-flat Major, Op. 64, No. 3, I.

When these digressions are set in close proximity, as here, the result is a fusion of different but complementary elements, obscuring the more distinctive qualities of each. It is probably more accurate to designate compositions in which elements of both major and minor appear consistently as *major-minor*.

Entire chords containing notes whose tonal roles are flexible may appear as a mutation. Both the mediant and submediant are particularly suited to mutation because their roles in the establishment of tonality are less direct. As mutated chords they add to the harmonic spectrum by making available sonorities that are more closely associated with other tonal contexts.

In Ex. 21-36 the elided phrases represent a prolongation of V. The deceptive harmonic activity in measure 4 is intensified by the appearance of the *B-flat* major chord, a mutation of the diatonic vi. It is created by the chromatic inflection of the third and sixth scale degrees, and changes the root and fifth of the triad by lowering them a half-step.

Ex. 21-36. Haydn: Quartet in D Major, Op. 64, No. 5, III.

Like its diatonic counterpart, the ♭VI prolongs harmonic activity when it is used to create a deceptive cadence. The marked difference between ♭VI and vi in the deceptive cadence is the result of several factors: (1) a major triad is heard instead of a minor triad, (2) the root motion is by minor second rather than major second, and (3) the inflected third and sixth scale degrees bring into play regional chromatic activity.

The non-cadential use of ♭VI is the same as the diatonic vi. If ♭VI is directly preceded by I, as in Ex. 21-37, both the diatonic and the mutated spellings of the third scale degree are juxtaposed. The resultant root movement is a major third. This combined with the chromatic inflection produces a *third relation*.

Ex. 21-37. Brahms: Symphony No. 3, II.

Third related chords are present when chord roots are a major or minor third apart. If the chords involved have two tones in common, a diatonic third relation exists, *e.g.*, vi—IV; on the other hand, if the chords involved only have one tone, or no tones in common, a "chromatic" third relation exists.

In Ex. 21-38 ♭VI both prolongs the influence of the tonic pitch and focuses attention on the plagal cadence. In part, this attention is a by-product of the lowered sixth scale step, both as root of ♭VI and as the third of iv in the cadential pattern.

The mutated mediant also is used in situations similar to its diatonic equivalent. To create the ♭III, both the root and the fifth of the mediant triad are lowered one half-step. Like the ♭VI, ♭III adds another sonority to the harmonic palette. When ♭III precedes V or V₇, a cross relation may be created by the juxtaposition of both the diatonic and the mutated seventh scale step, as in the second measure of Ex. 21-38.

Ex. 21-38. Dvořák: Quartet in A-flat Major, I.

The ♭III chord is in third relation to both I and V, and has one tone in common with each. The ♭III also bears an interesting relation to ♭VI because of their root relation of fifth and their common tone.

The purely coloristic roles of ♭VI and ♭III are sometimes regarded with less attention than their structural roles. In Ex. 21-39 the cadential activity is heightened by introducing ♭VI⁶ before proceeding to tonic.

Ex. 21-39. R. Strauss: *Die Nacht.* By permission of the International Music Company, New York.

At first glance it appears that the cadence is both deceptive and authentic. However, after the harmonic motion is completed, $^{\flat}VI^{6}$ is heard as a chromatic embellishment around I that is reminiscent of non-chord activity.

Earlier in the chapter we stated that consistent use of mutated chords produces the effect of elements mixed from two different tonal sources. The process we have seen thus far has always involved juxtaposition. In some rare instances the mixing involves both juxtaposition and superposition.

Ex. 21-40. Stravinsky: *Symphony of Psalms*, I. Copyright 1941 by Russischer Musikverlag, Renewed 1958. Copyright & Renewal assigned to Boosey & Hawkes Inc. Revised Version Copyright 1948 by Boosey & Hawkes Inc. Reprinted by permission.

The simultaneous mixing of different harmonic elements is also a possibility. Such stacking of diverse elements carries the practice of mixing to its logical further development. In Ex. 21-41 a harmonic groundwork of *A* major is clearly outlined by the cello chords. Stacked above this predominance of *A* major is the octave pattern of the violin that definitely outlines *a* minor.

Ex. 21-41. Bartók: Quartet No. 2, I. Copyright 1920 by Universal Edition; Renewed 1948. Copyright and Renewal assigned to Boosey & Hawkes, Inc. for the U.S.A. Reprinted by permission.

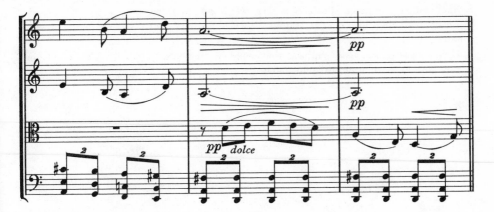

The following is a chart of common tonally directed harmonic progressions.

TONIC		PRE-DOMINANT (subdominant)	DOMINANT	TONIC
I, i	vi, VI iii, III, III⁺	IV, iv ii, ii° Secondary Sevenths, Secondary Dominants	V, V₇ vii°₆ (iii₆, iii III)	I, i (vi, VI)

The harmonic cycle may begin at any point.

Any step in the cycle may be omitted.

Any step or steps may be retraced before direction is resumed.

Exercises

For more detailed assignments see *Materials and Structure of Music I, Workbook,* Chapter 21.

1. Sing and spell the median and submediant chords in all diatonic keys.
2. Use the melodic material from measures 1 and 2 of Ex. 21-12 as the motivic basis for a sixteen-measure piano composition in ternary form.
3. Reduce Ex. 21-16 to a two-voice framework. Then elaborate this basic frame to create a "new" four-phrase work.
4. Reset the melody of Ex. 21-5 with a "faster" harmonic rhythm. Incorporate all of the diatonic chords into your setting.
5. Write an experimental composition that uses a preponderance of chords other than tonic, subdominant, or dominant. Make a formal plan, and sketch in the chordal forms that will serve as the basis for a phrase or section.
6. Write a three-phrase vocal composition. Use the following plan: first phrase, only root position chords; second phrase, parallel first inversion chords; third phrase, alternating root position and first inversion chords. Close the example with a median to tonic terminal cadence.

7. Spell and sing mutated chords (i, iv, III, VI) in all major keys.
8. Listen to compositions such as Brahms' *Rhapsody*, Op. 119, No. 4. Discuss the use of mutated chords.
9. Create various harmonic patterns that could be treated sequentially. Use one of the examples in this chapter as your model.

22

SECONDARY DOMINANTS

As we have seen, the presence of chromatic alterations in a passage may indicate one of several things: alterations of decorative tones (non-chord tones), usual altered tones of the minor scales, or modulation. Practically any page of music contains accidentals, either flats, sharps, or natural signs, which indicate inflections of notes within the diatonic scale system. Many such alterations result from the composer's desire to exploit one of music's strongest harmonic relationships, that of "dominant-tonic." Our foregoing study of harmony has shown the important role played by this relationship, a role emphasized by frequency of use, as well as structural prominence. It is also possible that composers simply developed a preference for such relations. In any event, a particular practice developed, namely that of creating "secondary dominant-tonic" relationships. This practice will be the basis of our study for the next two chapters.

In Ex. 22-1 the *d-naturals* that appear in the seventh measure create a half-step (leading tone) relation with *e-flat*.

Ex. 22-1. Mozart: Symphony in E-flat Major, K. 543, II.

The *d-natural* is part of a melodic sequence begun in measure 6 that leads to the focal point of *e-flat*, the dominant of *A-flat* major. The last chord in measure 7 is a Mm 7 chord on *b-flat*, the V_7 of *E-flat*. Mozart here heightens the effect of the cadence on the dominant by preceding the dominant with its own "dominant seventh" chord. In other words, he employed a "secondary dominant"[1] (more precisely, a "secondary dominant seventh"), the symbol for which is V_7/V. A further study of the second cadence in Ex. 22-1 reveals other interesting facts. Notice the third chord from the end. It is the dominant in second inversion, the V_4^6. This chord and the two following constitute a progression (V_4^6—V_7/V—V) that resembles one of the most common cadential patterns, I_4^6—V_7—I. In both instances the middle chord is the "dominant," which is preceded by its "tonic" in second inversion, then followed by its "tonic" in root position.

Using this example as a point of departure, and from observations made of musical practice, we may generalize about "secondary dominants" as follows:

1. Any diatonic major or minor triad may be embellished by its own dominant.
2. Such embellishment creates harmonic color and strengthens linear motion (leading tone effect), thereby heightening resolution tendency.
3. Their presence is sometimes indicated by the appearance of one or more chromatic tones of harmonic significance appearing in music that is basically diatonic. (Remember that chromatic notes may indicate other things as well.)
4. The secondary dominant *seventh*, because of the added dissonance and the resolution tendency of the members of the tritone, stands in stronger relation to its "tonic" than does the corresponding secondary dominant *triad*.
5. Secondary dominants and secondary dominant sevenths appear in inversions as well as in root position.
6. In four-voice textures the root of the secondary dominant is frequently doubled while the secondary dominant seventh usually appears in complete form; however, if not, the root is doubled.
7. Secondary dominants resolve *regularly* (to their "tonics"), *deceptively* (to a major or minor chord whose root is a step above the root of the secondary dominant), or *irregularly* (to a variety of other chords.)

It is easy to overlook the melodic significance of secondary dominants, since their harmonic effect is so pronounced. To do so is to ignore one very important aspect of their use. Ex. 22-2 (late sixteenth century) contains patterns of harmonic relation identifiable as "secondary dominant" in function. Through the use of the chromatic inflections *g-sharp*, *c-sharp*, and *f-sharp*, the composer has heightened the melodic drive to *a*, *d*, and *g*, respectively.

---

[1] In this sense, the dominant of a key might be regarded as the "primary dominant."

Ex. 22-2. Gesualdo: *Io pur respiro.*

In Ex. 22-3, composed some two centuries later, chromatic alterations are again used for line inflection, resulting in a secondary dominant chord function.

Ex. 22-3. Mozart: *Eine kleine Nachtmusik,* K. 525, Menuetto.

At the transient-terminal cadence in measure 4, perform either the viola or cello line as written and compare that result with a performance in which *c* is substituted for *c-sharp.* Obviously, either arrangement is possible; however, it is apparent that the original version drives more unequivocally to *d,* the dominant. Stressing the "progressive" nature of this interior cadence, the composer immediately cancels out the leading tone effect of the *c-sharp* by the use of *c*'s in the following passage, which terminates on tonic.

It is worth noting that secondary dominants are generally used to embellish and emphasize structural chords within a tonal framework. Consequently, their appearance is usually predictable. For example, one can expect to find V_7/V used with considerable frequency preceding the V chord in authentic cadences.

Ex. 22-4. J.S. Bach: *Wachet auf* (Cantata No. 140).

It is interesting to observe that of the three cadences in this excerpt, two are on the dominant. In both instances these important structural points have been emphasized by the use of secondary dominants. In so doing, Bach has stressed the dominant tonal area, and in the third phrase he is faced with the necessity of re-emphasizing the tonic in a convincing fashion. He accomplishes this by turning toward the subdominant through the use of its secondary dominant.

In seeking to create variety, composers are not always content to follow traditional patterns. We find secondary dominants used to obscure the tonic temporarily, thus creating an added element of suspense. For instance, Ex. 22-5 begins on a Mm_7 chord with E as root (V_7 of IV).

Ex. 22-5. Chopin: Mazurka in E Minor, Op. 41, No. 2.

Through hindsight we are able to hear the harmonic design and to establish the tonal focus of the passage. This is not immediately apparent upon a first hearing, at least not during the first few measures.

Secondary Dominant of the Dominant (V/V; V₇/V)

In major keys the appearance of the V/V or V₇/V is suggested by the presence of the raised fourth degree of the scale as a member of a chord. In such instances the chord will have as its root the second degree of the scale, and except for the altered note (the raised fourth scale degree, the third of the chord), will contain the notes of the diatonic ii chord. As a matter of fact, it is helpful to think of the V/V in both ways: as a *major triad* built on the second degree of the scale, and as a variant of the supertonic chord (with its third raised). (See Ex. 22-6.)

In minor keys the V/V or V₇/V is created by two chromatic alterations, the raised fourth and sixth degrees of the scale. Observe that two alterations are required to create a major triad or major-minor seventh chord on the second degree of the harmonic minor scale, because the supertonic triad is diminished. (See Ex. 22-6.)

Ex. 22-6. Secondary dominant of the dominant.

The V/V or V₇/V frequently is preceded by a chord that is common both to the original key and to the key in which the secondary dominant would be the primary dominant. For instance, in Ex. 22-7a the V/V is preceded by a chord common to the tonic (vi₆) and to the dominant keys (ii₆); in Ex. 22-7b, the V₇/V follows a minor triad that is i₆ in *a* minor and iv₆ in *e*.

Ex. 22-7. Approach to V/V.

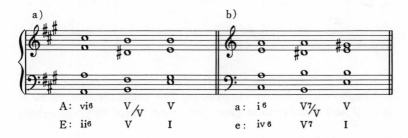

Although the approach to the secondary dominant indicated in Ex. 22-7 may result in a smooth melodic/harmonic progression, such progression is not always desirable or possible. Other cases may necessitate the creation of a chromatic relationship between members of the secondary dominant and the preceding chord; one tone of the scale may appear in its natural form in one chord followed by its chromatic alteration in the other.

Ex. 22-8. Chromatic relationships.

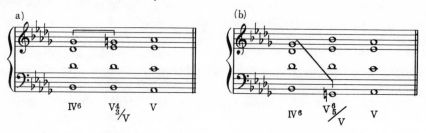

In Ex. 22-8a, note that the *g* is approached from the *g-flat in the same voice*. The result is an unbroken melodic ascent to the fifth degree of the scale. In Ex. 22-8b the *g-flat* appears in one voice and the *g* in another. This cross relation is somewhat rougher in that both notes are prominently located, and their relation is exaggerated by the fact that they do not appear in the same voice. Although the cross relation is not always undesirable, it is usually avoided when a less disjointed result can be obtained, as in Ex. 22-8a.

In connection with melodic movement in secondary dominant progressions one other observation should be made. It is often true that a chromatically inflected note progresses in the direction of the inflection. That is, if a diatonic note is raised by an accidental the melodic line tends to proceed upward; the reverse is true if the note is lowered by an accidental. In Ex. 22-9 this tendency is quite apparent. Note that the *f-sharp* is followed by *g;* the *f* by *e*.

Ex. 22-9. Schein: *Gelobet seist du, Jesu Christ.*

This rule of "tendency" corresponds to the functional relations of tones within the major-minor scale systems in that the leading tone (here represented by *f-sharp*) progresses up and the fourth degree (here represented by *f*) progresses down.

The principles of resolution of the V/V and V₇/V are not different from those of the V and V₇. The usual resolution is to their "tonic," that is, to a major chord whose root stands in a fifth relation below. The raised fourth degree, the "secondary leading tone" in the secondary dominant, generally progresses to the fifth degree. In other words, it follows the tendency of the inflection. See Ex. 22-10a. One exception occurs when the third of the chord (the inflected tone) proceeds to a note a third below, that is, to the fifth of the chord of resolution. This usually occurs in one of the inner voices (see Ex. 22-10b) in order that the chord of resolution be a complete triad.

Ex. 22-10. Resolution of the V/V.

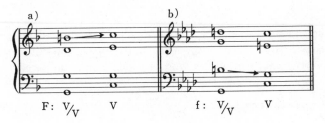

The notes of the tritone in the V_7/V usually resolve as do those of the V_7. The augmented fourth expands stepwise and the diminished fifth contracts stepwise. (See Ex. 22-11a). One exception to this appears where the third of the V_7/V proceeds to the fifth of V. (See Ex. 22-11b.)

Ex. 22-11. Resolution of the V_7/V.

The V/V or V_7/V is frequently used in transient-terminal cadences. In such instances the secondary dominant often appears in root position and progresses to V or V_7, which is also usually in root position.

Ex. 22-12. Mozart: Symphony in E-flat Major, K. 543, III.

Ex. 22-12 continued.

$$\text{vi}^6 \qquad \text{V}^6_4 \qquad \text{V}^7/\text{V} \qquad \text{V}$$

Note the similarity of the cadence pattern (vi_6—V^6_4—V_7/V—V) to the cadence "formula" previously discussed (ii_6—I^6_4—V_7—I). This similarity becomes more apparent when the two possible analyses of this kind of cadence are compared.

Ex. 22-13. Analyses of cadence pattern of Ex. 22-12.

$$E^\flat: \quad \text{vi}^6 \qquad \text{V}^6_4 \qquad \text{V}^7/\text{V} \qquad \text{V}$$
$$[\,B^\flat: \quad \text{ii}^6 \qquad \text{I}^6_4 \qquad \text{V}^7 \qquad \text{I}\,]$$

As illustrated in Ex. 22-13, the V_7/V is frequently "prepared" by the V^6_4, and in such instances, this chord is often preceded by vi or vi_6.

When used in the interior of a phrase, V/V or V_7/V frequently resolves to an inverted form of V, thereby contributing to the forward movement of the harmony. Note that in Ex. 22-14 the V/V is preceded by ii, its diatonic counterpart.

Ex. 22-14. Wagner: *Tannhäuser,* Overture.

$$\text{ii} \qquad \text{V}/\text{V} \quad \text{V}^7/\text{V} \quad \text{V}^4_3$$

One finds that there are no major differences in the use of V/V or V_7/V in minor; they are preceded and followed as in major.

Ex. 22-15. Chopin: Ballade in G Minor, Op. 23, No. 1.

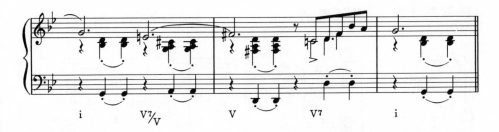

The dominant of the dominant is sometimes used in the minor mode to embellish the minor dominant chord. This is the function of the V_2^4/V in Ex. 22-16, in
which the minor dominant is introduced quite unexpectedly as the cadence chord
of a passage in which the major dominant has prevailed.

Ex. 22-16. Beethoven: Piano Concerto No. 3, in C Minor, Op. 37, III.

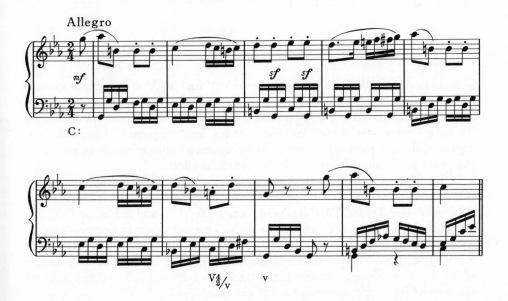

When working with V/V and V_7/V in minor in a choral style, care should be taken to avoid augmented intervals in the melodic lines containing the chromatic inflections. In instrumental performance these melodic intervals are not as difficult to produce accurately.

Inversions of V/V and V_7/V are used with considerable frequency, and generally in complete form. They may be designated by the following symbols:

V/V; first inversion, V_6/V; second inversion, V_4^6/V.
V_7/V; first inversion, V_5^6/V; second inversion, V_3^4/V;
third inversion, V_2^4/V.

Ex. 22-17. V/V, V_7/V, and inversions.

As indicated earlier in this chapter, the V/V and V_7/V often appear in connection with cadences on the dominant. This is equally true of the inverted forms. Inversions make possible a conjunct bass line that is more "melodic" in character. To some degree, the use of inversions stresses the "temporary" nature of such cadences, since in terminal cadences the penultimate chord is usually in root position, thus producing a more conclusive cadential effect.

In Ex. 22-18, IV precedes the cadence pattern V_5^6/V—V. The movement to V is heightened by the chromatic ascent of the bass *g-flat—g—a-flat*. A smooth connection between IV and V_5^6/V is possible because the third and fifth of the IV chord (*B-flat* and *D-flat* here) are common to V_7/V. This cadence may be considered as a variant of the simpler pattern, IV—V, here modified by the insertion of a passing V_5^6/V. The introduction of the chromatic leading tone (here *g*), and the presence of the dissonant elements in the Mm_7 chord (*g—d-flat* and *e-flat—d-flat*) increase the sense of inevitable movement to the cadence.

Ex. 22-18. Schubert: *Moments Musicaux,* Op. 94, No. 6.

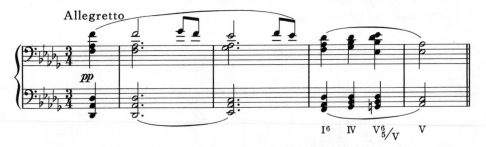

Ex. 22-19 contains another treatment of the V_7/V. Here the chord appears in second inversion preceded by vi. Such an approach is quite smooth, for there are notes in common between the two chords. As in Ex. 22-18, there is an acceleration of harmonic rhythm in the approach to the cadence. Notice also the simple step-progression in the middle pattern, *A-flat—B-flat—C—D—E-flat.*

Ex. 22-19. Beethoven: Sonata in C Minor, Op. 13, II.

Dominant of the Subdominant

The dominant is frequently the tonal goal of a phrase or larger melodic section, and the tonal movement to this goal is often intensified by the inclusion of secondary dominants, for example V/V. This relationship, in turn, can be strengthened by the addition of other secondary dominants which precede the V/V, for example, the V_7/IV and the V_7/ii.

Ex. 22-20. Mozart: Sonata in C Major, K. 279, II.

The dominant seventh of the subdominant (V_7/IV: V_7/iv) is a chord whose root is the tonic. Its appearance in minor requires a change of the tonic chord from minor to major, thereby creating the leading tone of iv.

Ex. 22-21. Dominant of the subdominant.

In terms of roots, I stands in relation to IV as V does to I. However, a "dominant-tonic" relationship is not so evident between the major tonic triad and its subdominant until a minor seventh is added to the former. The V_7/IV in Ex. 22-22 appears in conjunction with a short tonic pedal, and gives way to the subdominant in second inversion. Note the smooth introduction of the seventh of the V_7/IV in the tenor, where it functions as a passing tone between *g* and *f*.

Ex. 22-22. Gounod: *Faust*, "Salut! Demeure" (Act II).

The V_7/IV is often used to counterbalance emphasis on the dominant and, in many such instances, appears toward the close of a phrase, period, or section. Ex. 22-23 shows the last phrase of the second period of a theme, the first period of which ended with a transient terminal cadence, V/V—V. Through the use of a V_2^4/IV, the subdominant is emphasized at the climax of the phrase. The augmented fourth (*c—f-sharp*) expands by step to its typical resolution (*B—G*).

Ex. 22-23. Haydn: Sonata in D Major, III.

On the other hand the V_7/IV also occurs as in Ex. 22-24, at the beginning of a section before tonic has been established. Although tonic is not readily apparent at the beginning of this excerpt, it becomes clearly established in the ensuing measures.

Ex. 22-24. Chopin: Mazurka in E Minor, Op. 41, No. 2.

In Ex. 22-25, the subdominant is stressed by the V_7/IV, and by the prominent melodic use of the interval *d—g* at the head of the motive appearing in measures 1 and 3. Any tonal ambivalence between *d* and *g* which may have arisen by measure 4 is soon dispelled by the cadence pattern, ii_6—V—IV_4^6—I, in measures 7–8.

Ex. 22-25. Bartók: Little Pieces for Children, Vol. I, No. 11. Copyright by Edwin F. Kalmus. Reprinted by permission.

Because of the common pitch shared by I, V_7/IV, and IV (root, root, and fifth, respectively), these chords often appear in conjunction with a tonic pedal. This procedure offsets the weakening of tonality that otherwise can result from the use of a V_7/IV. In Ex. 22-26 the V_7/IV is preceded by tonic in a passage characterized by a rearticulated pedal. The harmonic movement to IV is heightened by the addition of the seventh, *d-flat*.

Ex. 22-26. Haydn: Sonata in E-flat Major, I.

The subdominant occasionally plays an important role as a cadence chord, and it frequently appears embellished by its secondary dominant. In Ex. 22-27 a transient-terminal cadence on the subdominant involves its dominant seventh.

Ex. 22-27. Schubert: Mass in G Major, Kyrie.

Ex. 22-28 illustrates another cadential use, but in this instance the subdominant is the penultimate chord of a plagal cadence. The *b-flat* pedal underlines the first two measures, above which a V_7/IV appears. The V_3^4/IV links the two forms of the same sonority, IV_6 and IV, which occur at the phrase's high point.

Ex. 22-28. Schubert: Octet, Op. 166, II.

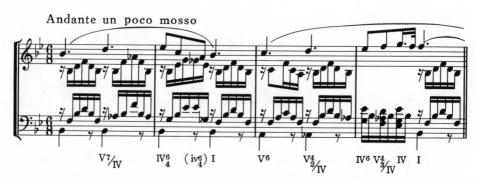

There are many other uses of this chord; obviously, any appearance of a subdominant could be embellished by its dominant. The standard "blues progression" of jazz cadences on a V_7/IV at the end of the first four-measure phrase.

Ex. 22-29. Arlen-Mercer: *Blues in the Night.* Copyright 1941 by Remick Music Corporation. Used by Permission.

Dominant of the Supertonic

The Use of V/ii is generally limited to the major mode, for the supertonic chord in minor is diminished and does not function satisfactorily as a "temporary tonic." Its root is the sixth degree of the scale, and its presence is suggested by the appearance of the raised first degree of the scale (leading tone of 2) that usually resolves upward.

Ex. 22-30. Dominant of the supertonic.

In Ex. 22-31, the *c-sharp* in the second measure is the third of an arpeggiated *A* major triad which moves to *D*. Similarly, a secondary leading tone is formed in the first and penultimate measures by the *F-sharp*.

Ex. 22-31. Brahms: *Ein deutsches Requiem,* "Herr, du bist würdig."

The V/ii is generally limited to the interior of phrases. It seldom appears at cadence points, except rarely when there is a transient-terminal cadence on the supertonic.

Ex. 22-32. Schubert: Octet, Op. 166, IV.

The sequential root pattern 6—2, 5—1 frequently involves a dominant embellishment of ii as in measures 2 and 3 of Ex. 22-32.

A noteworthy exception to the foregoing principle appears in Ex. 22-33 in which the V_7/ii serves as a climactic cadence chord (measure 4).

Ex. 22-33. Chopin: Prelude in A Major, Op. 28, No. 6.

An interesting use of the V_6/ii occurs in Ex. 22-34 where it appears as the opening chord forming the initial part of a sequence (V_6/ii—ii) that is completed by the pattern V_6/I.

Ex. 22-34. Mozart: Sonata in B-flat Major, K. 281, III.

It is not unusual to find the V_7/ii used in sequential patterns such as (V_5^6/ii—ii) (V_5^6—I), as exemplified in Ex. 22-35.

Ex. 22-35. Mozart: Sonata in B-flat Major, K. 333, I.

The V/ii is often used to prolong the action of the ii chord, as in the beginning of the second phrase of Ex. 22-36. In this passage the V_3^4/ii appears between successive occurrences of the ii in the forms of ii and ii_6. This treatment parallels the first three measures of the first phrase, where I and I_6 are linked by V_3^4.

Ex. 22-36. Beethoven: Sonata in D Major, Op. 10, No. 3, III.

In many instances the temporary "tonic" of the V/ii is altered, so that it too becomes a secondary dominant (V/V). In Ex. 22-37 V_5^6/ii progresses to V_7/V, which in turn resolves deceptively.

Ex. 22-37. Chopin: Nocturne in E-flat Major, Op. 9, No. 2.

The V_3^4/ii in measure 6 of Ex. 22-38 is approached in a conventional manner. However, it is followed not by ii but by its own dominant, the V_7/vi. This is then followed by V_2^4/ii which resolves to ii_6.

Ex. 22-38. Verdi: Requiem, *Requiem aeternam.*

Exercises

For more detailed assignments see *Materials and Structure of Music I, Workbook*, Chapter 22.

1. Scan new music rapidly, looking for chromatic inflections as possible indications of secondary dominants.
2. Indicate the major and minor keys in which *a–c-sharp–e–g* might appear as a secondary dominant seventh, and the appropriate identification of each.
3. Analyze some of the following, indicating keys, chords and non-harmonic tones:

    Haydn: Piano *Sonata in D major*, III (1–8)
    Mozart: *Piano Sonata in D major*, III, var. 12 (1–9)
    Beethoven: *Piano Sonata*, Op. 26, II (1–8)
    ‎   *String Quartet*, Op. 18, No. 5, IV (1–12)
    Schubert: *Quintet*, Op. 114, IV (1–8)
    Chopin: *Mazurka*, Op. 56, no. 2 (33–38)
    Wagner: *Wach Auf* (Die Meistersinger, Act III) (1–10)

4. Spell (from the bass up) the following:

    a. v_5^6/V, c   d. V_3^4/IV, G
    b. V_2^4/ii, E   e. V_5^6/ii, A-flat
    c. V_3^4/iv, d   f. V_2^4/V, B

5. Find examples of secondary dominants of dominant, subdominant and supertonic in the music for your instrument.
6. What is the third of each of the following:

    a. V_2^4/V, c sharp   d. V_7/V, B
    b. V_5^6/ii, B-flat   e. V_3^4/IV, D-flat
    c. V_2^4/iv, g   f. V_5^6/ii, A

7. Make an SATB setting of the following:

    $$I—V_2^4/V—V_5^6—vi_6—V_5^6/ii—ii—I_4^6—V_7—I—V_7/IV—IV_4^6—I$$

8. Using Ex. 22-36 as a model, compose a period (four-part texture) using at least one each of the following:

    V_3^4/V V_2^4/IV V_5^6/ii; arrange for 4 brass.

9. Add four measures to those in Ex. 22-28 using dominants of dominant and supertonic. When completed, arrange for oboe, two clarinets, and bassoon.
10. To continue the study of secondary dominants, analyze several of the following works, indicating key chords and non-chord tones:

    Haydn: *Symphony No. 6*, III. (1–18)
    Mozart: *Piano Sonata*, K. 284, I (1–10)
    ‎   *Piano Sonata*, K. 332, I (1–12)
    ‎   *String Quartet*, K. 387, I (1–6)
    Beethoven: *Piano Sonata*, Op. 7, I (59–61)
    ‎   *String Quartet*, Op. 18, No. 5, III (9–16)
    ‎   *Symphony No. 1*, Op. 21, II, (1–26)
    ‎   *Bagatelle No. 3*, Op. 33 (1–17)
    ‎   *Ich Liebe Dich* (song) complete work
    Schubert: *Octet*, Op. 166, II (1–5)
    ‎   *Octet*, Op. 166, V (trio) (1–16)
    ‎   *Symphony No. 5*, IV (1–16)
    Chopin: *Mazurka*, Op. 6, No. 2 (9–16)
    ‎   *Prelude*, Op. 28, No. 3 (1–34)
    ‎   *Nocturne*, Op. 37 (57–64)

23

CONTINUATION OF
SECONDARY DOMINANTS

Dominant of the Submediant (V/vi; V/VI)

There are two basic forms of the submediant chord, vi in major and VI in minor, with each having a related secondary dominant whose root is the third degree of the scale. The V/vi (major mode) requires that the fifth of the major scale be chromatically raised. The *c-sharp* in Ex. 23-1 is the third of a major-minor seventh chord whose root is *a* which has a dominant relation to the submediant.

Ex. 23-1. Dvořák: Symphony in D Minor, Op. 70, II.

In the minor mode no chromatic alterations are required for the triadic form V/VI, but the seventh chord (V₇/VI) necessitates the lowered second degree of the scale.

Ex. 23-2. V₇/VI, dominant of the submediant.

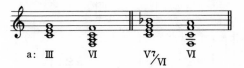

In measure 6 of Ex. 23-3, the *b-flat* creates the seventh of a chord that embellishes the submediant.

Ex. 23-3. Mendelssohn: Song Without Words, Op. 19, No. 2.

There are no new problems of resolution for the V_7/vi, because it resolves the same way as each of the secondary dominants discussed earlier.

The dominant of the submediant frequently appears early in a phrase following a dominant or tonic chord. When preceded by the dominant, as illustrated in Ex. 23-4a the result is an elaboration and chromatic reinforcement of the deceptive progression V_7—vi.

Ex. 23-4a. Progression V—V₇—V⅚/vi—vi.

Ex. 23-4. Brahms: *Ein deutsches Requiem,* "Herr, du bist würdig."

The progression of tonic to submediant is common, particularly at the beginning of a phrase, and the V_3^4/vi frequently serves as a connecting link between the two.

Ex. 23-5. Wagner: *Lohengrin,* Prelude to Act III.

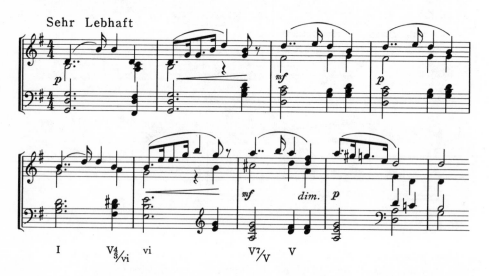

The dominant of the submediant in the interior of a phrase is often preceded by tonic or dominant, as the previous excerpts have illustrated. In Ex. 23-6 the V_6/vi is approached through the dominant and prepares the way to the half cadence.

Ex. 23-6. Verdi: *Aida,* "Su! Del Nilo," Act 1, Scene 1.

In the next quoted passage the submediant chord is prolonged through its repetition and its attendant secondary dominant. The result is the creation of a momentary tonal emphasis on vi prior to the progressive cadence on V.

Ex. 23-7. Wagner: Siegfried Idyll.

Except for occasional Phyrygian cadences in the major mode, it is unusual to find the V/vi serving as a cadence chord. When used as in the next excerpt the result is to strengthen the harmonic drive from the progressive cadence on the V/vi to the half cadence on V.

Ex. 23-8. Brahms: *Liebeslieder Walzer,* Op. 52, No. 8.

Dominant of the Mediant (V/iii; V/III)

As is true of the submediant chord, the mediant chord usually appears in one of two forms, iii in major and III in minor. Each has a related secondary dominant whose root is the seventh degree of the scale. To introduce a V_7/iii (major mode) requires the chromatic alteration of two diatonic tones; the second and fourth scale degrees both must be raised a semitone. In minor, the root of the V_7/III is the *subtonic* of the scale.

Ex. 23-9. V_7/iii, dominant of the mediant.

By raising the second scale degree (major mode) the leading tone of iii is created. The raised fourth scale degree permits a perfect fifth between the root and fifth of the chord.

Ex. 23-10 contains a passage in which V_7/iii follows V_6. Notice that this particular form of the progression uses the common tone between the two chords as a kind of pedal bass.

Ex. 23-10. Brahms: *Ein deutsches Requiem,* "Wie Lieblich."

As exemplified in Ex. 23-10 and Ex. 23-11, the V_7/iii frequently apepars in the interior of a phrase, generally resolving to iii and often being preceded by V or I. In Ex. 23-11 the step motion up to the dominant in the top voice is given added thrust by the *a-sharp*, the fifth of the V_7/iii.

Ex. 23-11. Schubert: Symphony in B Minor, II.

The inverted forms frequently occur in the course of a phrase and thus minimize the strong root progression. In Ex. 23-12 the V_3^4/iii appears in a short sequential passage, measures 3–4 being a melodic-harmonic sequence of 1–2.

Ex. 23-12. Beethoven: Quartet in F Major, Op. 18, No. 1, III.

One of the common functions of a secondary dominant is to reinforce various cadential patterns. Such a use of the V_7/iii may be found in Ex. 23-13. The period closes with a transient-terminal cadence on iii, followed by an immediate return to tonic upon the repetition of the period. Compare the treatment of the first and second phrases. Also note that the V_7/iii appears in root position, thereby creating a more decisive cadence on the iii chord.

Ex. 23-13. Haydn: Symphony No. 88, IV.

Ex. 23-13 continued.

The root of the V/III in the minor mode is the subtonic scale degree, hence a conventional fifth relationship exists between the roots of V_7/III and III. In Ex. 23-14 the V_7/III is used in the approach to the cadence on III, measure 4.

Ex. 23-14. Beethoven: Piano Concerto, Op. 58, No. 4, II.

Because the V_7/III in minor is identical to the V_7 of the relative major, it frequently is used to exploit this "duality." In Ex. 23-15 the V_7/III supports a transient-terminal cadence on III at the end of measure 4. The harmonic resources of g minor have been expanded here by this vacillation between these two closely related keys, each tonic is in turn supported by its own dominant. Since the passage does begin and end in g minor, the fleeting focus on *B-flat* as temporary tonic is best regarded as more a prolongation of the mediant than a true change of tonic.

Ex. 23-15. Beethoven: Sonata in G Major, Op. 79, II.

Dominant of the Subtonic

This survey of secondary dominants would not be complete without brief mention of the V/♭VII in minor. Since the leading-tone chord (vii°) is diminished and therefore never functions as a temporary tonic, its secondary dominant is not used. However, a major triad (VII) built on the seventh degree of the natural minor scale (subtonic) may be embellished by its dominant, the V₇/♭VII. In Ex. 23-16 note that the V₇/♭VII is used in a sequential pattern that begins in measure 3 and terminates in measure 6. (The sequential use of secondary dominants will be discussed in some detail later in this chapter.) Observe also the jolting effect of the root relation (tritone) in the progression V₇/♭II—V₇/V, in measures 6–7, in spite of the very smooth motion of *g-flat—g-natural* in the melodic line.

Ex. 23-16. Chopin: Mazurka in G Minor, Op. 67, No. 2.

Irregular Resolutions of Secondary Dominants

Thus far, our discussion of secondary dominants has been concerned primarily with "regular" resolutions. By definition, a secondary dominant stands in a fixed harmonic relationship to its "secondary tonic," a root relationship of a perfect fourth up or perfect fifth down; and its harmonic function is determined by the realization of this relationship (i.e., by its regular resolution). When such is not the case but the chord of resolution is still diatonic or a clearly related member thereof (another secondary dominant, for example), the embellishing sonority may still be considered a secondary dominant, and progressions of this kind as *irregular resolutions*.

Perhaps the most obvious irregular resolution is that in which the secondary dominant resolves "deceptively" (root progression up a second) as illustrated in Ex. 23-17 (mm. 3–4).

Ex. 23-17. Haydn: *The Creation,* "In Splendor Bright."

Ex. 23-18 is particularly interesting because it illustrates the use of simple chords in complex relationships. Note particularly the deceptive resolutions of the secondary dominants, V_7/vi—IV and V_7/iii—I in measures 3–4 and 7–8, respectively. The harmonic treatment in measures 1 and 2 is a progression of major triads whose root line is *d—c—b* and whose two-voice frame is organized mainly in contrary motion.

Ex. 23-18. Prokofiev: Classical Symphony, III. Copyright 1926 by Edition Russe de Musique. Copyright assigned to Boosey & Hawkes Inc. Reprinted by permission.

Another common type of deceptive resolution is that in which the chord of resolution is itself a secondary dominant. In such progressions the secondary dominant still resolves to a chord whose root is a step above, but the chord of resolution is a non-diatonic chord. In Ex. 23-19 the dominant of submediant is approached through the V_5^6/V which resolves deceptively to V_5^6/vi (measure 8) in the sequence begun in measure 5. Observe that the voices move in parallel motion from one seventh chord to the other, each "line" moving up a major second to the corresponding note of the next chord.

Ex. 23-19. Gounod: *Faust,* "Faites lui mes aveux" (Act III).

An alternate explanation of the above is possible if one assumes that the submediant region of C is established in measures 6–9. A logical analysis might then be IV_5^6—V_5^6—vi.

The subsequent discussion will be limited to a few other types of irregular resolutions with the assumption that more thorough knowledge of this practice will be acquired through continued observation of the works of various composers.

As a point of departure, consider the various resolutions appearing in Ex. 23-20.

Ex. 23-20. Some irregular resolutions of a Mm$_7$ chord

The irregular resolutions indicated as (a), (b), and (c) exemplify chromatic third relations. Of these three, (b) and (c) permit the simplest connection because there are two common tones between the first chord and its chord of resolution. It is apparent that such resolutions create various chromatic relationships, and as a general rule, cross relations between voices are avoided. The resolution by root movement down a second (example d) permits a conventional treatment of the leading tone; however, the seventh is retained as the root of the next chord.

In many ways Ex. 23-21 may serve as summation of the practice of irregular resolution, at least in regard to the harmonic materials thus far presented. Contained therein are six irregular progressions: (V_7—vi)—deceptive; (V_7/vi—V)—root movement up a third; (V—iv₆), (V_7/iii—vi₆), and (V_7/V—I₆)—root movement down a second; (V_6/V—V_7/iii)—root movement down a third. An important organizational feature is the contrary motion between the outer lines in the long melodic descent in measures 1–5. Through the use of secondary dominants the harmonic potential is increased, particularly through the irregular resolutions.

Ex. 23-21. Wagner: Prelude to *Lohengrin.*

Sequential Treatment of Secondary Dominants

Secondary dominants are used frequently in harmonic sequences of nonmodulatory nature. They add tones foreign to the basic key, and they make more cohesive the harmonies of which the sequences are comprised. In Ex. 23-22, the melodic sequence is accompanied with a succession of secondary dominant sevenths. The chord of resolution becomes a secondary dominant seventh that progresses to another, etc.

Ex. 23-22. Mozart: Symphony in C, K. 551, II.

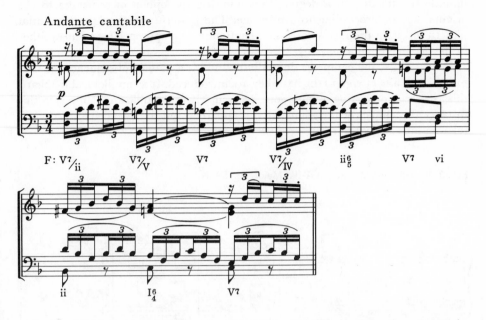

Ex. 23-23. Beethoven: Quartet in E Minor, Op. 59, No. 2, IV.

In Ex. 23-23 the beginning and end of the passage focus upon the same tonic, yet the composer runs the sequential gamut through the use of a two-note pattern beginning with V_7—I, progressing without interruption through $V_7/{}^{\flat}$II to the cadence on tonic. Since each Mm_7 chord resolves to its "tonic," regular voice leading is maintained.

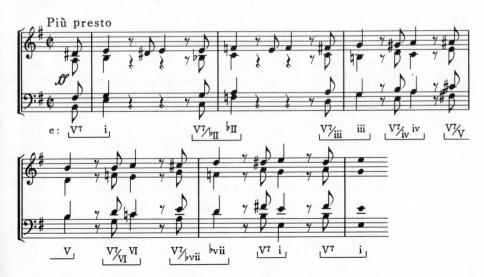

Passages such as these may or may not be modulatory in effect, but they do unsettle the tonality to a degree, thus allowing the option of returning to the original key or proceeding to a new one. The powerful unity of the sequential pattern sets up a propulsive force that continues to an appropriate cadence, either in the original or in a new key.

In Ex. 23-24, the composer doggedly maintains a pattern of sequences so that harmonies quite foreign to the basic key are introduced. It seems illogical to regard this as a series of fleeting modulations, particularly at the indicated tempo. In this instance the simple root relations are still apparent, but the so-called "functional" relationships are not so clear.

Ex. 23-24. Chopin: Mazurka in A-flat Major, Op. 59, No. 2.

From Ex. 23-24 we may generalize that to establish sequences of secondary dominants in which each "tonic" successively becomes a "dominant" of the next chord will weaken tonal stability. This is especially true if the sequential pattern is maintained so long that an overabundance of non-diatonic chords is introduced. This very factor made the harmonic sequence a popular modulatory device, for example, in the Classical period. A pattern of chord motion could be established and maintained until the original tonality had been obscured. Then, upon arrival at the desired new tonal region, a cadence pattern would establish the new tonality.

In Ex. 23-25 a modulation from C to a takes place. The original key is clearly established (mm. 1–4) and an imitative pattern begun which continues past measure 8 (where the key of C is reaffirmed) to measure 14 where it becomes part of a sequence of consecutive secondary dominant sevenths (exception, V in m. 15). This sequence is maintained to measure 18 where the pattern is interrupted in preparation for the cadence on the dominant of a. From measure 8 the key is a minor. However, the presence of the chain of secondary dominants creates an ambiguity that is unresolved until the arrival at the cadence on the dominant. Test this fact by substituting the optional cadence (No. 2) prepared by the authors to effect a return to C major.

Ex. 23-25. Beethoven: Quartet in A Major, Op. 18, No. 5, IV.

Although the secondary dominant concept generally provides a satisfactory explanation of the function of many non-diatonic Mm seventh chords, this is not always true. Consider Ex. 23-26, which contains a progression of tertian chords (predominantly Mm seventh chords) and consider the possible validity of the attendant analysis.

Ex. 23-26. Chopin: Nocturne in F Minor, Op. 55, No. 1.

True, there are some familiar root relationships as indicated by the symbols (V_7/V—V_7) and (V_7/ ♯ III—V_7/ ♯ VI); also, there are third relations (V_2^4/II—V_7/III) and (V_7/vi—i₆), as well as a tritone relation (V_7/VII—V_7/ ♯ III). As logical as such analysis may appear on paper, the question arises as to the information imparted by such an assortment of symbols, as they pertain to the unfolding of the harmonic materials. The rigid application of the secondary dominant classification to any and all Mm seventh chords can sometimes lead to naught, and the resultant symbolic representation may contribute little or even impede the understanding of the musical relationships involved. Generally speaking, the application of this concept should be limited to those relationships in which the chord of resolution is a recognized member of the diatonic family, or one clearly related.

The major-minor seventh chord, once used frequently as a secondary dominant, has fallen into disuse. Contemporary composers usually avoid it entirely, or treat it in ways different from those of previous composers. Its sound, as an isolated chord, is too reminiscent of major-minor music, and its implication of a simple tonal resolution is too compelling to enable it to fit into the more chromatic textures that have prevailed in music since the turn of the century.

Exercises

For more detailed assignments see *Materials and Structure of Music I, Workbook*, Chapter 23.

1. Spell the indicated chords from the bass up:
   a. V_3^4/vi, *A*   d. V_5^6/VI, *b-flat*
   b. V_2^4/iii, *E*   e. V_7/III, *d*
   c. V_5^6/♭VII, *c.*   f. V_2^4/vi, *D-flat*

2. Consider various pitches as root, third, fifth or seventh of dominant of submediant chords. Spell and sing the chord from the bass up, indicate the key and function and the chord of resolution. Do the same for the dominant of mediant.

3. Using the following harmonic progressions as models, create two different settings of each, one for piano, the other SATB. Use different harmonic rhythms, textures and keys for the two settings.

   a. I ii_6 V V^6_5/vi vi V^4_2/iii iii_6 V^6_5/IV ii V

   b. i V^4_3/VI VI iv_6 V^6_5/VII VII III_6 V^4_3/III III i^6_4 V_7 i

4. Invent phrases to follow those of Ex. 23-19, maintaining the same general texture. Employ at least one secondary dominant (other than V^6_5/V or V^6_5/vi) and cadence on tonic. Arrange the whole for woodwind quintet.

5. Analyze a number of the following, indicating keys, chords and non-chord tones.

Haydn:	*Symphony No. 85* (La Reine), II. (1–8)
Beethoven:	*Symphony No. 1*, Op. 21, I. (1–21)
Brahms:	*Variations on a Theme by Haydn*, Op. 56a (1–10)
Schubert:	*Der Erlkönig* (87–96)
Schumann:	*Symphony No. 2*, Adagio (1–9)
Chopin:	*Mazurka* Op. 67, No. 2 (1–16)
Liszt:	*Les Preludes* (70–80)

6. Practice resolving various forms of the secondary dominants of mediant and submediant at the keyboard. Establish a key and introduce and resolve the embellishing harmony in a smooth fashion.

7. Assuming that each of the following secondary dominants is to be resolved deceptively, spell the chord of resolution of each from the bass up.

   a. V^6_5/V, *E-flat*   b. V^6_5/iv, *b*   c. V^4_2/III, *c*

   d. V^4_3/vi, *D*   e. V_7/V, *e*   f. V^4_3/IV, *B*

8. Construct short progressions using different forms of the dominants of dominant, supertonic, mediant and submediant, and resolve them deceptively and irregularly (up a third, down a third, and down a second).

9. Write an instrumental and choral setting of each of the following progressions. Use different textures and harmonic rhythms for each.

   a. I vi_6 V_7/V iii vi_6 V^6_5/ii V^6_4 V_7/V V

   b. i V_6 V^4_3/VI iv_6 ii°_6 V V_7 VI V^4_3/III V V_7 i

10. Using a three-part texture similar to that in measures 4–12 of Ex. 23-25, develop an example employing imitation of short motives, using secondary dominants in deceptive progressions or in other types of irregular resolutions. Arrange for oboe, clarinet and bassoon.

11. Using the sequence pattern $(\text{V}^6_5/\text{ii}—\text{ii})$ $(\text{V}^6_5/\text{V}—\text{V})$ $(\text{V}^6_5—\text{I})$ $(\text{V}/\text{IV}^6_5—\text{IV})$ construct a phrase in which motivic treatment is a characteristic feature.

12. Analyze a number of the following indicating keys, chords and non-chord tones.

Beethoven:	*String Quartet*, Op. 18, No. 3, III (63–74)
	String Quartet, Op. 59, No. 1, IV (1–18)
	String Quartet, Op. 59, No. 2, IV (179–209)
Schubert:	*String Quintet in C major*, Op. 163, III (11–17)
Mendelssohn:	*Nocturne* (Midsummer Nights Dream) (91–100)
Chopin:	*Mazurka*, Op. 56, No. 2 (33–44)
	Mazurka, Op. 59, No. 1 (38–42)
Wagner:	*Lohengrin*, Prelude, Act III (1–16)
Verdi:	*Requiem*, Requiem and Kyrie (8–11)

24

TONALITY CHANGE

In this chapter we shall consider an important aspect of pitch organization, the change of key or tonality. Key change constitutes one of the most essential means for creating variety in tonal music, past and present. As such, it represents a primary agent of form delineation and tonal design.

Tonality change may be accomplished in a smooth, almost imperceptible way, concealing the actual point of change of tonic, or it may result from an abrupt and decisive shift from one to another key. In this book the former process is described as *modulation,* and the latter as *tonal shift.*

A key change may or may not be indicated by a new key signature,[1] but it may be recognized in notation by the appearance of "new" accidentals which,in a real sense "signal" the change of tonality. A change from *c* minor to *A-flat* major occurs in the next example.

Ex. 24-1. Schubert: *Erstarrung.*

---

[1] Changes of key within short sections are seldom indicated by a new signature.

The principal key of the song is *c* minor, and the change of key that occurs is a modulation to the *submediant* of *c*, *A-flat*. Schubert might have changed the key signature at measure 5; that he did not emphasizes the subsidiary relationship of *A-flat*, the new key, to *c* minor. The note *d-flat* occurs as an accidental, and *b-flats* replace the *b'-naturals* which were the leading tones in the original key of *c*.

Relationships of Keys

Subsequently, we shall deal in detail with many of the processes associated with key change. For the present we shall concentrate on developing a general picture of some of the most common key relations that have been used to create variety in tonal music.

The most frequent key relation is that of near-related keys. Near-related keys are those whose signatures differ by no more than one sharp or flat. For example, the key change in Ex. 24-1 occurs between near-related tonalities, since *c* minor and *A-flat* major are one flat removed. That is, the signature of *c* minor contains three flats, while *A-flat* major contains four.

Modulations from an initial key to the key of the dominant constitute the most common type of near-related key change. This seems logical and consistent when we consider the strong relationship between tonic and dominant tones.

Near relationship exists between major tonic and major dominant keys, and minor tonic and minor dominant keys. It does not exist between a minor tonic and a major dominant *key*, because of the lack of common pitches shared by the two keys. The foregoing discussion can be clarified by a study of Ex. 24-2.

Ex. 24-2. Tonic and dominant keys.

Near-related		*Near-related*	
C major	G major (♯)	c minor (♭♭♭)	g minor (♭♭)

Distant relationship	
c minor (♭♭♭)	G major (♯)

Applying the criteria described above to any major key, we can see several possibilities for creating near related modulations from an initial key. Using *C* major as a point of reference, modulations to *G* and *F* major and *a*, *d*, or *e* minor would represent changes to near-related keys. The tonic chord of each of the new keys is a diatonic chord of the key of *C*.

The same procedure can be applied to modulations from a minor key. Considering *c* minor as a key of reference, *E-flat* major, *g* minor, *A-flat* major, *f* minor and *B-flat* major are near-related keys. It is important to notice that the keys which form near relationships to an initial key are not always near-related to each other. For example, *d* minor and *e* minor are near related to *C* major, but not to one another.

Near related does not imply close intervallic distance; it merely denotes a relationship of keys, a relationship that results from common tones shared by different keys.

Several illustrations of near-related key changes follow. Play through Ex. 24-3 and study the changes of key therein.

Ex. 24-3. Frauenholz: *Der Herr gedenkt an uns,* for Voices, Strings, and Organ.

Ex. 24-4. Chopin: Mazurka in B-flat.

Ex. 24-5. Beethoven: Sonata for Piano, Op. 110, II.

Ex. 24-6. Beethoven: Mass in C Major.

Ex. 24-6 continued.

Ex. 24-7. Bach: Three-voice Invention in G Minor.

Ex. 24-8. Handel: Concerto Grosso, Op. 6.

This group of excerpts, which constitutes a variety of textures and styles, contains the following keys and key relations:

Example	Keys Established	Relationships
24-3	*D* major—*A* major	Modulation to the dominant
24-4	*B-flat* major—*F* major	Modulation to the dominant
24-5	*A-flat* major—*f* minor	Modulation to the submediant
24-6	*C* major—*a* minor	Modulation to the submediant
24-7	*B-flat* major—*d* minor	Modulation to the mediant
24-8	*g* minor—*c* minor	Modulation to the subdominant

Less Common Key Relations

Composers have by no means limited their choices of keys to near relations, since virtually any combination or sequence of keys may be found. Compositions written after the eighteenth century sometimes use relationships which bring into play many or all of the members of the chromatic scale. Consistent with the use of more distant key relations is the lessening of key stability and reduction of key duration. Sudden *shifts* of key, in contrast to the more gradual process of modulation, create an aura of tonal uncertainty that both broadens the tonal perspective and weakens the listener's feeling of principal tonic.

Third relationship describes a more distant key change involving two keys whose scales contain one or no common tones and whose tonic chords are a major or minor third apart. For example, *C* major and *E* major form a third relationship.

Their tonic chords possess one common tone, *e*, and a change from *C* to *E* (or *E* to *C*) is often described as a *third related* key change. The change to a third related key usually occurs as a sudden shift, rather than as a gradual change.

In Ex. 24-9 a third relation is introduced between *D* major and *F* major. Beethoven has employed the pitch *a* as a common link between the tonic chords of the two keys.

Ex. 24-9. Beethoven: Symphony No. 8, III.

Major and minor keys a half-step apart constitute the key relation in Ex. 24-10 in which a new key is introduced on the leading tone of the original key.

Ex. 24-10. Wolf: *Spanish Songbook*, 1, No. 4.

Since the system of "keys" is most prevalent in music written between the seventeenth and the beginning of the twentieth centuries (music with which we are most familiar), it is natural that we begin the study of tonality changes with this music. However, to form a more comprehensive picture of tonality change, we might examine some music in which modality prevails.

Two phrases from a composition by Landini, a fourteenth-century composer, are shown in Ex. 24-11.

Ex. 24-11. Landini: Two-voice Ballata.

The first phrase and the initial three measures of the second establish the mode of *g* Dorian (*f-sharp* occurs as a cadential leading tone alteration). The second phrase (the final phrase of the piece) asserts the principal tonal center of the work, *d.* The mode of the close of the composition is *d* Dorian, with a *c-sharp* introduced to create a leading tone in the 7—8 cadence pattern. The change of tonic is not felt until the final measure, and therefore is not so strong as it would have been if *d* had had more preparation. However, as the *last pitch heard*, *d* can hardly be discounted as a point of focus, and a definite change of tonic from *g* to *d* is perceived.

We are reminded, by glancing at Ex. 24-11 and Ex. 24-12, that alterations are common to compositions employing modal bases, just as they are to pieces written in major or minor keys. The designation of a specific mode is made on the basis of the most consistently recurring pitch material. Unlike most works in major or minor keys, many modal compositions begin and close on different tonics. In such examples, the closing tonic is usually considered to be the principal tonality of the work. The prevailing pitch material of Ex. 24-12 forms a natural minor (Aeolian) mode on *a*.

Ex. 24-12. Palestrina: *Adjuro vos filiae Jerusalem,* Motet.

In Ex. 24-12 tonal variety is created by a series of shifts from *a* to *C*, and the tonal plan of the example can be understood by singing the second bass part, measures 1–10. An analysis of the other parts will reveal that the notes *a* and *c* serve as terminal points for the various successive imitative entries which continuously overlap. At no point until the close of the excerpt can all five voices be found in cadential agreement, and the subtle shifts of tonality are not affirmed by strong cadences. The cadences are weak because they occur only in rhythmically staggered locations, rather than simultaneously in all the voices. The subtlety of tonal shifts in the excerpt must be related to the texture of the composition, which is quite contrapuntal, since strong tonality-defining cadences are avoided in favor of continuous motion in each part.

Our perception of *a* and *c* as zones of tonal focus in this passage is dependent upon three factors: (1) pitch repetition, (2) cadential leading tone patterns (i.e., *g-sharp*—*a* and *b*—*c*) and (3) V—I or vii₆—I chord progressions at cadences. *C* is not a strongly defined tonality, but as a study of the root relations (accompanying the example) will show, any description of its tonal organization would be incomplete without some mention of *c* as a subsidiary region. It is heard in a transitory relationship to *a*, but its duration as a tonic is such that it should be viewed as part of a continuously unfolding tonal pattern comprised of *a—c—a*, which creates unity and variety within the principal tonality of *a*. Vacillation between tonal areas is a significant aspect of much music.

The principal tonic (*a*) of the Palestrina Motet just discussed is the same as that of the passage in Ex. 24-13. Despite the similarity of tonic and prevailing minor mode, the two examples present a striking contrast of tonal material and organization. But since both examples illustrate shifting regions of tonal polarity, they are more alike in basic tonal design than they might appear to be.

Ex. 24-13. Wagner: *Tristan und Isolde,* Prelude, Act I.

In the concluding chapters of volume two of this book we shall deal extensively with some of the materials of more recent music. As we shall see, changes of tonality are as significant in the structure of some contemporary works as in music of past periods. Much twentieth-century music has a strong affinity for tonal relationships that are typical of earlier music. In Ex. 24-14 tonic and dominant relations constitute the principal means of delineating the tonality of the opening phrases.

Ex. 24-14. Hindemith: *Ludus Tonalis,* Interludium in E-flat (The March). (C) 1943 by Schott & Co., Ltd., London. Reprinted by permission.

Ex. 24-14 continued.

Modulation

As we have seen, key change is a common ingredient in all but the shortest compositions. Our objective in this unit is to study *how*, aside from melodic procedures, the change of key is accomplished. This involves more than observation of musical results; we must delve into the musical techniques used to modulate.

Modulation by Pivot Chord

One of the most frequent modulation procedures establishes the relationship between the two keys by means of a specific chord that they possess in common. The agent of modulation, then, is a chord that can be interpreted in both the old key and the new key. This process capitalizes on the potential ambiguity of chords, i.e., the fact that a single chord can possess a logical identity in more than one key.

Ex. 24-15 illustrates concisely the pivot chord modulation technique, in this case involving two distantly related keys, which is not uncommon in nineteenth century music.

Ex. 24-15. Schubert: *Die Winterreise,* Muth.

By measure 9 of this excerpt the change of key has taken place; *a* minor has been replaced by *E* major. From measure 8 the tonality is clearly *E* major; therefore, we must look immediately before this location to see the actual point of shift. The major triad on *E* in measure 7 is clearly V in *a* minor, *if we were to look no further*. In retrospect, however, we see that it can also be interpreted as I in *E* major. This triad is thus the pivot chord between these two keys; it is analyzed as shown on the example.

We can perceive this type of modulation only by looking back from the point at which the new key has been irrevocably established. Since any chord is capable of a number of interpretations in any number of keys, we would remain in a constant state of confusion if we were always conjuring up the many possibilities of each chord we hear. Fortunately, although we do make guesses as to the possible outcome of a musical situation, we guess only on the basis of the evidence at hand —in other words, we interpret each chord only in the light of the current key, *until this key clearly has been abandoned.*

Once this change has taken place, however, it is possible to identify the dual role of the pivot chord. Each modulation generally contains a signal or simple "clue" that the old key is no longer in effect. This is usually an accidental foreign to the old key but diatonic to the new key (often a new leading tone). Occasionally, though, the change of key occurs without additional accidentals, in which case other factors must be considered. Once this "clue" has been spotted, the pivot chord is easy to locate; it is usually the previous chord.

In Ex. 24-16 no accidental signals the advent of the new key. Instead, the Mm$_7$ chord in measure 6 (not a diatonic member of *b* minor but, as it turns out, clearly V$_7$ in *D* major) first indicates that *b* minor is no longer the prevailing key. The pivot chord is thus the previous chord—i in *b* minor becomes vi in *D* major.

Ex. 24-16. Haydn: Quartet, Op. 64, No. 2, Menuetto.

Any chord—diatonic or chromatic—can act as a pivot chord, and a situation may result in which a chromatic chord in the old key becomes a diatonic chord in the new key or vice versa. The V_6/ii chord in D major, for instance, can function as V_6 in E minor or major. Usually, however, the pivot chord is diatonic to both keys. The diatonic pivot chord possibilities are easily determined by pairing off the appropriate chords in the two keys involved, as in Ex. 24-17. If, as in this case, the modulation is to the dominant major key, the V will pair with I, vi with ii, and so forth.

Ex. 24-17. Modulation by pivot chord.

D Major:	I	ii	iii	IV	V	vi	vii°
A Major:	IV	V	vi	vii°	I	ii	iii

We can rule out several of these chord pairs: ii (a minor triad) will not serve as the chord equivalent of V (although V/V will); IV and vii° are likewise incompatible, as are vii° and iii. Four pairs remain: I and IV, iii and vi, V and I, vi and ii—all equally possible. It is obvious that the primary criterion is identity of chord quality.

Different pairs of keys display widely differing pivot chord potentials. In certain key relationships, as illustrated in Ex. 24-18, the possibilities are more limited than in Ex. 24-17.

Ex. 24-18. Relationships of pivot chords.

This process of common chord modulation does not require a harmonic texture of block chords. Ex. 24-19 is clear in its modulatory implications: *F* major is confirmed (although briefly) in measure 7; I becomes IV in the previous measure.

Ex. 24-19. Beethoven: Trio, Op. 97 ("Archduke"), Scherzo.

Ex. 24-20 contains a clear pivot chord modulation between two keys that are not near-related. The process is not more complex, though. The pivot chord occurs immediately before the first departure from *C* major—IV in *C* becomes V in *B-flat* major in measure 17.

Ex. 24-20. Schubert: Symphony in C Major, Scherzo.

Ex. 24-20 continued.

Pivot Tone Modulation

In some modulations the sole common link between the two keys is a single *tone*. Ex. 24-21 contains a pivot tone modulation between the keys of *F* major and *D-flat* major; the sustained tone *F* (introduced in m. 5) acts as a link between the two keys. Note that the harmonic motion is from the tonic of the original key to the tonic of the new key. Pivot tone modulation became more frequent in the nineteenth century than formerly, often as a link between distant related keys.

Ex. 24-21. Beethoven: Trio, Op. 1, No. 3, Finale.

This principle is equally apparent in Ex. 24-22. The pivot tone here is the reiterated *G* in the viola part; its role changes from that of tonic in *g* minor (in m. 8) to that of mediant in *E-flat* major. Here the change is better described as a tonal shift than as modulation because of its abruptness.

Ex. 24-22. Shostakovitch: Quartet, Op. 49, I. (C) Used by permission of MCA Music, a division of MCA Inc., New York, N.Y. All rights reserved.

Modulation by Chromatic Inflection

In another common process the relationship between two keys is established by melodic inflection—a voice that moves (or voices that move) up or down a minor second, leading smoothly to a diatonic pitch in the new key. In this relationship, of course, there are no diatonic elements in common between the two keys. Therefore the connection is through the stepwise melodic action of one of the lines.

Ex. 24-23 contains a modulation by chromatic inflection in the fourth and fifth measures.

Ex. 24-23. Mendelssohn: Symphony No. 3 (*Scotch*), I.

The Mm_7 chord on F in measure 4 no more suggests G major than does the same chord type on D suggest the F major of the preceding section. The agents of modulation are the bass line, moving chromatically from tonic of the old key to the leading tone of the new key, and the movement from tonic F through *E-flat* to D, the fifth of the new key.

An extension of this technique may be seen in Ex. 24-24, in which the two tonics (F and C) are connected by the chord in measure 126. Although this *d-flat* minor triad is foreign to both keys, its use as a connecting link is obvious and relates it to the technique described above.

Ex. 24-24. Bartók: Concerto for violin, No. 2, I. Copyright 1938 by Hawkes & Son (London) Ltd.; Reprinted by permission of Boosey & Hawkes Inc.

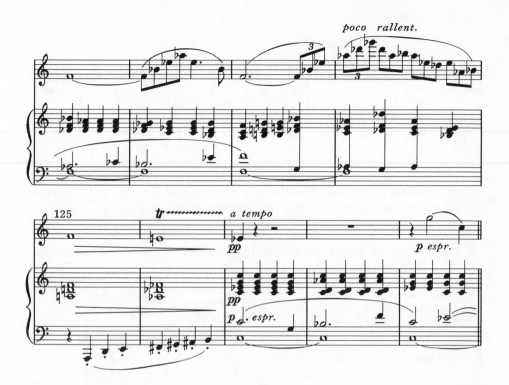

Modulations by chromatic inflection frequently involve the dominant as at least one of the chords. Composers often have modulated to the supertonic or submediant keys by this procedure. For example, the raised tonic pitch of a key becomes the leading tone of ii; the raised dominant becomes the leading tone of vi.

Ex. 24-25 contains a further example of this type of modulation, in this case involving a chord that is not diatonic to either old or new key. The upward chromatic inflection in the bass at measure 6 leads our attention from i in f minor to V_5^6/V in c minor.

Ex. 24-25. Purcell: *Dido and Aeneas,* Prelude, Act I, Scene 2.

Ex. 24-25 continued.

c

Descending chromatic inflection establishes the modulation in Ex. 24-26, again in the bass line, in measures 2 and 3. It is interesting to note that the two tonics in this excerpt lie a tritone apart, *A—E-flat*; they are distant relations.

Ex. 24-26. Hindemith: Sonata for Organ, I. (C) 1937 by B. Schott's Soehne, Mainz. Reprinted by permission.

Enharmonic Modulation

Composers occasionally have found it necessary to relate the two keys of a modulation through enharmonic spelling. This does not necessarily imply a remote modulation, however, since the enharmonic spelling is often used merely for the performer's convenience. The keys *F-sharp* major and *D-flat* major seem distantly related at first glance, but they are in fact no more distant than *C* major and *G* major. It is as natural, when in *F-sharp* major, to modulate to the dominant as when in *C* major, and most people would find *D-flat* major easier to read than *C-sharp* major, because of the notational complications of the latter.

The modulation in Ex. 24-27 is not between keys as closely related as *F-sharp* and *D-flat*, but it does demonstrate that convenience of spelling can take precedence over a more notationally consistent indication of key relationships. Measures 5 and 6 of this excerpt are actually notated in *F-flat* major, although the accompaniment appears in the enharmonic key of *E* major. The pivot chord is also unusually interesting, for it is not diatonic. In the last half of measure 4, V in *A-flat* major becomes V/iii in *F-flat* major and resolves deceptively to the tonic of this new key. However, a more musical interpretation of this modulatory relationship would recognize the common pitch bond between the two keys; *A-flat* (tonic) of the initial key becomes mediant of the new key.

Ex. 24-27. Schumann: *Frauenlieben und Leben,* "Helft mir, ihr Schwestern."

Chordal texture is absent from the enharmonic modulation in Ex. 24-28 from *e-flat* minor to *b* minor; the change of key is brought about solely by the change in function of the pivot tone: *G-flat/F-sharp* (3 in *e-flat* minor—5 in *b* minor). Schubert has cleverly expedited the modulation by the running chromatic scale in the piano, effectively blurring the recollection of the previous key.

Ex. 24-28. Schubert: Trio in E-flat Major, Op. 100, I.

Abrupt Tonality Changes

Disguising a change of tonic through a subtle relating of two keys has not always been the composer's goal. A sudden shift of key can produce a stunning effect, one that many composers have obviously considered desirable at times. We will not dwell on the manifold effects of this procedure except to note that this lays bare the relationship between the two keys, emphasizing their contrast, particularly when they are not near-related.

Measure 11 of Ex. 24-29 contains a cadence on V of *c* minor, but measure 12 begins with the tonic triad in *E-flat* major. Despite the cross-relation created by this succession of chords (*B/B-flat*), the effect is only mildly abrupt. We are well able to accommodate seemingly unrelated juxtaposed sounds as long as each possesses a logical and well-defined tonal identity in a clearly-established tonal system. There is no appreciable abruptness about this key change because the two are near-related.

Ex. 24-29. Haydn: Quartet, Op. 64, No. 6, I.

Ex. 24-30 and Ex. 24-31 contain shifts of tonal center that are not only abrupt but, at times, of distant relations. In the Beethoven, for example, the rapid tempo contributes to the effect of merely sliding the tonic down a minor second—from *f-sharp* minor to *F* major. The succession of keys in the Brahms excerpt is no less unusual.

Ex. 24-30. Beethoven: Symphony No. 8, Finale.

Ex. 24-31. Brahms: Symphony No. 4, III.

Although its harmonic style is less accessible than in the previous examples, Ex. 24-32 contains a similar abrupt shift of tonal center from *C* in measure 3 to *E-flat* in the next measure. The two sections are related thematically through the sequence of perfect fourths in the bass, the first note of which forms a step-progression of *g—f—e-flat*. But there is an unmistakable change of tonal center after the double bar.

Ex. 24-32. Stravinsky: *Symphony of Psalms,* III. Copyright 1941 by Russischer Musikverlag; Renewed 1958. Copyright & Renewal assigned to Boosey & Hawkes Inc. Revised version Copyright 1948 by Boosey & Hawkes Inc. Reprinted by permission.

Ex. 24-33 contains a succession of tonal regions too brief to classify as full-fledged modulations, since none is established by a cadence and subsequently confirmed. In their succession, however, the sequence of tonal areas on *C*, *E*, *G*, *B*, and again *C* is organized by the chromatically ascending bass line. Each region serves as a momentary point of focus in an unstable, constantly shifting tonal context.

Ex. 24-33. Schumann: Symphony No. 2, Adagio.

Ex. 24-34 represents the ultimate in abrupt tonal shifts. The regions in this excerpt, *E-flat*, *D-flat*, and *C* majors, succeed one another through the successive descents of the major triads that act as their tonics.

Ex. 24-34. Beethoven: Symphony No. 3 (*Eroica*), I.

Harmonic sequences are often involved in the process of modulation. As in Ex. 24-35 the sequence can be a stabilizing factor, the repeated pattern sustaining the ear through a series of distantly related tonal regions.

Ex. 24-35. Wagner: *Die Walküre*, Act I.

Ex. 24-35 continued.

Mutation

We recall that modulation requires an actual change of tonal center. The process of *mutation*—a change in *mode*—retains the same tonic pitch and should not be confused with modulation. Although many aspects of one key are changed through mutation (e.g., the quality of most of the diatonic triads, the roots of several diatonic chords—notably mediant and submediant), the most important factor, the tonic pitch, remains unchanged. Mutation's primary effect is a change in the "color" of the key from predominantly major to minor, or vice versa. Such a passage occurs in Ex. 24-36.

Ex. 24-36. Brahms: Intermezzo, Op. 118, No. 2.

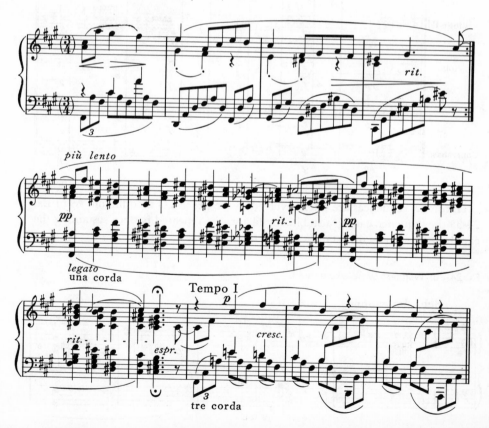

Although not in itself modulatory, mutation often serves as an easy vehicle for modulating to more remote keys. The following diagram demonstrates that, when the tonic triad is altered through mutation, a variety of new near-related keys are made readily available.

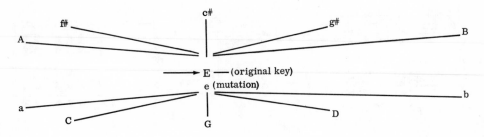

In Ex. 24-37 Schubert twice uses this technique to accomplish relatively remote modulations: *A* modulating to *F* major through *a* minor, and later *F* modulating to *D-flat* major through *f* minor. In each case the second form of the chord undergoing the mutation is the pivot chord, i in the old key becoming iii in the new.

Ex. 24-37. Schubert: *Sehnsucht.*

Ex. 24-37 continued.

F: I   { fm
                        { Db: iii   Db

Exercises

For more detailed assignments see *Materials and Structure of Music I, Workbook,* Chapter 24.

1. Explore the diatonic pivot chord possibilities of the following pairs of keys:
   a. *E-flat* major and its supertonic
   b. *A* major and its mediant minor
   c. *F* minor and its subdominant minor
   d. *F-sharp* minor and its submediant major

2. What are some possible pivot tones between the following pairs of keys? Write a melody containing such a modulation.
   a. *C-sharp* minor and *C* major
   b. *A-flat* major and *D* major
   c. *E* major and *A-flat* major

3. Using roman numerals plot a modulation from a major key to a near-related key. Improvise at the keyboard, or vocally, a melody that fits this harmonic pattern. Such a melody could be a simple arpeggiated version of the chords, or a more complex line.

4. Choose a simple melody and effect a modulation 1 to 2 measures long that leads to a restatement of the same melody a major third higher (or lower).

5. Using the following harmonic scheme, construct a number of 3- or 4-part textures and arrange the best for some instrumental combination.

   F: I V_2^4/IV   IV$_6$ V_7/vi $\binom{\text{vi}}{\text{a:}\ \text{iv}}$ ii$_6^\circ$ V_7 VI   i$_4^6$ V   III

6. Find other examples illustrating the various types of tonality changes illustrated in this chapter.

25

BINARY FORM

A two-part or *binary* formal plan is one of the most significant structural designs in music history. From the early days of monophonic music until recent times, one can find compositions demonstrating this two-section pattern of tonal organization. Medieval composers of instrumental dances favored a grouping of such dances in pairs: pavane-galliard, passamezzo-saltarello, and others. One must conclude that a convincing and satisfying psychological basis must exist to account for the popularity of the binary principle over such a great span of time.

Bernart de Ventadorn's graceful "Be m'an perdut," a masterpiece of the twelfth-century Troubador genre, is organized in an important early manifestation of the binary design: the Bar form (a a b). The song clearly divides into two sections at the end of measure 10; within the first section we find two almost identical statements. Typical of the binary principle is the absence of strong contrasts; virtually all binary compositions display this thrifty use of the musical materials.

Ex. 25-1. Ventadorn: *Be m'an perdut.*

Ex. 25-1 continued.

morn:— car en s'a - mor me de - leih em — so - jorn! _____ Ni

de —— ren ats nos ran - cu - ra ___ nis cla - ma.

This principle of two-part organization is often found as the basis for *sections* of compositions as well as for entire pieces. The themes of variation movements, for example, often display the binary structure. Example 25-2 shows such a theme. The subsequent variations retain the structure, harmony, and melodic outline of the passage quoted.

In this later version of the binary design *both* sections are designated to be repeated. The second section then represents both a logical "answer to" and a continuation of the first section. We can diagram this pattern as *a a b b*—there are slight but perceptible contrasts between the sections in rhythm, contour, harmonic progression, and texture.

Ex. 25-2. Beethoven: Sonata in F Minor, Op. 57, II.

Andante con moto

Baroque Binary Form

A particular manifestation of the binary principle appears in much music written during the Baroque period. This is the only specific type of binary construction to achieve widespread currency, and then only in the seventeenth and eighteenth centuries.

This formal design is significant not only because it was *the* prevailing small form for over 200 years, but also in that it was the direct precursor of the sonata-allegro form. In these centuries the binary form was widespread, appearing in the separate movements of the dance suite (allemandes, courantes, sarabandes, gigues, bourrees, forlanas, menuets, etc.) as well as in the various movements of the instrumental sonata and the concerto.

Many of our observations on the nature of this form will apply equally to other compositions in two-part structure. It should be understood, however, that these specific descriptions are based upon Baroque binary compositions such as Ex. 25-3.

Two general aspects are almost always present in this type of form: an obvious parallel between the two sections in their use of themes, and an absence of strong contrasts such as those found in the ternary form. A certain basic "sameness" of themes, texture, register, tonality, etc. often characterizes the binary form. This quality is readily apparent to the listener. Both of these attributes are clearly demonstrated in Ex. 25-3, a keyboard sonata by Domenico Scarlatti.

Ex. 25-3. D. Scarlatti: Sonata in B Minor.

Ex. 25-3 continued.

In many respects the above example is quite similar in its organization to Ex. 25-2. Like the earlier example, its bi-partite design is confirmed visually by the double bars at the end of each section; likewise each section is repeated.

The Thematic Design

An understanding of the formal design is facilitated by extracting the important thematic fragments. The fragments (or "motives") shown in Ex. 25-4 are not complete *themes*, but they comprise the significant musical ideas in the first section (mm. 1-47), and they recur in the second section in recognizable form. A comparison of the thematic outlines of these two large sections will make clear the similarities (and differences) between them.

Ex. 25-4. Significant thematic fragments from Scarlatti: Sonata in B Minor.

The thematic outlines of each section are very similar. Fragment (a) occurs in much the same form at the beginning of each part (mm. 1 and 48). Similarly, fragment (d) is the thematic basis for the last part of each section (mm. 35 and 75). The principal difference between the two halves of the form is the order of appearance of fragments (b) and (c); they are reversed in the second section. Compare measures 7 and 67 and also measures 29 and 62.

From this analysis we can conclude that the two sections of this binary movement are quite similar—almost parallel in many cases. The interchange of position of the two middle motives in this example is not typical of the form, although other examples of the same arrangement do exist. Our analysis has not accounted for every melodic fragment, but it has been thorough enough to disclose the basic thematic similarity of the two sections.

The Tonal Design

Before leaving this example, we must consider the tonal organization, an equally important factor in the complete analysis. We can chart the tonal progress of the composition as follows:

Section #1   Section #2

Tonic to contrasting key   Contrasting or   } returning to tonic
                              indeterminate key

It is apparent that the key scheme of the two sections does not duplicate the same neat parallelism of the thematic design. Section 1 begins in the key of *b* minor, changes to *D* major in measures 25 and 26, and remains in that key until the double bar. The tonality at the beginning of section 2, however, is not clearly defined (*G* major and *D* major are both possibilities), but it becomes stabilized in *b* minor, arriving there in measure 55, and it remains there until the end of the sonata. The tonal direction of the second section is reversed, in a sense.

The apparent tonal indecision or instability at the beginning of the second section is present in the majority of binary movements. In many cases it is not possible to rule out all but one key at this point. In the analysis of compositions showing this characteristic tonal ambiguity it is sufficient to point out the general key area.

The relationship between keys is somewhat different when the composition begins in a major key. In that event the contrasting key is almost always the dominant (for example *D* major to *A* major). The minor key to relative major key progression of the Scarlatti is the rule, however, when the basic key of the composition is minor.

Other Formal Considerations

The above elements hardly exhaust the list of possible factors which contribute to the perception of form in this or any other composition. Considerations such as changes of texture, register, cadences, phrase structure, phrase extensions, contrapuntal factors, sequences, melodic contour, harmonic implications, and many others affect our mental image of the structure of a piece of music. These may not all be of equal importance in any given composition, but all of them— along with countless other factors not mentioned—contribute in some degree to the total experience of musical form.

Among the other significant form-producing factors in Ex. 25-3 is texture. A change of texture is often the signal that a new formal or thematic unit has begun, and this occurs in measures 29 and 62. The addition of the octave in the right hand against the continuous sixteenth notes in the left hand marks an important change from the previous texture and attracts attention in both of these locations. Aside from this one change, however, the remainder of the composition does not use this method of delineating formal sections.

Cadences play an important role in defining the breaks between sections. An obvious example occurs in measure 34 and again in measure 75, each bringing the previous material to a terminal cadence. These mark the points of arrival for the keys in which each of these sections concludes.

An element that is not readily apparent often serves as a unifying formal device. Such is the case in measures 1–10 where the left hand part is an *ostinato*, repeating the same two-measure fragment again and again. Similar figures appear in at least two other locations in each section, particularly near the final cadence. Notice also the use of augmentation in measures 7 and 8; both hands play the same melodic fragment but in differing note values. Suggestions for further analysis of this composition will be given at the end of this chapter.

Binary and Ternary Forms Contrasted

The characteristic features of these two prominent formal types are summarized below. Where the external evidence is not clear, enough of these distinctions should be present to enable one to place the composition in the appropriate category.

BINARY	*TERNARY*
1. In two sections, each set off by double bars and repeat signs.	1. In three sections, the third of which is a literal repeat of or is similar to the first.
2. Each of the two sections ends in a different key from that in which it begins.	2. Each of the three sections usually ends in the same key in which it begins.
3. There is little thematic contrast between the two sections.	3. There is considerable thematic contrast between the first two sections.
4. In the conventional binary, the opening thematic material does not recur in the tonic key.	4. The opening thematic material invariably returns in the tonic key—at the beginning of the final (A) section.

Rounded Binary

A basic element of almost all musical forms is the return or restatement of opening material near the close of a composition. This element, prominent in the ternary design, is absent (except in terms of key return) from the binary form as described above. In the Scarlatti sonata, the opening theme does not return intact in the tonic key. The only reprise of this opening pattern appears at the *beginning* of the second section.

After the Baroque era some composers began to display in their binary compositions traces of a partial or even complete restatement of the opening thematic material near the end of the movement. Ex. 25-5 demonstrates how a movement that is basically binary integrates this principle of a *recapitulation*.

Ex. 25-5. Haydn: Quartet in C Major, Op. 76, No. 3, III (Trio).

Ex. 25-5 continued.

The first three of the four criteria suggested above apply to this composition. Significant alterations have been made, however. The two sections are not approximately the same length as in the Scarlatti sonata; the second section here is more than four times the length of the first. We also find a restatement of the opening material in measures 93–100, where the mutation of the parallel major key returns to minor. In contrast to measures 56–64, these measures are not modulatory but remain solidly in *a* minor. Another example of tonal instability occurs following the double bar at measure 64. This additional factor contributes to the recognition of the binary structure. The rounded binary form, of which this composition is a typical example, must be viewed as a hybrid form. Although it reveals traces of the ternary form, notably in the restatement it contains, it belongs clearly to the binary category.

Song Form and Trio

Ex. 25-5 is the middle part, or "trio," of the third movement of Haydn's "Emperor" Quartet, a movement that illustrates clearly the song form and trio principle. This formal arrangement was used frequently by composers of the Classical period as one of the middle movements in large works such as the symphony, string quartet, sonata, and concerto, and it was cast in the spirit of a dance or at least a movement of a relatively light nature. The *menuet and trio* and the *scherzo and trio* are the most frequent names given to these movements which are moments of relaxation in the midst of the weightier and more serious movements that surround them.

Actually this formal design incorporates two different small compositions (the so-called "trio" is merely a second menuet or scherzo). The trio apparently derives from the Baroque practice of lightening the texture in sections such as this, sometimes even to three voices; hence the name "trio."

Exercises

For more detailed assignments see *Materials and Structure of Music I, Workbook*, Chapter 25.

1. Listen to a recording of Ex. 25-3, noting each formal change and comparing the two large sections. Analyze further for the following details:
   a. Examples of repetition, sequence, imitation, phrase extension, motivic development
   b. Cadence types
   c. Points of contrapuntal interest
   d. Points of contrapuntal sterility
2. Play Example 25-5 from the score at the piano. Analyze for the following points:
   a. In what ways does this example exhibit principles of effective counterpoint?
   b. Analyze for phrase and period construction; analyze and label each cadence by key, roman numerals, and cadence type.
   c. Make a harmonic analysis of measures 76–92.
   d. Discuss the intervallic structure of the theme in measures 1—8 and how this is developed in the remainder of the trio.
   e. Find examples of stretto and of imitation.
3. Follow a recording of Beethoven's String Quartet, Op. 18 No. 5, II. After listening to the full movement at least twice, make a diagram of the form. Try to incorporate the broad details at first, then perfect by noting smaller details. Listen once again and check for accuracy. Then answer the following questions:
   a. Are there contrasts of homophonic and contrapuntal textures? If so, where do they occur?
   b. Are there examples of sequence, melodic inversion, and repetition? Where do they occur?
   c. Where do the main cadences occur and what types are represented?
4. Following exercise 3 above, study a score of the movement, taking note once again of the above points. Then make a harmonic analysis of selected passages.
5. Write a brief composition for piano that is cast in simple binary form. Make each section no longer than sixteen measures, and retain a simple texture of two voices throughout (prominent top line, accompanimental bass voice).

INDEX OF MUSICAL EXCERPTS

A

America, 65
Anonymous: *Angelus ad Virginem*, 208;
    Sumer Is Icumen In, 81
Arlen-Mercer: *Blues in the Night*, 383

B

Bach, C.P.E.: Keyboard Sonata, 136, 190;
    Prussian Sonata, 180
Bach, J.C.: *In dich hab ich gehoffet, Herr*,
    126; Symphony in B-flat Major, II,
    73
Bach, J.S.: *Aria With 30 Variations* (Gold-
    berg Variations), Var. 27 (Canon),
    185; *Art of the Fugue*, 114, Contra-
    punctus IX, 204; B minor Mass,
    "Cum sancto spiritu," 122; Bran-
    denburg Concerto No. 3, I, 67;
    Cantata No. 140 ("Wachet auf"),
    372
    Chorales: *Alle Menschen müssen ster-
    ben*, 223; *Aus meines Herzens
    Grunde*, 349; *Christ lag in Todes-
    banden* (outer voices), 178; *Ermun-
    tre dich, mein schwacher Geist*, 306,
    349; *Herr, ich habe missgehandelt*,
    352; *Vater unser in Hummelreich*,
    204
    Inventions: (*three-voice*) B Minor, 98;
    D Major, 99; E Major, 198; A Ma-
    jor, 210; G Minor, 408; (*two-voice*)
    A Minor, 143; C Minor, 113; D
    Major, 135–36, 152, 173, 174, 187;
    D Minor, 127, 128, 142; E Minor,
    120, 181; F Minor, 137, 167; G Ma-
    jor, 128, 186; G Minor, 153, 161–62
    *Little Notebook of Anna Magdalena
    Bach*: Gigue, 107; Minuet, 133;
    Musical Offering, The, Six-voice
    Ricercar, 299; *Orgelbüchlein*, "Puer
    natus in Bethlehem," 281; Over-
    ture in F Major for Harpsichord,
    Bourrée, 123–24, 158–59; Passaca-
    glia in C Minor, 100
    St. John Passion: "Ruht wohl, ihr
    heiligen Gebeine," 73; "Wäre dieser
    nicht ein Übeltäter?" 111
    Sinfonia in E-flat, 246; Sonata No. 3
    for Flute and Harpsichord, II, 83
    Suites: A Major, Courante, 133; No. 2
    in B Minor, Allemande, 128–29,
    Rondeau, 213; French, No. 2, Men-
    uet, 186, French, No. 3, Menuet,
    277
    Twelve Little Preludes, Prelude No.
    1, 157
    Well-Tempered Clavier (Book I)
    Fugues: A-flat Major, 137; B-flat Ma-
    jor, 30; C Minor, 207, 269; D Mi-
    nor, 179, 211; E Major, 203; E
    Minor, 139; F Major, 98; G Major,
    97, 207; G Minor, 246

Bach, J. S. (*cont.*)
  Preludes: A-flat Major, 137; C Major, 257-58; D Major, 181; E Minor, 101; G Major, 285
  Well-Tempered Clavier (Book II)
  Preludes: A-flat Major, 134; E Major, 202
Barber: *School for Scandal*, Overture, 95, 96
Barret: Keyboard Sonata, 181
Bartók: Concerto for Orchestra, 95, 304; Concerto for Violin, No. 2, I, 422–23; Improvisations, Op. 20, I, 274; Little Pieces for Children, Vol. I, No. 11, 381
  Mikrokosmos: 143; 159–60; (*Vol. IV*) "From the Island of Bali," 88; "Playsong," 73; (Vol. V) "Boating," 71; "Fourths," 104; "Staccato and Legato," 56; No. 139, 356
  Quartets: No. 1, 120; No. 2, I, 366–67
  Violin Duets, No. 11, *Cradle Song*, 46
Beethoven: *Coriolan* Overture, 319; Mass in C Major, 407–408
  Missa Solemnis: 230; Gloria, 256; Kyrie, 300
  Piano Concertos: No. 2, Op. 19, II, 345; No. 3, in C Minor, Op. 37, III, 75, 377; No. 4, Op. 58: I, 303; II, 394; III, 305
  Quartets: F Major, Op. 18, No. 1: I, 102, 228–29; III, 393; G Major, Op. 18, No. 2, 246; IV, 87; C Minor, Op. 18, No. 4, I, 70; F Major, Op. 59, No. 1, I, 239; A Major, Op. 18, No. 5, IV, 401; E Minor, Op. 59, No. 2: I, 280; IV, 339; Septet, Op. 20, Menuetto, I, 323
  Sonatas: (*for Piano*) F Minor, Op. 2, No. 1: I, 90f; III, 82; C Major, Op. 2, No. 3: I, 80; III, 301; D Major, Op. 10, No. 3, III, 385; C Minor, Op. 13: II, 66, 379; III, 320, 360; Op. 14, No. 1, III, 191; Op. 14, No. 2, I, 110; C-sharp Minor, Op. 27, No. 2, III, 109; E-flat Major, Op. 31, No. 3, 76; III, 113; C Major, Op. 53: I, 82, 288-89, 290; III, 88; F Minor, Op. 57, II, 436; G Major,

Op. 79: II, 394; III, 249; E-flat Major, Op. 81a, III, 359; E Minor, Op. 90, II, 108; A Major, Op. 101, I, 111; A-flat Major, Op. 110: 187; I, 107, II, 407; Fugue, 245; (*for Violin and Piano*) Op. 23, II, 12–13; F Major, Op. 24, 361
  Symphonies: No. 2, II, 84; No. 3 (*Eroica*), I, 3, 104, 431; No. 5: II, 87; III, 100; No. 8: I, 77; III, 410; Finale, 428; No. 9, IV, 54
  Trios: E-flat Major, Op. 1, No. 1, II, 50; Op. 1, No. 3, Finale, 420–21; B-flat Major, Op. 11, I, 350; Op. 97 ("Archduke"), Scherzo, 419
Bégue, Le: Bourrée, 86
Binchois: *De plus en plus*, 246
Bloch: Concerto Grosso for String Orchestra with Piano Obbligato, 73
Brahms: *Alto Rhapsody*, 324; Concerto (Violin), II, 294
  Ein deutsches Requiem: "Der gerechten Seelen," 296; "Herr, du bist würdig," 383, 390; "Wie lieblich," 88, 392
  Es ist ein Ros' entsprungen (chorale prelude), 270–71
  Intermezzi: E-flat Major, No. 1, 95; Op. 10, No. 3, 349; Op. 118, No. 2, 432
  Liebeslieder Walzer, Op. 52, No. 8, 391; *Salamander*, 73; *Sehnsucht*, 282
  Sonatas: F Minor, Op. 5: I, 359; V, 309; C Major, Op. 1, II, 347–48; (*for Violin*) A Major, I, 321; G Major, I, 266
  Symphonies: No. 1, IV, 80; No. 2, I, 100; No. 3: I, 319; II, 82, 364; No. 4: III, 345, 428; IV, 309
  Variations and Fugue on a Theme by Handel, Op. 24, Var. I, 355; Variations on a Theme of Haydn, theme, 56–57
Bruckner: Symphony No. 7, II, 318
Buxtehude: *Herzlich thut mich verlangen*, 321; Instrumental Sonata, *Jesu, Meine Freude*, 323; Prelude in E Minor, 239, 286–87
Byrd: Madrigal, 235

C

Cannabich: Sinfonia in B-flat Major, II, 302

Carter, Elliott: Piano Sonata, II, 81, Woodwind Quintet, I, 110

Chopin: Ballade in G Minor, Op. 23, No. 1, 377; *The Maiden's Wish*, 49

    Mazurkas: A-flat Major, Op. 59, No. 2, 400; B-flat, 407; C Major, Op. 33, No. 2, 328–29; E Minor, Op. 41, No. 2, 372, 381; G Minor, Op. 67, No. 2, 395; Op. 7, No. 2, 309

    Nocturnes: E-flat Major, Op. 9, No. 2, 386; F Minor, Op. 55, No. 1, 402; Op. 37, No. 1, 361

    Prelude in A Major, Op. 28, No. 6, 384; Sonata in B Minor, Op. 58, I, 111; Valse brillante, Op. 34, No. 2, 67; Waltz in A-flat Major, Op. 64, No. 3, 46

Chorales: *Ermuntre dich, mein schwacher Geist*, 59; *Valet will ich dir geben*, 49, 59; *Wer weiss, wie nahe mir*, 228

Ciconia: *Et in terra pax*, 61

Copland: *Appalachian Spring*, Bride's Dance, 212; Concerto for Clarinet, I, 94; Sonata for Violin and Piano, 292

Corelli: Concerto Grosso, 101; Concerto Grosso, Op. 6, No. 11, Sarabande, 301; Sonata, Op. 2, No. 4, 271; Sonata in D Minor, Giga, 238; Violin Sonata in C Major, III, 308; Sonata da camera for Violin, Sarabanda, 188

D

Debussy: *Bruyères*, 310; Prelude, Book I, "Les sons et les parfums tournent dans l'air du soir," 356

Dello Joio: *Song of Affirmation*, Part 1, 256

Dufay: *Craindre vous vueil*, 76; *Le jour s'endort*, 39; *Mon chier amy*, 92

Dunstable: Sancta Maria, 60

Dvořák: Symphony in D Minor, Op. 70, II, 388; Symphony in E Minor, II, 93; Quartet in A-flat Major, I, 365

F

Fischer, J.C.: Fugue in E Major, 243

Folksongs: American, 55; Comin' Round the Mountain, 24; German, 21, 56; *Die Lorelei*, 69; *Have You Ever Seen a Lassie?* 220; Hungarian, 32; Irish, 21, 59–60; Italian, 24; Russian, 47; Scotch (*My Bonnie Lies Over the Ocean*), 32; Swedish, 47–48; United States, 38

Foss, Lukas: Invention for Piano, 124

Franck: Pastorale in E Major, 287; Symphony in D Minor, I, 199, 297

Frauenholz: *Der Herr Gedenkt an uns*, for Voices, Strings, and Organ, 406

Frescobaldi: *Canzona dopo l'Epistola*, 165; Canzona for Organ, 203; Organ Ricercare, 189; Toccata, 237

Froberger: Gigue, 51

G

Gesualdo: *Io pur respiro*, 371

Giovanni da Florentia: (Phrygian Mode), 147

Glazunov: *Carnival* Overture, 98

Gounod: *Faust*, "Faites lui mes aveux," 397; Faust, "Salut! Demeure" (Act II), 380

Greek: Epitaph of Seikelos, 38

Gregorian Chant: Responsorium, *Libera me*, 21; *Sanctus*, 336–37

H

Handel: 148; Air with Variations, Var. 3, 60

    Concerti Grossi, Op. 6: 408–409; No. 1, I, 282; No. 2, 325

    Fughetta, 151; *Judas Maccabaeus*, "Rejoice, O Judah," 280

Handel (*cont.*)
   Organ Concerti: Op. 4, No. 4, 99; F
      Major, II, 358
   Sonata No. 6 for Flute and Continuo,
      186
   Suites: Allemand, 154, 155; D Minor,
      Fugue, 199; E Minor, Gigue, 209;
      No. 7, Allegro, 117; Clavier Suite
      in E Minor: Courante, 206; Sara-
      bande, 202
      Trio Sonata, Op. 5, No. 4, Passacaille,
      200
Haydn: Capriccio in G Major, 279
   Creation, The: "In Splendor Bright,"
      396; "Now Vanish Before the Holy
      Beams," 347
   Quartets: Op. 9, No. 2, Menuet, 299;
      E Major, Op. 20, No. 6, I, 282; D
      Major, Op. 50, No. 6, I, 268, 317;
      C Major, Op. 54, No. 2, II, 317; D
      Major, Op. 64, No. 2: Menuetto,
      418; IV, 268; Op. 64, No. 3, I, 362–
      63; Op. 64, No. 5, III, 364; Op. 64,
      No. 6, I, 427; F Major, Op. 74, No.
      2, I, 112; Op. 74, No. 3, III, 301;
      D Minor, Op. 76, No. 2: III, 193;
      IV, 350–51; Op. 76, No. 3, III
      (Trio), 443–44; Op. 76, No. 6, I,
      184
   Sonatas: D Major, II, 135; D Major,
      III, 380; E-flat Major, I, 179, 382;
      E-flat Major, II, 62, 242; E-flat Ma-
      jor, III, 118; E-flat Major, Menuet,
      133, 182; E-flat Major, Finale, 160;
      No. 6, II, 94; No. 18, I, 223–24
   Symphonies: No. 86, I, 278; No. 88, IV,
      393–94; No. 93, I, 77; No. 95,
      Menuetto, 278; No. 102, IV, 302
Hindemith: *Ludus Tonalis*: Fugue No. 4
      in E, 138, 188, 198, 219; Fugue No.
      8, 240; Interludium in E-flat (The
      March), 415–16; *Marienleben*, 127;
      Mathis der Maler: I, 114; II, 330,
      331–32; Sonata for Organ, I, 424;
      Third Piano Sonata, I, 93
   Theme and Four Variations, 30, 63;
      *When Lilacs Last in the Dooryard
      Bloomed*, 63
Hovhaness: *Prayer of Saint Gregory*, for
      Trumpet and String Orchestra, 76

I

Ingegneri: *Ecce Quomodo*, 293

J

Josquin des Près: Chansons, 141, 142;
      (Dorian Mode), 147; *Homo quidan
      fecit coenam magnam*, Motet, 192;
      Tu pauperum refugium, 122

K

Kuhnau: *The Battle Between David and
      Goliath*, 307

L

Landini: *Amor dal tuo suggétto*, 61; Bal-
      lata, 209; Two-voice Ballata, 411
Lantins, de: *Puisque je voy*, 93
Lassus: *Cantiones*, No. 1, 62: Penitential
      Psalm No. 3, 200, 205; *Sequentur
      Cantiones* (First Part), 194
Leonin: Organum, 117
Liszt: Hungarian Rhapsody No. 9, 94
Loewe, Carl: *Der Pilgrim vor St. Just*, Op.
      99, No. 3, 305
Lully: Overture to *Alceste*, 97

M

Machaut: *Mes esperis*, 61
Marenzio: Madrigal, 232
Marini: Sonata for Violin and Organ (two
      outer parts), 117–18
Maschere: Canzona, 74
Massenet: *Manon* (Act III, Scene I), 354
Mendelssohn: *A   Midsummer   Night's
      Dream*, Intermezzo, 110; Songs
      Without Words: Op. 19, 198; Op.
      19, No. 2, 389; Op. 85, No. 5, 307;
      Op. 102, No. 3, 258; Symphony No.
      3 in A Minor (*Scotch*), I, 323, 422
Milhaud: Quartet No. 9, III, 163
Monteverdi: *Ohimè, se tanto amate*, 315;
      Toccata, from *L'Orfeo*, 222

Mozart:
Concerti: G Major, K. 453, I, 314; F Major (Piano), K. 413, I, 353; C Minor (Piano), K. 491, I, 240; A Major (Piano), K. 488, I, 244; (Two Pianos) K. 365, III, 74
Eine kleine Nachtmusik, K. 525, Menuetto, 371; *Mass in C Minor*, K. 427, "Domine Deus," 324; Motet, *Ave verum corpus*, 272; *Nozze di Figaro, Le*, "Deh vieni, non tardar," 265
Quartets: A Major, K. 464: I, 112; II, 307; D Major, K. 499, I, 81; D Major, K. 575, IV, 130
Quintet, K. 516, III, 318; Requiem, K. 626, *Domine Jesu Christe*, 323, 346–47; Rondo in A Minor, K. 511, 311
Sonatas: (*Piano*) C Major, K. 279: II, 379; III, 355; B-flat Major, K. 281, III, 385; E-flat Major, K. 282, I, 31; D Major, K. 284, III (Variation 12), 109; D Major, K. 311, I, 272; A Major, K. 331, I, 75, 93; F Major, K. 332, I, 4, 22, 24, 29, 34; B-flat Major, K. 333: I, 385; III, 288, 310; Finale, 187; F Major, K. 533, I, 62; C Major, K. 545, I, 92, 156; D Major, K. 576, III, 108; (*Violin and Piano*) E Minor, K. 304, I, 298; K. 376, II, 205
Symphonies: A Major, K. 114, Menuetto, 323; E-flat Major, K. 543: II, 369; III, 375–76; G Minor, K. 550: III, 258–59; IV, 91f; C Major, K. 551 (*Jupiter*): II, 399; IV, 66–67
Variations on a Menuet by Duport, Var. I, 265

N

National Anthem, The, 24

O

Obrecht: Agnus Dei, *Missa Sine Nomine*, 147, 178

Ockeghem: *Agnus Dei*, 118–19; Motet, 241; *Ut hermita solus*, 241

P

Pachelbel: *An Wasserflussen Babylon*, 319; *Aus tiefer Not*, 321; *Nun lasst uns Gott, dem Herren*, 267
Palestrina: *Adjuro vos filiae Jerusalem*, Motet, 412–13; *Adoramus te Christe*, 249; *Missa In dominicus quadragesima*, 62; *Missa Vestiva i colli*, Kyrie, 61, 97; *Sicut cervus*, 122; *Veni, Sancte Spiritus*, 293
Pergolesi: 32
Perotin: Three-voice Organum, *Alleluia*, 267
Piston: Sonata for Violin and Piano, III, 119; Symphony No. 4, I, 68
Praetorius: Chorale Prelude, *Ein feste Burg ist unser Gott*, 173; *Ich dank dir, lieber Herre*, 252
Prokofiev: Classical Symphony, III, 396; Rigaudon, Op. 12, No. 3, 80; Violin Concerto No. 2, I, 68
Puccini: *Il Tabarro*, Frugola's aria, 355
Purcell: *Dido and Aeneas*, Prelude, Act I, Scene 2, 423–24; *Dido and Aeneas*, "Shake the Cloud," 279

R

Rameau: Rigaudon, 280
Ravel: String Quartet in F, I, 74; Trio, IV, 346
Reger: Toccata in D Minor, 269; *Kyrie eleison*, 295
Reveille (Bugle Call), 222

S

Satie: Fifth Nocturne, 86
Scarlatti, D.: Sonata in B Minor, 437–39, 440; Sonata in C Major, 235
Scheidt: *Allein Gott in der Höh sei Ehr*, 314; *Gelobet seist du, Jesu Christ*, 201

Schein: *Gelobet seist du, Jesu Christ*, 374

Schoenberg: Piano Pieces, Op. 11: No. 1, 333, 334, 335; No. 2, 105

Schubert: Impromptu in A-flat Major, Op. 90, 257, 277; Impromptu Op. 142, No. 3, 85; Mass in G Major, Kyrie, 382; *Moments Musicaux*, Op. 94, No. 6, 379; Octet, Op. 166: II, 382; IV, 384; Sonata in A Major: II, 83; Rondo, 283; Sonata in G Major, IV, 283–84

Songs and Cycles: *An die Leier*, 75; *Alpen Jäger, Der*, 85; *Erstarrung*, 404–405; *Frülingssehnsucht*, 9; *Jüngling auf dem Hügel, Der*, 337–43; *(Schöne Müllerin, Die)* Morgengrüss, 197; *Müller und der Bach, Der*, 223; *(Schwanengesang)* "Ständchen," 248; Sehnsucht, 433–34; *(Winterreise, Die)*: "Der Leiermann," 269; "Muth," 416–17

Symphonies: C Major, Scherzo, 419–20; B Minor: I, 93; II, 393; No. 5: I, 68; II, 352

Trios: B-flat Major, Op. 99, II, 85–86; E-flat Major, Op. 100: I, 426; III, 56

Schuman, William: Symphony No. 3, Fugue, 199

Schumann, Robert: *Album for the Young*, Folk Song, 326–27; *Album Leaf*, Op. 124, No. 4, 359; *An den Sonnenschein*, Op. 36, No. 4, 48; *Carnaval*, "Reconnaissance," 89; Concerto (Piano), Op. 54, II, 318; Dichterliebe: "Die alten, bösen Lieder," 346; "Im Wunderschönen Monat Mai," 79; *Einsame Blumen* (Waldszenen), 273; *Frauenlieben und Leben*, "Helft mir, ihr Schwestern," 425; *Freue dich, O Meine Seele*, 261; Fugue on B.A.C.H., 211; Quintet in E-flat Major, Op. 44, II, 283; Symphony No. 1, II, 71; Symphony No. 2: Adagio, 430; Finale, 282

Shostakovitch: Quartet, Op. 49: I, 207, 421; III, 270

Symphonies: No. 1, Op. 10, II, 190; No. 5, Op. 47, I, 189; No. 7, I, 94

Siamese Orchestral Piece: *Kham Hom* (Sweet Words), 217

Spain: Chant to the Virgin, 38

Stamitz: Sinfonia in E-flat Major, 301

Strauss, J.: Emperor Waltz, 98

Strauss, R.: *Breit über mein Haupt*, 317; *Die Nacht*, 365

Stravinsky: *Le Sacre du printemps*, "Dance of the Adolescents," 357; Octet for Winds, III, 179; Octet, Sinfonia, 105; *Symphony of Psalms*: I, 366; III, 429; Symphony in Three Movements, I (piano part), 139

Sweelinck: Fantasia (for organ), 134; Organ Toccata (cadence), 143–44

T

Tansman: "Berceuse" (*Pour les Enfants*, Set 4), 72

Taulipang melody (after Hornbostel), 20

Tchaikovsky: Symphony No. 5, II, 100, 114; Violin Concerto in D Major, I, 317

Telemann: Fantasia for Harpsichord No. 1, 94; *Christus, der uns selig macht*, 212

Trouvére Songs: *C'est la fin*, 72; Virelais, *Or la truix*, 71

Tye: *Come, Holy Ghost*, 314

U

Uitoto Indian melody (after Bose), 20

V

Vaughan Williams: *Mass in G Minor*, Kyrie, 281

Ventadorn: *Be m'an perdut*, 435–36

Verdi: *Aida*: "Ritorna Vincitor," 303; "Su! Del Nilo," Act 1, Scene 1, 390; Requiem, *Requiem aeternam*, 386

Viotti, Violin Concerto in A Minor, I, 293

Vivaldi: Violin Concerto in C Minor, III, 95

W

Wagner: *Lohengrin*: "Ha, dieser Stolz," 319; Prelude to, 398; Prelude to Act III, 390; *Meistersinger, Die,* Prelude to Act III, 83; *Parsifal,* Grail motive (Act I), 348; Siegfried Idyll, 391; *Tannhaüser,* Overture, 376; *Tristan und Isolde*: Prelude, Act I, 414–15; Act II, 132; *Walküre, Die,* Act I, 431–32

Walther, J.G.: Concerto in B Minor, 296, 297; *Herzlich thut mich verlangen,* 236, 244

Weber: Overture to *Euryanthe,* 266

Webern: Five Pieces for String Quartet, Op. 5, II, 195

Wilder, Alec: Concerto for Oboe, String Orchestra and Percussion, I, 70

Willaert: (Aeolian Mode), 146

Wolf: *Spanish Songbook,* 1, No. 4, 410–11

Z

Zachau: *Vom Himmel hoch, da Komm ich her,* 126

INDEX

A

Accent:
  contoural, 4
  dynamic, 4
  metric, 2–4, 92, 100, 113, 127f
Accidentals, *15f,** 369, 404, 417f
Alberti bass, *249fn*
Ambiguity:
  in the Baroque binary form, 441
  of chords, 218
  in melody, 30, 92, 137
  in modulation, 416
  of secondary dominants, 400f
Anacrusis, *93ff*
Antecedent-Consequent, *75*
Anticipation, *113*, 178f, 245–247, *263ff*
Appoggiatura, *108–111*, 179–181, 245–247, *263ff*
Arpeggiation of chord. *See* Chord, pro-
  longed
Augmentation, *87*, 194, 442
Augmentation dot, *11*

B

Bar form, *435f*
Basic duration, *2*, 5ff, 169, 177, 201ff
  beaming of, 9f
  in compound meter, 6
  rest equivalents, 10
  subdivision of, 8

Basic melody, *90–102*, 104f, 158
Basic pitch, *104ff*, 159f, 165, 167, 172, 178, 188, 241
Beam, *8*
Beat (as rhythmic pulse), *1f*
Bichord, *272*
Binary form, *435–445*
  Baroque binary, *436–442*
  rounded, *442–444*

C

Cadence:
  authentic, *322ff*, 371f
  deceptive, *152*, 350, 362, 364–366, 389
  dominant-tonic, 148–151, 154, 220. *See
    also* Cadence, authentic
  half, *151*, 324f, 347, 390
  harmonic, *322–325*
  imperfect terminal, *58*
  interior, 153f, 354
  Landini, *61*
  melodic, 53ff
  modal, 145–147, 152
  musical style and the, 60ff
  Phrygian, *147, 324f*, 391
  plagal, *324*, 361, 365, 382
  progressive, *53–55*, 57, 79, 151f, 324f, 350
  rhythmic characteristics of, 142f
  terminal, *53–55*, 57, 61, 65, 79, 148–151, 322ff, 348

*Note: *Italic* type indicates pages on which the definition of a subject appears.

Cadence (*cont.*)
   in tonal music, 142
   tonic-dominant. *See* half
   transient-terminal, *58–61*, 84, 151–154,
      238, 371, 380, 382, 384, 393f
   in two-voice textures, 144–158
Cadential tonic six-four, *298–300*
Cadenza, 303
Caesura, *54*
Canon, 141, 185, *189*, 193
Changing tone, 77, *244*
Chorale prelude, *201*
Chord, *206*, 215–219
   chromatic, *218*, 418
   diatonic, *218ff*, 262, 418
   dominant, 220ff, 251, 276–281, 286ff,
      300f
   dominant seventh, 313–320
   doubling. *See* Doubling
   embellishing. *See* Embellishing chord
   fundamental position, *224f*
   inversion. *See* Inversion
   leading tone, 320–322
   mediant, 344–355, 362–367
   mutated, 280f, 311, *362–367*
   neighbor. *See* Neighbor chord
   passing. *See* Passing chord
   pivot, *416–420*
   position, 224f
   prolonged, *228–230*, 283f, 285–290, 364,
      391
   relationship, 360–362
   secondary dominant, *369–402*
      of dominant, 369–379
      irregularly resolved, 395–398
      of mediant, 392–394
      in sequences, 398–402
      of subdominant, 379–383
      of submediant, 388–391
      of subtonic, 395
      of supertonic, 383–386
   subdominant, 251, 281–284, 302
   submediant, 344–355, 362–367
   succession. *See* Harmonic succession
   supertonic, 304–311
   tonic, 220ff, 251, 276–281, 286ff, 298ff
Chromatic half-step, *17fn,* 106ff, 369ff,
   374f, 378f
Circle of fifths, *45*, 360

Clef:
   alto, 14f
   bass, 13f
   c, 14f
   movable, 14f
   tenor, 14f
   treble, 13
Closed score, *250*
Codetta, *143*
Common tone relations, *261f*, 347ff, 360f,
   381, 397
Conductor's beat patterns, 5
Consonance, *122–124*, 159, 167, 215, 217,
   237, 266f
   basic, 123f
   cadential, 123f, 126, 144f, 169, 171, 208,
      238
   decorative, 123f, 145, 169, 171, 238
Contrary motion, *125f*, 130, 144, 150, 186,
   259, 309, 345, 351
Contrast, 79, 84f, 326, 435, 437
Contrasting phrase construction, *75*
"Corelli clash," *271*
Counterpoint/contrapuntal, 99, *116*, 123,
   126, 156ff, 161, 194, 198, 202, 235ff
Cross relation, *138–141*, 398

D

D.C. (da capo), *328*
D.S. (dal segno), *328*
Decorative chords. *See* types under Chord
Decorative pitch, *105–115*, 151, 164ff, 239–
   247. *See also* specific types, e.g., es-
   cape tone
Density, 216
Diad, *228*, 236
Diatonic half-step, *17fn,* 106ff
Diminution, *87*, 194
Direct fifth, *145*, 259f
Direct octave, *145*, 259f
Dissonance, 123f, 134, 159, 164ff, 167ff,
   215, 241, 266f, 314, 370
Dominant, scale degree, 41f, 59, 92, 220,
   268f. *See also* Chord, dominant
Dominant-tonic cadence. *See* Cadence,
   dominant-tonic

Doubling:
  in augmented mediant chord, 352
  in deceptive resolutions, 351
  in dominant seventh chord, 320
  in four voices, 251f, 261
  in leading tone chords, 321f
  in secondary dominants, 370
  in submediant chord, 351
  in suspensions, 245, 267
  in three voices, 237–239
  in tonic six-four chord, 300
Durchkomponiert. *See* Through-composed
  form

E

Echappee. *See* Escape tone
Elaboration, melodic, 101f, 104ff
Elision, *83*
Embellishing chord, *302*
Enharmonic, *17fn*, 46fn, 424ff
Escape tone, *108*, 111f, 181, 245–247, *263ff*
Extended melody, 79ff
Extension:
  cadential, 81f
  internal, 83
  by interpolation, 82
  by variation, 87

F

False relation. *See* Cross relation
Fauxbourdon, *208*, 354
Fermata, 82
Figured bass symbols:
  for seventh chords, 316
  for triads, 226f
Flag, *8f*
Form:
  binary, *435–445*
  diagramming of, 84, 436
  harmonic rhythm and, 296f
  key relations and, 327, 333, 441f
  melody and, 65ff
  phrase structure and, 68ff
  song form and trio, *444f*
  ternary, *326-336*, 442

  texture and, 329, 333, 335, 441
  through-composed, *336–343*
  tonality and, 31
Free tone, *272*
Function, tonal. *See* Root, relations; Harmonic succession
Fundamental pitch, *27f*, 224

G

Gamut, 14
Great staff, 14

H

Half cadence. *See* Cadence, half
Harmonic parallelism, *354–357*
Harmonic progression. *See* Harmonic succession; Root, relations
Harmonic rhythm, 235f, 257–259, *293–298*, 344, 347, 353, 379
Harmonic series, *26f*, 232
Harmonic succession, 154–158, 216, 220ff, 257, 276–284, 292f, 304ff, 346ff, 360–362, 367
Harmony. *See* Chord
Hemiola, *4*
Homophonic, *116*, 182fn, 191, 197, 235–237, 248ff, 257–259
Homorhythmic, 116fn

I

Imitation, 119, 136, *189–195*, 199ff, 236, 413
Intensity, *1*
Interim progression, *278f*
Interval:
  abbreviations for, 17
  approach, *126–128*, 144f, 152
  augmented, 17f, 132
  cadential, 126–128, 144f
  classification of, 17f, 123f
  defined, *16*
  diminished, 17f, 132
  harmonic, *16*, 28, 122f, 209f

Interval (*cont.*)
  harmonic succession of, 130
  inversion of, 28
  melodic, *16*, 28
  perfect, 17f
  perfect fourth, treatment of, 128ff, 170,
    239, 243f
  quality and melodic organization, 29
  roots, *28*, 122f, 153–155
  scale and, 36ff
  stable, 123, 126
  table of, 17
  ultimate, *144f*
  unstable, 132–134
  vertical, 122ff
Inversion:
  chord, 225–228, 279ff
  first:
    dominant seventh, 316–320
    dominant triad, 279f
    leading tone triad, 320–322
    mediant triad, 352–354
    secondary dominant, 370, 378ff
    subdominant triad, 282–284
    submediant triad, 352–354
    supertonic triad, 307ff
    tonic triad, 279f
  as a melodic device, 67, 88
  second:
    dominant seventh, 316–320
    dominant triad, 298, 300–304
    secondary dominant, 370, 378ff
    subdominant triad, 298, 300–304
    tonic triad, 298–304
    triads, 298–304
  third:
    dominant seventh, 316–320
    secondary dominant, 370, 378ff

K

Key, *34*, 292f
  distant related, *405*, 409f
  near related, *405–409*, 441f
  parallel, *45*
  relation, 405–416, 441f
  relative, *45*
  signature, *42–46*, 404ff
  in two-voice textures, 137f

L

Leading tone, *39f*, *42*, 62, 132, 147ff, 150,
  220, 239, 252, 279, 317, 320
Leaning tone. *See* Appoggiatura
Ledger lines, *14*

M

Major-minor seventh (Mm7). *See* Chord,
  dominant seventh
Mediant, 42, 59, 92
Melodic contour, 96ff, 134–136, 206ff
  in two-voice textures, 134–136
Menuet, 445
Meter, *2f*
  compound, *6*
  signatures, *5–7*
  simple, *5*
Metric rhythm, *3*
Metronome markings, *5*
Mode, *37ff*, 145–147, 152, 411–414
  change of, 47
Modulation, *47–51*, 153f, 220, 328, 369,
    400, 404f, 416–426
  by chromatic inflection, 421–424
  enharmonic, 424–426
  in melodic form, 84
  by pivot chord, 416–420
  by pivot tone, 420f
  by sequence, 431f
  transitory, 50f
Monophonic, *116*
Motive, *57*, 66–68, 184f, 194
Mutation, *47f*, 88f, 140, 328, 362ff, 432–
    434, 444

N

Neighbor chord, 241, 270, 349
Neighbor group, *112*, 166, *263*
Neighbor tone, *107f*, 165–167, 240f, *263ff*
Non-chord tone, *263–274*. *See also* Decora-
    tive pitch
  accented, 270f
  simultaneous, 271–273
  twentieth-century usage of, 273f
Note head, *8*
Note stem, *8*

O

Oblique motion, *125f*, 259, 309
Octave:
  as interval, 26f, 144, 147, 215
  segment, 15
Organ point. *See* Pedal
Ostinato, 207, *357*, 442
Overtone series. *See* Harmonic series

P

Parallel motion, *125f*, 129f, 233f, 259, 309,
  329, 354–357
Parallel phrase construction, *75*, 79, 85
Partials, 27, 232
Passing chord, 230, 241f, 270, 295, 300f
Passing tone, *106f*, 164f, 240f, *263ff*
Pedal, 98, *182f*, 207, 235, 263, 267–270,
  286–290, 295f, 300, 302f, 381
Period, *57fn*, 76ff
  double, 77
Phrase, *57*, 66, 68–78, 336ff
  asymmetrical, 76
  contour, 71ff
  elision, *83*
  extended, 81ff
  in modulation, 48, 49fn
  rhythmic content of, 68–71
  symmetrical, 76
  truncated, 83
  in two-voice textures, 134–136
Pitch, *1*, 13–15
Pitch spectrum, 15
Point of imitation, *192*
Polyphonic, *116*. *See also* Counterpoint
Prime, *218fn*, 226f, 305, 320
Prolongation. *See* Chord, prolonged
Propulsion, 202, 222, 277, 291
Pulse, *1*
  in compound meter, 7

R

Range, voice, 121, 250
Recapitulation, *442*. *See also* Restatement
Repetition, 48, 67f, 70f, 79–81, 100, 104,
  184–189
  in establishing tonality, 21

Resolution:
  change of bass, *174f*, 244f
  deceptive, *350ff*, 370, 395f
  of dominant seventh, 320
  irregular, *370*, 395–398
  ornamental, 172–174, 244f
  of secondary dominants, 370, 395–398
Restatement, 84, 189, *326*, 328, 330, 333,
  336, 442
Rests, 10f
Retardation, *176f*
Rhythm, *1ff*
  accent. See Accent, metric
  in the cadence, 54
  metric, *3*
  phrase structure and, 68–71
Rhythmic association:
  in three voices, 197–205
  in two voices, 116–121
Rhythmic diversity, 201–206
Rhythmic notation, correct, 8–13
Rhythmic unity, 201–205
Root, *25ff*
  chord, 156, 219, 224ff
  doubled, 238
  of incomplete chords, 228
  interval, *28*, 123, 153–155
  motion in two-voice cadences, 152
  pitch, *25–27*
  position, 224ff
  relations, 150, 154–158, 216, 220ff, 304ff,
    360–362, 367, 413ff

S

Scale, *34*
  chromatic, 46, 138, 215, 409
  degrees, 41
  diatonic, 36–41, 140
  harmonic minor, *40*
  heptatonic, *39*
  key signature of, 42–46
  major, 34, 37, 43
  melodic minor, *39f*, 139
  minor, 37, 40, 43
  modal, 37ff, 43
  parallel, 45
  relative, 45

Scherzo, 445

Secondary pitch, *104f*, 110, 159, 272

Sequence:
  harmonic, 278f, 353f, 357–360, 385, 398–402, 431f
  melodic, *67*, 80, 186–189, 240, 370
  modulatory, 154
  real, *80*
  of secondary dominants, 395, 398–402
  tonal, *80*

Seventh chord, *313. See also* Chord, dominant seventh; Chord, secondary dominant

Similar motion, *125f*, 128, 145

Sixth chords (parallel), 208, 354

Slur, *11*

Song form and trio, *444f*

Sonority, 215ff, 219

Spacing:
  close, 253–256
  in four voices, 252–256
  heterogeneous, *213*, 254–256
  homogeneous, *213*, 253–256
  in three voices, 210–213, 232–235
  in two voices, 121f

Staff, 13f

Statement, 189, 326, 336

Step-progression, *96–100*, 102, 105, 109, 158, 160, 165, 173, 187f, 379

Structural interval, 125ff

Structural pitch, *25*, 107ff

Subdivision, 7f

Subdominant, 42, 59, 132, 251, 281ff

Subject, 189

Submediant, 42, 59

Subtonic, 39, 41f, 145, 150, 281, 392, 394

Supertonic, 42, 145, 148

Suspension, *113–115*, 167–178, 243f, 263, 266f. *See also* Resolution
  chain of, 177
  in four voices, 263, 266f
  naming of, 169f
  in three voices, 245
  in two voices, 167–178
  2–3, *170*, 172, 243, 245, 267
  4–3, *170*, 243, 245, 266
  6–5, *171*, 245
  7–6, *169f*, 245, 266
  9–8, *171*, 243, 245, 266

Syncopation, *3f*, 61f, 167f, 177, 179, 194, 204

T

Tempo, *1*
  as a factor in harmonic analysis, 296

Ternary form, *326–336*, 442

Tetrad, *313*

Texture, 116, 197, 204ff, 222f, 248–256, 329, 441

Theme, 439f

Third relation, *364f*, 397f, 409f

Through-composed form, *336–343*

Tie, *11*

Tierce de Picardie, *280f*

Timbre, *1*, 27

Tonal direction, 277–279, 282, 345

Tonal function. *See* Root, relations; Harmonic succession

Tonality, *20ff*, 31, 142–163, 220ff
  analysis of in melody, 31f
  change of, 47–51, 416–426
  form and, 99ff

Tonality frame, *20–25*, 51, 74, 90–93, 101, 240f

Tonal region, 50, 430f

Tonal relation, in major and minor keys, 360–362, 367

Tonal shift, *404*, 409, 413, 421, 426–431

Tonal stability and instability:
  of chords, 215ff, 277, 314, 352
  of intervals, 123ff, 132ff
  of keys, 409, 412ff, 441, 444

Tonic, *20ff*, 41, 47, 57, 92ff, 151, 220ff, 251, 268f, 279

Transposition, *35fn*

Triad, *28f*, 216ff, 251f
  augmented, 29, 217–219, 224fn, 227
  diminished, 29, 217–219, 224fn, 227, 305, 320
  fundamental, 225
  implied, 155–158, 160–163, 224, 237
  major, 29, 217–219, 280, 304, 344, 346
  minor, 29, 217–219, 280, 304, 344, 346
  nomenclature, 219, 223f, 226f

Trio, *444f*

Tritone:
  resolution of, 130, 132f, 152, 239, 260, 309, 315, 320, 322, 375
Truncation, *83*
Two-voice framework, *158–163*, 197, 206, 208, 248, 260f, 396

V

Variation, *85–89*, 436
Voice:
  crossing of, 234f
  leading, 259–262
  overlapping, 260
  ranges, 121, 250